Michael Cox first discovered the townlands of Edymore and Cavanalee fifty years ago when he installed milking machines on two farms there. After his marriage a few years later, he and his wife moved to Edymore, staying there for over twenty years. In the 1960s he started to explore the history of the townlands following the discovery of old maps of the district among the Abercorn Papers at PRONI. After moving to Scotland he continued his research during annual visits to the Strabane district. He was later persuaded by two friends, both Ulster local historians, to write down the story of the two townlands.

Overlooking the River Mourne

An early twentieth century view of Strabane and the River Mourne
Illustration courtesy of Gray's Museum, Strabane

Overlooking the River Mourne

*Four Centuries of Family Farms
in Edymore and Cavanalee in County Tyrone*

MICHAEL COX

ULSTER HISTORICAL FOUNDATION

This publication has been supported by the Ulster Local History Trust.
Ulster Historical Foundation is also pleased to acknowledge support for this
publication provided by the Strabane District Council and Strabane History Society.
All contributions are gratefully acknowledged.

Front cover: *farmers attending the Strabane Show in 1911*
Courtesy of Cooper Collection, PRONI
Back cover: *a 1990 view of the River Mourne and part of Strabane,
looking south eastwards towards Edymore and Cavanalee*
Courtesy of Michael G. Kennedy and Strabane History Society

First published 2006
by Ulster Historical Foundation
12 College Square East, Belfast BT1 6DD
www.ancestryireland.com

Except as otherwise permitted under the Copyright, Designs and Patents Act 1988,
this publication may only be reproduced, stored or transmitted in any form or by
any means with the prior permission in writing of the publisher or, in the case of
reprographic reproduction, in accordance with the terms of a licence issued by The
Copyright Licensing Agency. Enquiries concerning reproduction outside those
terms should be sent to the publisher.

© Michael Cox

ISBN 13: 978 1 903688 44 1
ISBN 10: 1903688 44 2

Printed by Cromwell Press
Design by December Publications

CONTENTS

	ACKNOWLEDGEMENTS	x
	INTRODUCTION	xi
	LOCATION	xv
1	IN THE BEGINNING An O'Neill Cattle Ranch?	1
2	FARMS AND FARMERS from 1600 to 1750	6
3	HAND TOOLS AND ACHING BACKS Farms and farmers from the mid-eighteenth to the mid-nineteenth century	10
4	FARMING FAMILIES from the mid-eighteenth to the mid-nineteenth century	35
5	A CENTURY OF CHANGE Farms and farmers from the mid-nineteenth to the mid-twentieth century	45
6	SOCIAL LIFE AND LIVELIHOODS Farming families from the mid-nineteenth to the mid-twentieth century	70
7	THE TRACTOR AND THE ELECTRONIC AGE Farms and farmers from 1945 to 2000	86
8	CONCLUSION	110
	BIBLIOGRAPHY	111
	INDEX	149

APPENDICES

1	Finding sources and the search for information	114
2	1756 Rent Assessment and Land Valuation Survey	119
3	Land Description and Valuation Survey 1833	124
4	Land Assessment and Valuation map 1833	126
5	Robert Wilson's will 1836	127
6	Griffith's Valuation map 1858/60	129
7	Griffith's Valuation: Published Versions 1858 and Amendments 1860	130
8	1901 Census – farming families only	134
9	Brief extracts from original documents	138
10	Farms and farmers from 1756 to 1827 showing rents and tithes	140
11	Farms and farmers from 1838 to 1900 showing rents and tithes	142
12	Farms and farmers in the twentieth century excluding the mountains	146

MAPS

Part of Sir William Petty's County Tyrone sheet of *Hiberniae Delineatio* 1685	x
Location of townlands	xvi
The area around Strabane	xvii
Strabane and Lifford at the end of the sixteenth century	1
Part of Bodley's 1609 Plantation Survey map of the Barony of Strabane	2
Abercorn Estate map of Edymore and Cavanalee *c.*1710	4
Abercorn Estate map of Edymore, Cavanalee and their 'mountains' 1777	16
Abercorn Estate map of Edymore, Cavanalee and their 'mountains' 1806	17
Extract from the County Tyrone map by McCrea and Knox 1813	22
Ordnance Survey map of Edymore and Cavanalee 1834 edition – surveyed in 1833	28
Ordnance Survey map of Edymore and Cavanalee 1855 edition – surveyed in 1854	29
Ordnance Survey map of Edymore and Cavanalee 1907 edition – surveyed in 1905	60
Ordnance Survey map of Edymore and Cavanalee 1951 edition – surveyed in 1951	61
Edymore and Cavanalee farms in 2000	108

ACKNOWLEDGEMENTS

There are three groups of people to whom I am greatly indebted for help, advice and forbearance when researching and writing about the farms, farmers and their families in Edymore and Cavanalee. Firstly there are the professional historians, archivists and librarians who pointed the way and told me of the many avenues that had to be explored. Principal among these are Bill Crawford, Bob Hunter and Johnny Dooher – they have all become good friends and have endured many hours of answering endless questions. In this group, I would also include Brian Trainor, John Bradley, Michael Kennedy, John Mills, Valerie Wallace and especially the current and former staff of PRONI (David Lammey, Roger Strong and Heather Stanley); the Ulster Folk and Transport Museum (Jonathan Bell), as well as the local studies sections of the libraries in Omagh, Derry and Coleraine, all of which were visited many times over the years.

The second group is the farmers and their families – my farming friends – in the two townlands whom I have known for over fifty years. They also had to answer many questions, but when doing so we had some great craic. Finally, sincere and grateful thanks to my family who have had to put up with my many absences and the countless times when I disappeared to the 'office'.

Photographic sources and acknowledgements

Part of Sir William Petty's County Tyrone sheet of Hiberniae Delineatio 1685

Thanks are extended to PRONI for allowing the reproduction of photographs in the Cooper Collection, as well as to the Ulster Folk and Transport Museum for the use of the Green Collection; to Estyn Evans' estate; to Aerofilms Ltd; and to the Strabane History Society for the use of photographs from their publications. Grateful thanks to the following who supplied original photographs and illustrative material – Michael Kennedy, William Fulton, Jackie Davis, Roland Houston, Bertie Huston and Doone Taylor-O'Callaghan. Archaeological information provided by the Monuments and Buildings Record, Environment Heritage Service was appreciated. Permission was obtained from the Ordnance Survey NI for the use of their maps post 1955 and from PRONI for the use of their historical OS maps before that date.

INTRODUCTION

This book relates the course of change on the farms and for the farming families in two townlands, Edymore and Cavanalee, in the north of County Tyrone, during the last four hundred years. Since the beginning of the seventeenth century, no historical event either at a national or county level has taken place there. Today, there are no actual or ruined castles, churches, 'big houses', or even pre-historic or medieval remains to be seen. So why should anyone wish to find out what has taken place on a hilly two thousand acres in northwest Ulster? For me, the reason is two-fold. I lived there and have known the area for over fifty years and I wanted to find out how my friends and their forebears came to be living there.

Many changes have taken place in the economic and social life of farming communities in northwest Ulster over four centuries. The most significant change was the early seventeenth century Plantation (colonisation) of Ulster. This resulted in the dispersal of Irish landowners, the introduction of new laws covering the ownership and leasing of land, and the arrival of new settlers from Britain. During this period there have been two agricultural revolutions. The first lasted for about one hundred years from the middle of the eighteenth century; the second during the last fifty years. I have been able to show in Table 1 (overleaf) that in this small part of Ulster there has been continuity, with farming families living on the same land for upwards of 250 years.

The townlands of Edymore and Cavanalee, with about 2,000 acres (800 ha) of land, lie immediately to the southeast of Strabane in County Tyrone. They lie to the east of the River Mourne, bounded on the north side by the Cavanalee River, and rising to the foothills of the Sperrin Mountains at 1,000 feet (300 m). Until 1800 there was only one track, later road, leading to them. After 1800 the new road from Strabane to Plumbridge passed through the upper part of Cavanalee. Later in the nineteenth century new roads were constructed providing access to neighbouring townlands.

All through the centuries it has been possible to walk to Strabane in an hour or less from most parts of the two townlands, so farmers and their families were able to avail themselves of the services, fairs, markets (later shops) and take part in the social life of the town. The latter was usually linked to their churches. Strabane developed into an important market town following the development of the national road network; the opening of the Strabane Canal (1796) providing water transport for goods to and from Derry; the arrival of the railway (1847) providing an even quicker journey to and from Derry, and later, when extended beyond Omagh, to many towns throughout Ireland.

As will be seen, a wide range of sources of information has been used. The most important of these was the extensive collection of the Abercorn Estate Papers and Letters, deposited at the Public Record Office of Northern Ireland

EDYMORE

++ *Wilson > H(o)uston* (by marriage/inheritance 1873 and a member of the Cavanalee Houston family)	1782–2000	218 years
++ *Davis* (see Cavanalee)	1795–2000	205 years
++ *Fulton* (Rabb's farm – see below)	1816–2000	184 years
Conway	c.1827–2000	c.173 years
++ McCrea > *H(o)uston* (by marriage/inheritance 1914 – same H(o)uston family as above)	1845–2000	155 years
Gordon (family died out)	1806–1957	151 years
Rabb	c.1666–1816	c.150 years
Aiki(e)n	c.1827–1939	c.111 years
Sa(w)yer	c.1777–1880	c.103 years
Finlay	c.1666–c.1766	c.100 years

CAVANALEE

++ *Houston* (on the same land to 1934 and then bought another farm in Cavanalee	c.1753–2000	c.247 years
Barnhill > Mutch (by marriage 1913)	c.1756–2000	c.244 years
Dooher	c.1765–2000	c.235 years
Graham (family died out)	c.1756–1934	c.178 years
++ Cuthbertson > *Davis* (by marriage/inheritance 1882 - same family as Davis, Edymore)	c.1841–2000	c.159 years
McNamee	c.1777–c.1903	c.126 years
++ *Davis* – see above: this was a different farm (same family as Davis, Edymore)	1873–2000	127 years
** Lowry > Smyth (by inheritance 1915)	1879–2000	121 years

Note: The first dates in the above table are the first verifiable dates obtained from records. Most of the seventeenth and eighteenth century, and some of the nineteenth century, dates could have been earlier. This would apply to Aiken, Conway, Finlay, Rabb and Sa(w)yer in Edymore, and Barnhill, Cuthbertson, Dooher, Graham, H(o)uston and McNamee in Cavanalee. These dates are preceded by 'c.' (circa = about).
** A member of the Lowry family, Robert Lowry, was a tenant in Edymore from 1858, possibly earlier. He moved to one of the best farms in Cavanalee in 1879.
++ The families in bold italics are the main ones featured in the book. The others appear in the narrative from time to time.

Table 1. Farming families from 1666 to 2000 who lived in the two townlands for more than 100 years
Sources: Hearth Tax 1666; Estate papers 1756–1900; and information supplied by the families

(PRONI), which cover many facets of Ulster's history, especially that of the northwest of the province, from the seventeenth to the twentieth century. The estate records show how and when the farms were created and developed. Farms in Edymore were well-established by the early eighteenth century. Most of the farms in Cavanalee were not set out until the middle of that century, whilst those on the 'mountain land' did not appear until the nineteenth century.

Government records also play their part. The most important of these are the large scale Ordnance Survey (OS) maps which date from 1834, with subsequent editions up to the end of the twentieth century.* Equally important is the information obtained from the Censuses from 1841, and especially that of 1901 where the enumerators' books were consulted. Before 1841, Abercorn estate records provide clues to population changes. The rise and fall in the population is given in Table 2 (overleaf). In the two townlands, a peak of 608 people was reached in 1841. Following the Great Famine there was a considerable fall in the population over the next two decades. The population declined, albeit unevenly at times, right through to 2000 when only 112 people lived in the two townlands. In 2000, there were only six children living in Edymore.

Documents describing various events and activities in the lives of some of the farming families came to light. These range from a will made by a farmer in 1836, through to notebooks kept by a farmer between 1868 and 1872 describing some of the activities on his farm. One disappointment was the limited amount of oral reminiscence handed down to their children by the farmers active between the two World Wars. This, however, was more than made up for by the detailed information provided by the present generation of older farmers when describing life on the farms during the last fifty years.

This book is dedicated to fellow local historians. As a group, their horizons rarely extend beyond their townland, village, parish or town. In Ulster, national or provincial history is beset by the interpretations of professional historians and politicians. The role of the local historian is to collect facts that have to be interpreted by being related to other facts.

---

* In this book the dates given for the OS maps are the survey dates (see page ix).

EDYMORE

Year	No. of houses	Population	Male	Female	Persons per house
c.1600	c.12**	60*			
1756	20	100*			
1777	30	150*			
1806	52	260*			
1833	54	270*			
1841	56	310			5.5
1851	46	236			5.1
1861	36	185	98	87	5.1
1871	30 + 2e	166	98	87	5.5
1881	22 + 1e	130	77	53	5.9
1891	22 + 4e	126	58	68	5.7
1901	23 + 1e	121	59	62	5.3
1911	23 + 3e	99	48	51	4.3
1926	18 + 3	83	42	41	4.6
1937	17	91			5.3
1951	19 +3e	88	41	47	4.6
2000	16	39	19	20	2.4

CAVANALEE

Year	No. of houses	Population	Male	Female	Persons per house
c.1600	c.15**	75*			
1756	25	125*			
1777	29	145*			
1806	43	215*			
1833	54	270*			
1841	59	298			5.0
1851	60	291			4.9
1861	49 + 1e	221	95	126	4.5
1871	34 + 3e	163	77	86	4.8
1881	32	176	88	88	5.5
1891	29 + 3e	171	95	76	5.9
1901	27 + 2e	139	75	64	5.1
1911	25 + 3e	136	84	52	5.4
1926	22 + 1e	103	48	55	4.7
1937	22	70			3.2
1951	19 + 1e	59	32	27	3.1
2000	18 + 1e	73	39	34	4.1

Note: In the tables above 'e' indicates the number of empty but habitable houses
** A guestimate! Based on the number of sessiaghs in each ballyboe (townland) – see page 2
* Population based on the presumption of 5.0 persons per house

Table 2. Population and houses in Edymore and Cavanalee 1600–2000
The table gives the approximate number of houses and the population in each townland from 1600 to 1833 and the actual number of both houses and population from 1841. This information was obtained from seventeenth century records, estate records and maps, early Ordnance Survey maps, census returns from 1841 and from a personal survey in 2000.

LOCATION

Edymore and Cavanalee are two adjacent townlands situated between one (1.5 km) and four miles (6.5 km) southeast of Strabane as featured on a variety of maps shown on the following pages. The area of Edymore is 947.5 acres (383 ha), whilst Cavanalee is 1098.5 acres (444.5 ha). Edymore stretches for 2¼ miles (3.5 km), with Cavanalee covering 3 miles (5 km) from the river Mourne to the 1,000ft (300m) high television transmitter mast, just beyond the eastern boundary of the townland, a landmark since the early 1960s.

The Strabane to Plumbridge road enters Cavanalee at the Cavanalee Bridge, passes through the higher parts of the townland, past the television transmitter mast at a height of 900ft (275m) on its way to Ligfordrum, Plumbridge and the Glenelly valley. At the western end of the townland is the Strabane to Victoria Bridge road (B72) at Milltown, the location of the Strabane Grammar School, established in 1967. Only minor roads pass through Edymore. The road named by the Post Office as Bearney Road continues to Douglas Bridge, whilst the Carrigullin Road meets the road which links Douglas Bridge to the Strabane to Plumbridge road at Ligfordrum.

The townlands are at the western end of the foothills of the Sperrin Mountains, an area of metamorphic rock overlain with deposits resulting from the melting of the glaciers at the end of the last ice-age some 10,000 years ago. The glacio-fluvial deposits choked most of the valleys, resulting in steep-sided valleys, even gorges, being formed by the melt-water. An example of this can be seen in the last mile of the Cavanalee River before it reaches the River Mourne. In the lower reaches of the valley of the Cavanalee River are some significant, almost drumlin-like, hills of gravel and sand. Remains of some small gravel quarries can still be seen at various locations in both townlands. The vagaries of the Cavanalee River are noted in the 1756 Rent Assessment and Land Valuation Survey (Appendix 2), where it records that along its upper reaches the Cavanalee River often changed its course annually and sometimes after every new flood. The results of such changes can be seen on later Ordnance Survey maps, where the townland boundary is not always shown as the centre of the river.

Edymore is a steep hillside, with mostly shallow soils, rising from 100ft (30m) to 800ft (245m). The slope is not continuous as the Back Burn crosses the slope from south to north, falling from the 400ft (120m) to the 300ft (100m) contour, and continuing through Cavanalee to the Cavanalee River. A nearby remnant of a melt-water channel can be seen in the narrow flat valley parallel to and immediately adjoining the western boundary of Edymore in Drumnaboy townland. The Carrigullin Burn was prevented from flowing directly westwards into the river Mourne by a glacial deposit and forced to flow for 1¾ miles (2.75 km) along this depression in a northerly direction to reach the river Mourne. Before this low-lying land was drained it had been a significant area of bogland

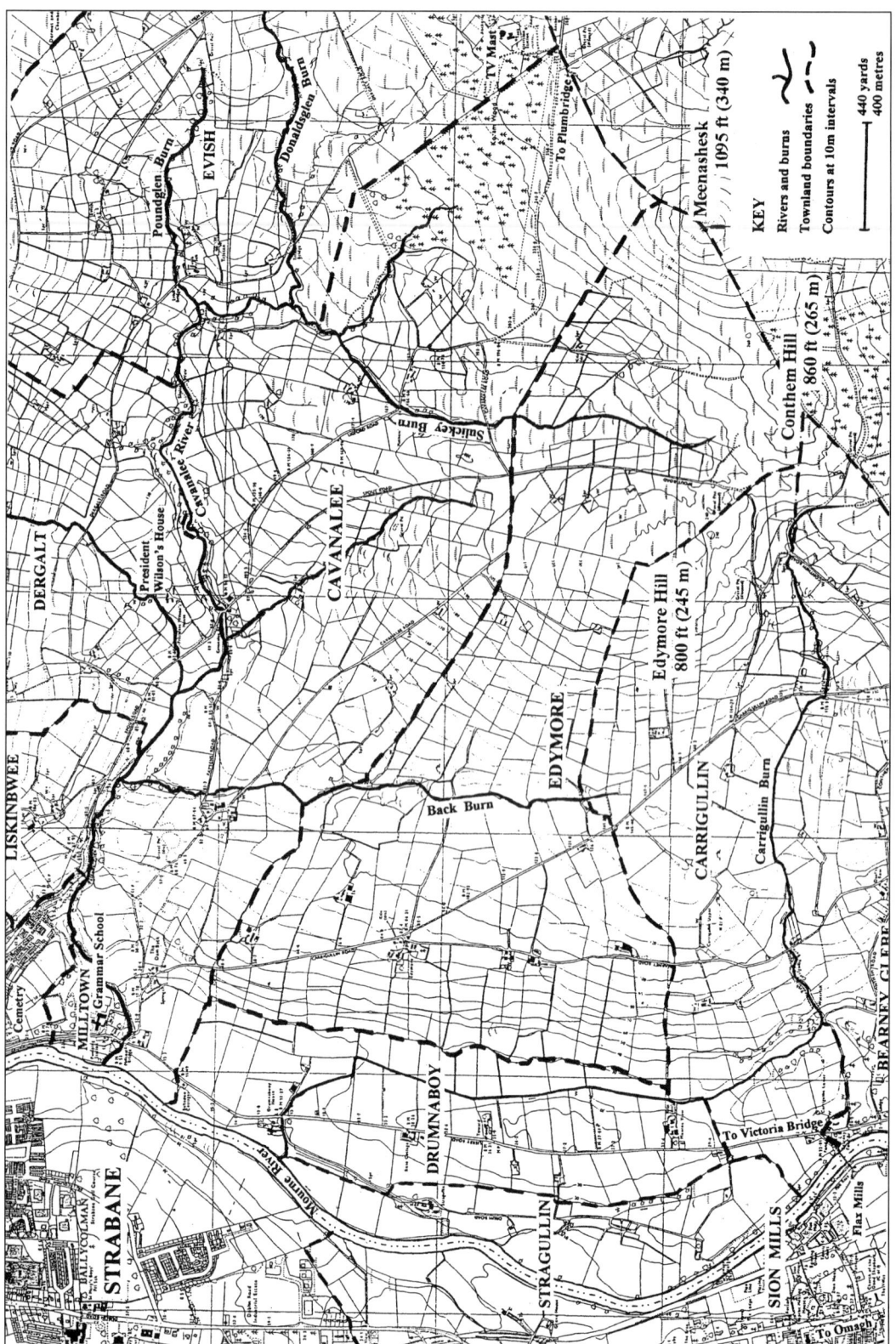

Location of townlands

which is shown on Petty's map of 1685 on page x.

All this post-glacial activity moulded the landscape we see today and virtually created the boundaries of the two townlands. The Cavanalee River forms three-quarters of the northern boundary of Cavanalee. The northeastern boundary is an artificial boundary agreed following a dispute between the Abercorn estate and the neighbouring Spotiswood estate, which was settled about 1800. The very small western boundary is the River Mourne. Three minor waterways form much of the boundary between Edymore and Cavanalee. One rising below Meenashesk runs into the Sulicky Burn; the second joins the Back Burn and the third rising near the Back Burn runs direct to the River Mourne. The western boundary of Edymore runs along the 100ft (30m) contour. The southern boundary of Edymore follows no existing natural feature. The earlier natural ones have been drained and/or ploughed out. The upper boundaries of the two townlands are 'lines on a map', possibly determined by the Abercorn estate surveyors in the eighteenth century. These link the tops of hills, the Edymore Hill (not named on OS maps – 800ft, 240m) with the named ones being Conthem Hill (860ft, 265m) and Meenashesk (1,095ft, 340m).

The views from the upper parts of the two townlands are outstanding. Some 30 miles (50 km) to the northwest, Errigal (2,460ft, 750m) and Muckish (2,200ft, 670m) mountains can be seen. Due west lies the valley of the river Finn with Stranorlar and Ballybofey some 15 miles (25 km) away, and the Blue Stack mountains beyond. Bessy Bell can be seen eight miles (13 km) to the south.

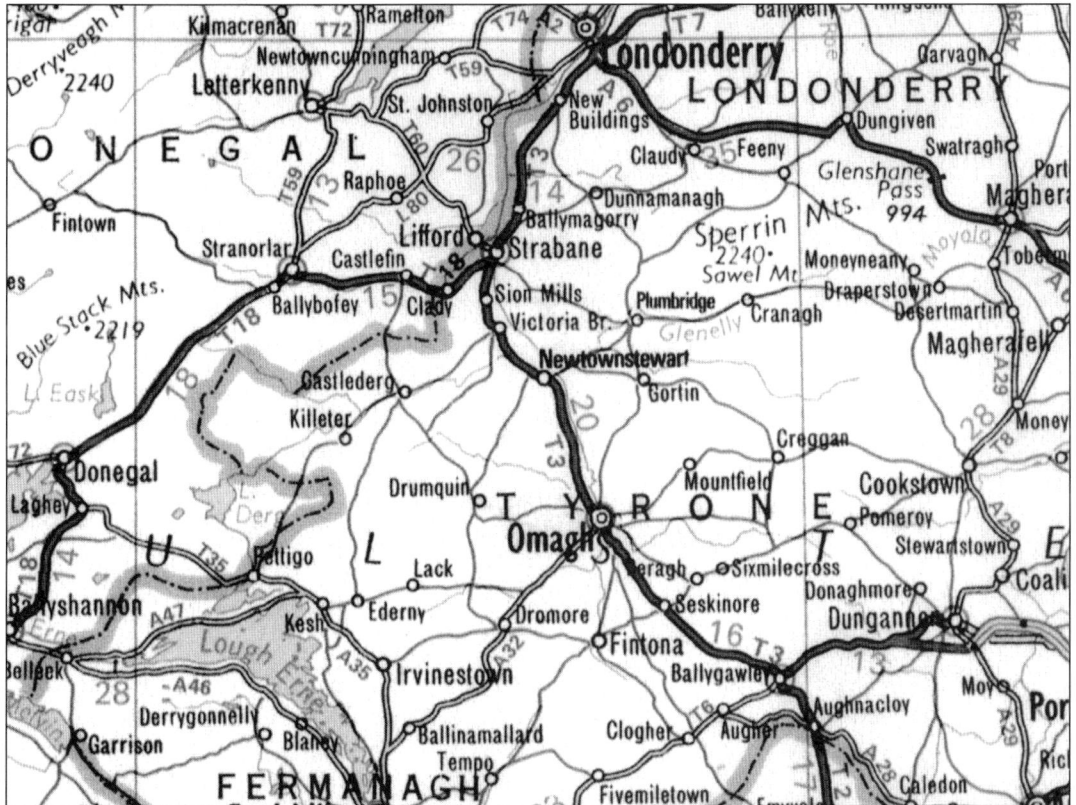

The area around Strabane

1

IN THE BEGINNING
An O'Neill Cattle Ranch?

At the end of the sixteenth century Strabane was just a small village surrounding the O'Neill castle, one of three in the area. The castle was destroyed in 1583 and after its rebuilding in 1591 Turlough Luineach O'Neill, who was The O'Neill from 1570 to 1593 and who died in 1595, owned the three castles at Strabane, Dunnalong and Newtownstewart. It was destroyed again in 1598 – see map below. In the early 1570s, after becoming The O'Neill, he married Lady Agnes McDonnell, daughter of the Earl of Argyll. She brought mercenaries (New Scots) from the west of Scotland who would first have been based at the Dunnalong fort and used to supplement O'Neill's and his successors' own forces during the various encounters which occurred before and during the Nine Years' War, 1594–1603. Like mercenaries over the centuries, many stayed on and married local women. Whilst Turlough's successor, Sir Hugh O'Neill, Earl of Tyrone, was based at Dungannon, members of Turlough's family continued to play varying roles in north Tyrone during the latter part of the Nine Years' War.

After the Flight of the Earls, Tyrone and Tyrconnell (Donegal), to permanent exile on the Continent in 1607, much of Ulster was ripe for plantation (colonisation). One more event speeded up the process. This was the revolt by Sir Cahir O'Doherty of Inishowen, who with about 100 men attacked both Derry and Strabane in 1608. Strabane was again burnt down and the colony of between

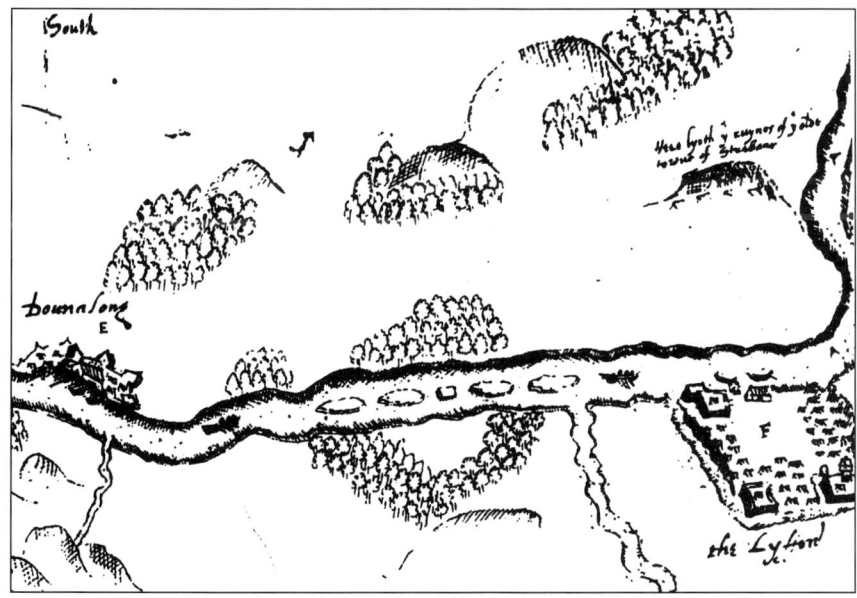

Strabane and Lifford at the end of the sixteenth century

60 and 80 Scots living there fled across the river to the fort at Lifford. This revolt was put down by a force of 200 soldiers sent from Scotland under the command of Captains William Stewart and Patrick Crawford.

It has proved impossible to find out how Edymore and Cavanalee were farmed or who lived there before 1600. Some indication of the number of resident families and the kind of land on which they lived can be gleaned from the seventeenth century Record of the Rolls 1639 (in the Lodge MSS in the National Archives of Ireland), mirrored in the Court of Claims of 1662–3. In these are listed the pre-Plantation ballyboes (later usually the townlands) and sessiagh divisions. The latter often formed a third of a ballyboe but it would seem there was no conformity regarding how many sessiaghs were to be found in a ballyboe. Sessiagh names fall into three main groups – topographical descriptions, a location for agricultural activity and places where named people lived or had lived. It would seem that the number of sessiaghs in any particular ballyboe would, by the later sixteenth century, relate to some extent to the economic and social activity within a ballyboe – the larger the number of sessiaghs, the greater number of people living there.

From information supplied by the Northern Ireland Place-Name Project of the Department of Irish and Celtic Studies, Queen's University Belfast, it can be established that the sessiagh names for Cavanalee and Edymore include all three elements referred to above. However it has been possible, following 'walkovers' in the two townlands from time to time, to suggest that the Irish versions of some of the sessiagh names do show that Cavanalee with Edymore might well have played an important agricultural role for the O'Neills.

On Bodley's Plantation Survey map of 1609, below, Cavanalee is shown surrounded by hills, whilst Edymore stretches from the River Mourne to the hills surrounding Cavanalee. We have seen that the boundaries and extent of the two

Part of Bodley's 1609 Plantation Survey map of the Barony of Strabane

townlands are somewhat different from these early seventeenth century sketches. However, for the ballyboes of Teadanmore and Cauaneley, we find from the Lodge MSS that they had eight and nine sessiaghs respectively. This is more than for other ballyboes in the Strabane district, which usually had between three and six sessiaghs.

Gaelic chiefs counted their wealth by the size of their herds of cattle. It was recorded that in 1601 Cormac O'Neill, the half brother of Sir Art O'Neill (died 1600), the son of Turlough Luineach, together with his nephew Turlough McArt and cousin Neal possessed 2,000 cattle each, some of which may well have been given to Turlough Luineach by minor chiefs as tribute. He and his successors would have needed suitable places where they could keep the cattle, a place to raise calves, keep horses, and practise basic husbandry to provide food for family and followers. Cavanalee, linked to the sheltered valley of the Back Burn in Edymore, with its boundaries of river, streams, steep and boggy hills, the occasional ravine and narrow lowland entrance was a naturally secure location needing the minimum of enclosure for a substantial agricultural operation. It was an ideal location for a cattle-ranch type of operation able to accommodate a substantial herd. Clues to substantiate this are to be found in the pre-1600 Irish names of the Cavanalee ballyboe and sessiaghs. Cavanalee, the anglicised *Cabhán na Laoigh*, could be translated as 'hill/hollow of the calves'. In this sense it would include all ages and kinds of cattle.

A study of the sessiagh names in Cavanalee adds weight to this. Knockganiffe – *Cnoc Gainimh* – hill of sand. There are a number of drumlin-like gravel/sand hillocks in the lower reaches of Cavanalee which would have provided good grazing and patches for the growing of oats. Then there are Knockedaghtan – *Cnoc an Dachtáin* – hill of mud; and Fallagherin – *Fáladh Iarainn* – field/enclosure of the iron. The latter could have resulted from the runoff deposits from the peat bogs which would have left an iron-coloured silt in the flat lower reaches of the burns before they joined the Cavanalee River. One of these areas might be the sessiagh of Straghrey – *Srath Réidh/Ré* – a valley bottom/smooth holm/holm of level ground. The latter can be seen today in the lower reaches of the Back Burn. Two sessiaghs with an agricultural connotation are Straghnemucke – *Srath na Muc* – holm of the pigs, and Corlegaskin – possibly *Corr* (round hill) *Eascann* (of the eels).

Two sessiaghs link a topographical feature with a person: Crosmi(ck)gillyvane – *Cros Mhic Giolla Bháin* – MacGillavane's cross(roads?) for which there is no obvious location, and Alltydyarry – *Allt Uí Dhaighre* – O'Deery's place of the steep glen. Patten's Glen of modern times is steep! Nearby would have been Downemellegan – *Dún Uí Mhaolagáin* – O'Mulligan's fort. The 1854 Ordnance Survey map shows a substantial fort/rath site a little under half a mile up the Cavanalee River from its confluence with the River Mourne. It was on the top of a substantial drumlin-like hillock and it would have had a commanding view up and down the River Mourne. It has long since been ploughed out and was not shown on the 1905 OS map. The last one to consider is Tempillam – *Teampall* – church? Could this be the place where mass was celebrated and the location of what came to be known as the 'Priest's Bush' of the mid-seventeenth century?

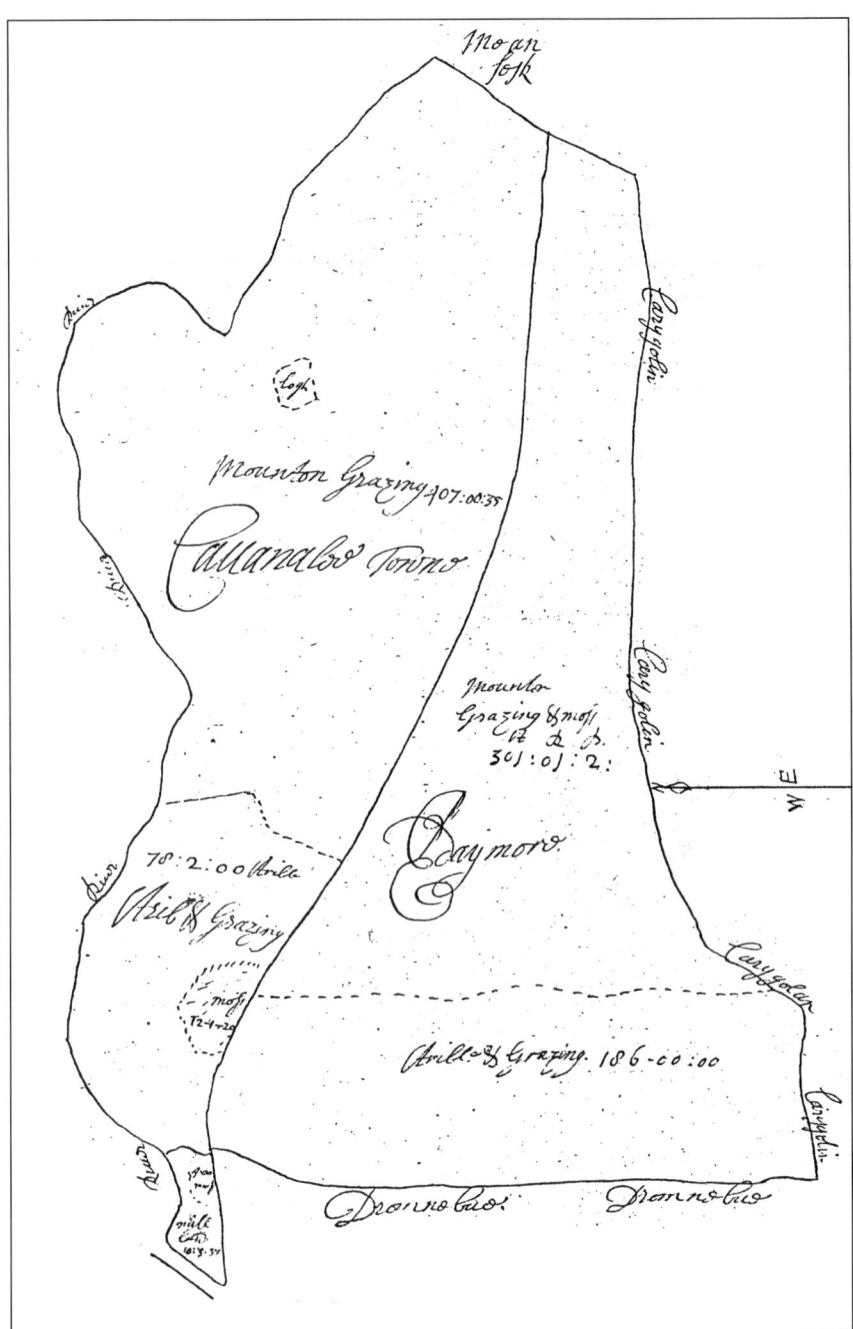

Abercorn Estate map of Edymore and Cavanalee c.1710

Edymore – *An tÉaden Mór* – the big (hill-) brow is an apt description for this townland – see location map on page xiv. Most of the Edymore sessiaghs relate to topographical features. Tawnaghnehaskelly – *Tamhnach na hAscaille* – field of the recess could be next to Altconoleve – *Ard/Allt* – steep glen which is at the western part of the Back Burn at the Cavanalee boundary. A little to the east would have been Tawnaghenagh – *Tamhnach Eanach*(?) – field of the bogs. There was a boggy area alongside this part of the Back Burn right down to the twentieth century, as shown on the 1905 OS map on page 60. Nearby might have been Tawnalohan – *Tamhnach an Locháin* – field of the small lake.

Further east in the higher reaches of the Back Burn could have been Tawnaghranny – *Tamhnach Raithní* – field of the ferns. Perhaps on scrubby land would have been the location of Cooleneshanagh – *Cúil/Cúl na Sionnach* – back of the foxes. No doubt with all the agricultural activity taking place foxes would have been ever present. Two sessiaghs with person linkages were: Lissdownmorry – *Lios Dún Muirígh* – Muirioch's enclosure of the fort, and Corrikerrygan – *Corr Uí Chiaragáin* – O'Kerrigan's round hill. There are no features on the ground today or on early OS maps that would suggest a location for these.

On the north bank of the Cavanalee River in its lower reaches is the townland of Liskinbwee. It had two sessiaghs: firstly, Gortegaddery – *Gort Gadraigh* – field of the withies. These are tough flexible shoots of willow, which when dried can be used for making hurdles for fencing. They would have been essential for use on the Cavanalee/Edymore cattle ranch. Secondly, Dromrollaghe – *Droim Roilleach*? – ridge of the oyster-catchers, or *Droim Rollach* – rolling ridge. A 1777 Abercorn estate map confirms the latter's location and certainly the topography is a 'rolling ridge', whilst the alternative meaning would certainly have been a possibility. This name survives to the present time, as the district of Strabane to the north of Milltown is known as Drumrallagh. None of the sessiagh names in Cavanalee or Edymore have survived.

As part of the Plantation distribution of lands in six of the counties of Ulster by James VI and I, the O'Neills in the Strabane area were transferred to South Tyrone and Armagh. The Cavanalee/Edymore cattle ranch would have then ceased to operate. We do not know how many families had lived there, but if each sessiagh name indicates at least one family unit living there then the pre-Plantation population may well have been more than 100 in the two townlands.

2

FARMS AND FARMERS
from 1600 to 1750

The townlands of Edymore and Cavanalee were part of the Earl of Abercorn's Strabane Proportion (estate) which James VI and I granted him in 1609. Planters (settlers) from Scotland started arriving during the next few years. Only two records have survived which identify people leasing land in the two townlands up to the mid-seventeenth century. In 1641 both townlands were leased from Claud Lord Hamilton, Second Baron of Strabane (the second son of the First Earl of Abercorn) by James Hamilton, Scottish Protestant, for the duration of his life. His name does not appear on the 1630 Muster Roll – there were ten Hamiltons listed on the Roll living in Strabane and district at that time! No information was given about his sub-tenants. The Muster Roll for Strabane lists 208 settler men, both Protestant and Catholic, and the arms they held. Unfortunately the Muster Rolls do not identify the places where people were living.

The second source was the Hearth Tax returns for 1664 and 1666 which list some of the tenants in the two townlands, giving the names of tenants who lived in houses with a single chimney. The occupants of such houses would have been relatively better off than the rest of the farming families. In Edymore there were five such houses occupied by John Rabb, James Nichol, Robert Cunningham, George Finlay and Sean O'Machry. The first three surnames all appear in the 1630 Muster Roll, suggesting that they might have arrived in the Strabane area during the early days of the Plantation. In Cavanalee we find Donald McColgan, Donald oge M'Cartan, Manus O'Haran, Donaghy boy O'Fadachan and John Magee 'younger'. This shows that there was only one native Irish family listed in Edymore and one Scottish family in Cavanalee. Later we find Rabbs in Edymore until 1816 and Finlays until at least 1766. These two families appear on the list in Table 1 – Farming families from 1666 – 2000. McColgans were later found on Edymore Mountain until 1780.

The exceptionally rare outline map on page 4, featuring Edymore and Cavanalee, dating to about 1710, shows the limited extent of the farmed land in the two townlands at the beginning of the eighteenth century. Its shape approximates to the actual boundaries on later maps, except for the higher mountain land where the boundaries are somewhat shortened. On this map the areas are given in Plantation acres which are equivalent to approximately 1.6 statute acres. The map shows that about 40% of Edymore and 15% of Cavanalee were reckoned as arable and grazing land, with two areas in the lower part of Cavanalee shown as bogs. The smaller of these is located at the mill-pond found on later maps, whilst the 'mill land' is separately noted. The boundary between the arable and grazing land and the mountain grazing in Edymore approximates to the Back Burn. In Cavanalee the arable and grazing land lies in that part of the townland where there was (and still is) good naturally drained soil.

Trials and tribulations

Farming families faced many difficulties during this time as a result of recurring periods of severe weather. There were periodic harvest failures in the seventeenth century, notably those in the 1630s, 1642, 1650, 1664 and 1674. In the next century there were periods of severe weather leading to crop failures and famines in 1728–9, 1740–1, 1744–5 and 1756–7. The famine of 1740–1 was probably worse than the famine in the 1840s. During this period the linen industry expanded which meant that more flax could be grown providing additional cash income for farmers. A report by Abercorn's agent describing a textile exhibition, held in 1700, in the 'large apartment of the Town Hall' to promote good spinning techniques, shows that linen was produced in the district.

An annual problem facing farmers was the payment of tithes to the established Church of Ireland rectors: one-tenth of a farm's output, usually at this time paid in kind. In the 1740s the Church Vestry of Strabane had initiated standard cash payments in addition to payments in kind. The cash payments took into consideration the livestock kept on the farm and even gardens and turf stacks. This caused much discontent as the total outgoings from a farm could be as much as one-fifth of the rent. The farmers in the two townlands would no doubt have discussed this with other farmers when they met at the Strabane market, or at Sunday worship and especially at the May and November fairs when rents were due for payment.

Edymore

The 1756 Rent Assessment and Land Valuation Survey, hereafter called the '1756 Survey' (see Appendix 2) and the 1777 Abercorn estate map, on page 16, provide clues to the possible location of the seventeenth century farms. If the Rabb and Finlay families had been tenants of the same farms from 1666, then the Finlay farm was the first farm, on the northern boundary of Edymore and the Rabb farm was the sixth. It might also have been possible that the Nichol and Cunningham farms lay between them. The original pre-1641 farmsteads were most likely to have been in the Back Burn valley, away from the prevailing westerly winds – the O'Machry farm might have been one of them. The land on the farms located on the hillside was probably broken in after the unsettled times of the 1640s, with the houses and yards making use of a line of springs with a median around the 300ft (90m) contour line; this will be discussed later.

The 1777 estate map shows a cluster of buildings serving four farms that included the Rabb farm. Although there is only one farm there today, Ordnance Survey maps have always called this location 'Edymore', possibly because these adjacent farmsteads were located at the centre of the townland. The 1756 Survey lists two or more houses on all but one of the Edymore farms. Cottiers would have lived in those houses not occupied by the farmers' families. (Cottiers were labourers paid in kind rather than cash. The farmer provided a dwelling, a small plot of land and pasture.) No names other than those of the farmers are given in the 1756 Survey.

In some of the long-settled low-lying land in the district there were rundale holdings. These were usually farmed on a collective basis by extended families on a joint tenancy arrangement. They were often divided among the sons of a farmer, leading to uneconomical units. Such holdings had potato ground, small permanently cultivated infields, occasionally cultivated pastoral outfields, with access to mountain land for summer pasture for cattle. From the mid-1730s the estate proposed that such farms should be put into individual holdings. In 1744, the agent, John McClintock, advised the Earl to allow rundale holdings to continue for another year when access problems would be resolved.

There is no evidence that rundale holdings had existed in Edymore. The settlers, some of whom were paying hearth tax in 1666, slowly developed the land on the steep hillside into productive farmland. These farms would have been single holdings from the beginning, having the benefit of long leases. This set the pattern for the continuity of farming families in the two townlands.

Cavanalee

It is not possible to say where the farming families in Cavanalee were located in 1666 as none of the surnames of that year appear in the mid-eighteenth century records. The 1756 Survey plus the estate and Ordnance Survey maps provide some clues to where people were living before and after 1700. In Cavanalee, as in Edymore, there was a cluster of three farmsteads, located in the zone described as 'arable and grazing' on the 1710 map, which was named Cavanalee on Ordnance Survey maps up to 1951 and was situated above the Back Burn and halfway between the southern boundary of the townland and the Cavanalee River. The 1756 Survey notes houses at this location and also four more alongside the upper reaches of the Cavanalee River.

The first mention of any agricultural event in Cavanalee appears in the Abercorn Letters in July 1736. Abercorn's agent reported that: 'George McGee of Strabane impounded some of his lordship's tenants' cattle at Cavanalee grazing on land at Dergalt'. In the upper reaches of the Cavanalee River, where the Cavanalee and Dergalt townlands are on opposite sides of the river, the land is quite flat, with the river being fordable in dry seasons, so it was quite easy for cattle to cross over the river to sample new pastures. George McGee had been a burgess of the Strabane Corporation. He was deposed in 1732, but apparently continued to wield some influence in the district during the following years. He died in 1743. No other references to Cavanalee have been found for the first half of the century.

Strabane and further afield

During the latter part of the seventeenth century Strabane was still little more than a village with probably around 500/600 residents. Towards the end of the century the whole area played a part in the Williamite wars, culminating in the Siege of Derry in 1689. At that time many people of Scottish origin returned to their homeland. Strabane was torched by the retreating army of King James and the town had to be rebuilt. Did the farmers keep a low profile during this period of unrest? We have seen that the Rabb and Finlay families remained in Edymore beyond this period. It is possible that the Cunningham and Nichol families were amongst those who returned to Scotland at that time.

The rebuilding of Strabane was a slow process. By 1692 a new Church of Ireland church was being built, and in the following year a Presbyterian Meeting House was opened. Between 1695 and 1699 there was a period of famine in the southwest of Scotland. During that period into the early 1700s, many young men, with their families, came across to Ulster where they were able to obtain the tenancies of farms on the Abercorn estate. The only local example of this was a reference in the Abercorn Letters to a James Huston living in Cavanalee in 1753, who had previously farmed at Artigarvan up to 1715. He was born in 1677 in Ayrshire according to family tradition. The 1756 Survey provides the names of nine new farmers in Edymore and two in Cavanalee. As half of them had been succeeded by another member of the family, probably a son by 1777, it would seem likely that some of these families had obtained their leases by the 1720s/1730s.

The building of the Lifford bridge in 1730 made access to County Donegal much easier with greater contact possible between farmers in north Tyrone and east Donegal. In 1745 and 1746 a topic of discussion on market day or after church would have been the Jacobite rising in Scotland. Landlords were afraid that trouble would flair up in Ulster. A militia was mobilised and Abercorn's agents carried out a review of the arms held by its members. Nothing developed in Ulster, but trade was affected, especially linen. In 1752 with trading conditions improving and the expansion of the linen industry, the Strabane Corporation built a market house and brown linen hall.

3

HAND TOOLS AND ACHING BACKS
Farms and farmers from the mid-eighteenth to the mid-nineteenth century

Everyone an improver – hand tools to the fore!
The eighth Earl of Abercorn (1712–1789), after succeeding his father in 1744, initiated a programme of improvements for all parts of his extensive estates. He employed some very capable agents and surveyors who would have assessed what should or might be done to improve the farms and farming methods of that time. If successful they hoped that it would eventually be possible to increase the rental income of the estate. Surveys of farms were initiated. The 1756 Survey (Appendix 2), covering Cavanalee and Edymore, provides information on the size of the farms, condition and valuation of the land, the rent assessed, together with the names of the tenants and the number of houses.

The estate records do not describe how the farmers improved their farms. Hand-tools, such as spades (the essential tools used for breaking in land), shovels, forks, sickles, hooks and scythes were in use throughout this hundred-year period. In 1796, Robert Stephenson, a farmer and flax mill owner living near Raphoe, in a letter sent to an enthusiastic improver, John Foster, the Speaker of the Irish House of Commons, describes the use of the spade in improving the mountain land of Donegal some years previously. This would have been the method used by the farmers in Edymore and Cavanalee.

In his letter Robert Stephenson notes that 'according to the slope of the ground, ridges would have been prepared in the autumn. The farmer would trench up his ground, as if planting potatoes, turning the moss or grass to meet each other and proportioning his furrow to the breadth of the ridge. He would dig so deep in the furrow with the spade as to bring up some of the subsoil to throw on the tops of the ridges. In early spring he would place whatever manure he had on the ridges. In April oats or barley would be sown on the top of the ridges. This would be repeated in the second year with a change of the ridges and potatoes grown (on lazy beds) in the third year'. Sometimes the paring (cutting) and burning of the moss on boggy land was carried out, with the ash spread on the ridge. By changing the position of the ridges, drainage would be helped with the removal of the surface water to nearby minor watercourses, of which there were many in the two townlands.

Farmers with better naturally-drained light-land may well have used the wooden Irish ploughs and harrows. With the hilly land, often with heavy soils, in the two townlands, ploughing was unlikely to have occurred until the arrival of the metal Scotch ploughs in the nineteenth century. Harrows used for breaking up soil before seed-sowing also moved from wood to metal construction. By the middle of the nineteenth century the ridge and furrow

'Lazy bed' techniques employed to produce wide ridges on which potatoes were planted

Slipe

Slide car

Early Scotch cart

Wheel car

system had mostly gone, organised drainage systems were in place, and much of the land was cultivated by ploughs. Slide cars or slipes (wooden sledges pulled by horses) were mainly used on the higher land with wheel cars (carts) used on virtually all farms. In the nineteenth century there was an increase in the number of more substantial Scotch carts seen on the farms.

John McEvoy in his *Statistical Survey of the County of Tyrone,* published in 1802, provides a great deal of information on the farming scene in the county at that time. He was an active improver and exhorted farmers to use the latest methods. The main crops were oats, potatoes, hay from grass and on many farms, flax. All the farms in the two townlands would have kept cattle, pigs and poultry. The womenfolk on the farms would have looked after the poultry, selling the eggs and the butter they churned in the Strabane markets, a tradition which continued into the twentieth century. They would also have helped with milking the cows and with the haymaking and harvest.

Flax needs a special mention as its husbandry and harvesting remained virtually unaltered for two hundred years up to the Second World War. Flax was a greedy crop needing significant amounts of farmyard manure. The fields used for flax were usually located in the lower fields in Edymore near the water courses descending from springs, or near the Back Burn; and near the various streams in Cavanalee, where flax (lint) dams were constructed. These were usually three or four feet (about one metre) deep, of varying length and width. A great deal of effort and time was involved in harvesting the crop. The ripe flax was pulled by hand by early September, tied into small bundles (beets) and left to dry out for a few days in stooks. The dried out beets were then placed in the lint dams for upwards of two weeks. Removing the wet, heavy and stinking beets from the lint dams was probably the worst job done on any farm. The beets were then spread over nearby fields and turned occasionally to assist drying out which might take another two weeks. The flax stems would be broken in the scutch mill so that flax fibres could be separated out and prepared for spinning into linen yarn. The nearest scutch mill was at Douglas Bridge, a journey of between 3 and $5^{1}/_{2}$ miles (5 and 9 km).

Farms in Edymore to the beginning of the nineteenth century
The 1777 estate map shows a series of ladder-type farms throughout the townland. They extended from the western boundary of Edymore, at the 100ft (30m) contour, up the steep hillside to some 650 yards (600m) east of the Back Burn and up to the boundary with the Common Mountain at around the 600ft (180m) contour. It was just over a mile (1,600m) climb from the bottom to the top for five of these farms. In 1777 most of the farmhouses and yards were located on a spring line, which is at a height of 350ft (110m) at the southern boundary of the townland, falling to around 275ft (85m) towards the northern boundary. The writer dug a shallow well on this spring line (a nominal contour line joining the places where springs break out at ground level) in the early 1950s. From this spring line a number of minuscule watercourses descended to the western boundary of the townland. Some of these formed the lower boundaries of most of the ladder farms, with these boundaries, some of which survived to the

The flax plants, complete with roots, were pulled by hand – it was very hard work

Retted flax being taken from a flax dam

Scutched flax being hackled (combed) ready for spinning

end of the twentieth century, narrowing as they extended up the hillside.

All the farms in Edymore had named tenants in the 1756 Survey. We have seen that two of these farming families, Finlay and Rabb, had been living there since 1666, possibly earlier. Their farms are described in the 1756 Survey with their location shown on the 1777 map – farms Nos. 1 and 7. The Finlay family had gone by 1777, whilst the last date for a member of the Rabb family was 1816. It would seem likely that these two families had been tenants on the same land for 90 years before 1756 and that these farms or some semblance of organised farms may well have been in existence well before 1700. In addition to the minuscule watercourses there would have been plenty of stone removed from the land to form stone banks or hedged ditches.

In the 1756 Survey we see that the smallest farm was 24 acres (10 ha), whilst the largest was 103 acres (42 ha). Five of them were around 40 acres (16 ha). The Survey shows that all the farms had very little good land (best arable and pasture), usually in the range five to eight acres (2 and 3.5 ha). It was noted that all the farms were 'improvable', a difficult task as much of the land was 'cold, wet and springy'. The land was steep with small areas of 'stript bog' above the

Back Burn – land from which most or all of the peat had been extracted. Such land needed a lot of effort to farm it, let alone improve it.

Comparing the 1756 Survey and the somewhat brief information accompanying the 1777 and 1806 estate maps – see pages 16 and 17 – it can be seen that improving the land was a slow process. Most of the changes in the condition of the land seem to have taken place between 1756 and 1777, with the coarse arable land of 1756 becoming good arable by 1777. Most of the pastureland was alongside or near the Back Burn, clearly seen on the two maps. These improvements are reflected in the substantial increase in rents set in 1787, at which level they continued for fifty years. The changes between 1777 and 1806 seem to have been mainly the reclaiming of the mountain land – the steep land above the Back Burn. The maps show that there were very small areas of arable land near houses above the Back Burn, which might suggest that these were the houses of cottier families. The people living there may also have been descendants of the families who had lived there in the seventeenth century or earlier, having found that the location sheltered them from the prevailing westerly winds.

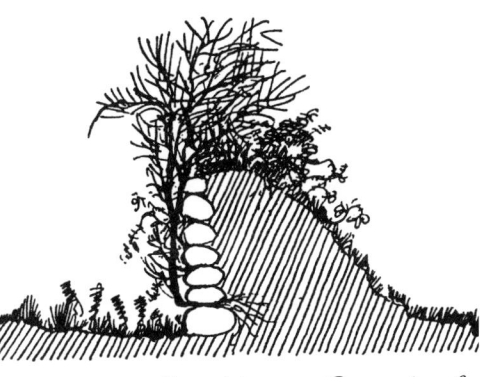

Cross section of a 'hedged ditch'

The 1806 map shows that some of the 1777 farm boundaries had been slightly altered. In one case, three farms had been created out of two farms: farms Nos. 12 (Galbraith Thompson) and 13 (George Orr) in 1777, became farms Nos. 11/12 (Nathanial Thompson), 13 (Joseph Thompson) and 14 (James Hamilton) in 1806. There were some other minor changes where short stretches of the Back Burn had been straightened.

'Buying and selling' farms and shared tenancies

Only one farm in Edymore, the Simison farm (No. 3 in 1756), was divided during the second half of the century. In 1777, we find that it had been divided between John Simison senior, and his sons, John Simison junior and Alex Simison. We will see later that Alex emigrated to America. By 1787, John Junior had taken over both Alex's and his father's farm, whilst his own farm had been 'sold', under the Ulster Custom system, to Thomas Sawyer, who was the tenant of farm No. 7, occupying higher land near to and above the Back Burn. By 1806, the original 48 acres (19 ha) had been divided in two equal parts. One half was tenanted by William Sawyer, possibly a son of Thomas Sawyer, and the other half tenanted by Joseph (1)* Davis.

Ulster Custom gave tenants an option for renewal of leases, or, on termination of leases, the right to receive from incoming tenants the value of improvements carried out by the outgoing tenant, as well as a monetary payment for the outgoing tenants' interest. The estate's agreement for such a sale had to be sought

---

* The number in brackets indicates that Joseph Davis is the first member of that family who had Joseph as his first (christian) name. Subsequent generations of all the main farming families having the same first names are indicated by (2), (3), (4) and so on.

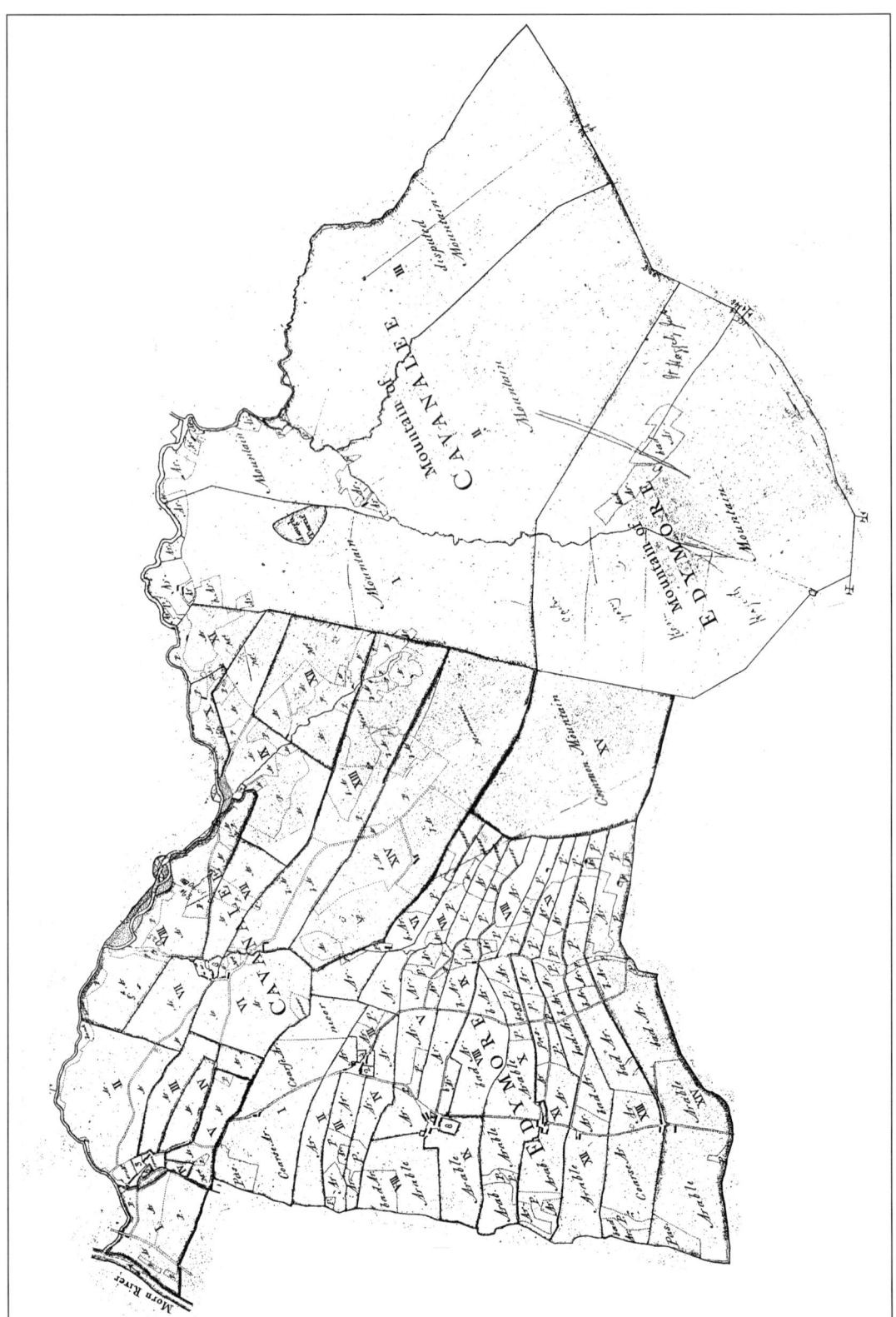

Abercorn Estate map of Edymore, Cavanalee and their 'mountains' 1777

Abercorn Estate map of Edymore, Cavanalee and their 'mountains' 1806

and it considered that the payment should be five times the annual rent. In the Strabane area it could be as much as ten years' rent. In 1778, James Hamilton in a letter to the Earl of Abercorn commented that 'every tenant thinks himself as secure as to title as if he had a fee farm' – tenants acted as though they owned the farms they occupied. Another 125 years would pass before this became reality.

Only one example in Edymore was found in the Abercorn Letters. This was the purchase of William Stilly's farm by John (1) Fulton in December 1816. For the last quarter of the eighteenth century the tenant of this farm had been John Rabb junior. In 1806, it was then a joint tenancy – John Rabb junior and William Stilly. By 1806, John Rabb junior would have been getting on in years and by sharing his farm he would have lessened his workload. When John Rabb junior died William Stilly probably found that he did not have sufficient cash to pay the debts incurred by John Rabb and himself. By selling (assigning) the lease he would have been able to pay these and possibly have a surplus to enable him to move to a smaller farm. The rent in 1806 was £20.60. John (1) Fulton paid £240 in December 1816 to obtain the tenancy with a 21 year lease. This was almost twelve times the rent paid by William Stilly. John Fulton found that he would have to pay an annual rent of £27.30, an increase of over 30%. This increase reflects the inflation that occurred during and immediately after the Napoleonic Wars, which ended in 1815.

Another problem facing farmers was highlighted when John Rabb junior's father died in 1782. Abercorn's agent reports that 'John Rabb of Edimore is dead he left but one child a son who has a holding in Edimore. His widow is very old and poor – she consents to sell'. No doubt she went to live with her son. A young man, Robert Wilson, who had come from the Castlederg district, purchased the farm, presumably in 1782 – his family features in the next chapter. Robert Wilson's neighbours were Widow Brown and her son William Brown, noted as joint tenants. In 1787, after the death of his mother, William Brown entered into a joint tenancy with Robert Wilson, an arrangement that continued to the end of the century.

During the latter part of the eighteenth century other farms had shared tenancies. After the death of her husband, Widow Knox and her son William became joint tenants. By 1787, William's mother had died and he shared the farm with his brother Alex. William paid 60% of the rent and Alex the rest – had they divided the farm in that proportion, farming each part separately? At the end of the century we find Alex, Ezekiel and George sharing the tenancy. No information was given regarding the relationship of Ezekiel and George with William or with Alex, or whether they farmed the whole of the farm as a complete unit.

From 1756 until at least 1777 Samuel Gillilan and William Lowther also shared the tenancy of a farm. By 1787 William Lowther was the sole tenant; Samuel Gillilan had probably died. In 1806, we find that William Lowther had joined forces with his near (but not adjacent) neighbour of some thirty years, James Porter. A similar case could have been that of the tenancy shared by George Orr and Galbraith Thompson noted in 1787. Thompson was also the sole tenant of the neighbouring farm; after his death in 1795 it would seem that this was the time when the two farms were reorganised and made into three farms as described earlier.

Farms in Cavanalee to the beginning of the nineteenth century

Only three farms with named tenants in Cavanalee are described in the 1756 Survey, located at the lower western end of the townland, with its boundary the River Mourne, on the naturally well-drained drumlin-type gravelly and sandy hills, sometimes with boggy areas at their base, lying between the Cavanalee River and steep hillside of Edymore. These farms all had a high percentage of good land. The three tenants were The Miller, John Barnhill (see below) and Thomas Graham. It would seem that in 1756 the Mill Pond (see later) was not watertight. This affected the nearby land tenanted by The Miller and John Barnhill. Thomas Graham also had a problem with his 'steep oak bank' alongside the river. The surveyor observed that it is 'precipitous and ought to be inclosed as it occasions the loss of some cattle to the Tenants'. This is the first and only mention of enclosure in the two townlands found in the Abercorn Papers. It is interesting to see that oak trees were growing along the steep bank, beside the river. These trees belonged to the estate and Thomas Graham would have had to pay the estate for any mature trees he wished to use for construction purposes on his farm. The 1806 map shows that alongside the Graham farmstead there was a large orchard. The 1833 Ordnance Survey map shows that there were extensive orchards around Strabane.

The 1777 map shows that Abercorn's agent, James Hamilton, proposed to divide the rest of the townland into a number of farms. From the 1756 Survey we see that the best land, with six houses, was in Upper North Cavanalee within the 'arable and grazing' zone shown on the 1710 estate map. On the 1777 and 1806 estate maps this cluster of houses was centred on what the Ordnance Survey continued to name Cavanalee up to 1951. The 1756 Survey also lists houses adjacent to the middle course of the Cavanalee River. They were somewhat isolated and no doubt hard to reach. The 1777 map shows that they were located between a quarter and half a mile (400m–800m) from the nearest tracks. In view of their remoteness they may not have featured in the estate records at that time.

Hamilton had decided to establish farms with defined boundaries where none had existed before, and to agree leases with the prospective tenants. The 1777 map also shows that many of these new boundaries did not follow natural features and it is not known what form the boundaries took. It is most likely that they were stone-faced banks of sods in the side of which quick-thorn is planted – the 'hedged ditches' which have been widely used during the last two centuries.

From the Abercorn Letters we see that there was already an occupant on one of these apparently new farms. James (1) Huston was a tenant in Cavanalee in 1753 (see later). By comparing the 1777 map and the 1787 rental, we find that he had been allocated a farm in the Upper South Division in the 1756 Survey. This was the largest farm in the townland, 110 acres (46 ha). On this farm there were 18 acres (7 ha) of arable land: 'about three-quarters of this is tolerable, the rest a very wet mossy indifferent sort of land perishing the seed and not ripening properly'. 47 acres (19 ha) of 'Bogg & heathy pasture' contained 11 acres (4.5 ha) of 'uncut Turf bog, the rest is mostly stript & barren'. This farm, like most of the others, was 'very improvable', and they all had uncut turf bogs. A great deal of hard work faced the Huston family when attempting to improve their farm.

Cavanalee also had a farm that was divided amongst three members of the same family. In 1756, James Barnhill had a 43 acre (17 ha) farm, which by 1777 had been equally divided between James, John and Joseph Barnhill. Their relationship to each other is not known. By 1787, the three farms had become two equal sized farms, with only John Barnhill on one of them. James Weir and James Hunter farmed the other in partnership. James Hunter was the sole tenant in 1806. James Barnhill succeeded John Barnhill with this family continuing into the twentieth century. Some of the new regularly shaped farms shown on the 1777 map had been radically reorganised by 1806. Farms No. 7, 8, 9 and 12 in 1777 became No. 6, 7, 8, 11 and 11a in 1806, with differing boundaries. No reason for this was found.

The turn of the century – roads, tracks and planning the future

A major event affected Cavanalee at this time. This was the construction of the Strabane to Plumbridge road. Although the precise date is not known, the new road is clearly shown on the 1806 estate map on page 17. The Cavanalee Bridge was built at the first easy crossing place above the lower gorge-like stretch of the river. The road then passed through the upper part of the townland, through the gap between the Meenashesk and Koram hills, descending to Ligfordrum crossing the Douglas Burn on its way to Plumbridge. The farmers in the middle and upper parts of Cavanalee then benefited from a shorter journey to Strabane and on a better road. On the other hand they would, and did, have less contact with farmers in the lower part of Cavanalee and Edymore.

Before 1800 there had been only one way to reach the two townlands from Strabane. Half a mile (0.8 km) after leaving the town on the then Strabane to Douglas Bridge road (now the B72 Strabane to Victoria Bridge road – Victoria Bridge was a nineteenth century creation) all the farmers and their families would have turned left at the bridge over the Cavanalee River. 250 yards (225 m) along this road there was (and still is) a choice of roads – turn left for Cavanalee and right for Edymore. A steep climb was (and still is) then required to reach both townlands, which were difficult to negotiate before the appearance of cars and tractors.

On the 1806 estate maps a number of proposed changes were pencilled in by the agent or his surveyors. The most significant was the proposal for a new road through Edymore. Until that time the roads went from farm to farm. After the first steep rise to the Davis farm the road then divided, one branch going to the farms on the spring line leading to the lower part of Carrigullin townland, and the other wending its way towards the upper part of Carrigullin. The proposed new road started at the lower northern townland boundary of Edymore, going directly to the Fulton farmstead, connecting with the lower road to Carrigullin following a straight line to upper Carrigullin. In effect it was the line of the present road named by the GPO as the Carrigullin Road. This road is shown on the 1833 map on page 28.

In Cavanalee townland we can see that until 1806 there were two roads going from the farms at the western end of the townland to the central group of farms. From there one road went to the southeastern tip of the townland, whilst another went towards the farmsteads near the new Cavanalee Bridge. A short length of new road connected them with the new Strabane to Plumbridge road. With the exception of the road going from the centre of Cavanalee to the southeastern tip of the townland, all had disappeared by 1833. The roads that replaced them, shown on the 1833 map, survived, with minor alterations, right through to the end of the twentieth century.

The estate maps show two tracks in Edymore that climbed the steep land above the Back Burn providing access to the Common Mountain. However the maps also show that most of the houses on each side of the Back Burn had no tracks in their immediate vicinity. Lower down the hill two tracks which survived until the latter half of the twentieth century had been constructed by using large stones as a base, over which were placed smaller stones and gravel. Often the top layer got washed away after heavy rain but it was easily replaced as there were gravel pits in both townlands.

No tracks to any of the houses in Cavanalee and Edymore Mountain are shown on the 1777 map. Without tracks the development of the Edymore and Cavanalee Mountain land would be a bigger problem. The map does show pencilled lines for proposed roads/tracks, land divisions and names of proposed tenants. By 1806 the houses were all accessible by tracks leading to the new Strabane to Plumbridge road. The two houses on Edymore Mountain also had a track access to the Strabane to Plumbridge road.

Edymore and Cavanalee Mountains 1745 to 1855

The first mention of Edymore Mountain, in the eighteenth century, is in the Abercorn Letters where in March 1745 it is noted that William Starrat, Abercorn's surveyor, had 'separated Edymore Mountain from the farm it first belonged to' – no further details are given. A letter of 30 March in the following year notes that 'Edymore Mountain set at £2'. Two months later the agent changed his mind: 'Thought better to keep it waste. Strabane folk get turf (peat) from it'. To win turf (cut, dry, stack and then transport the peat) was a time consuming task. Strabane was over 3 miles (5 km) from Edymore Mountain, which could be reached only by steep tracks. At that time there were peat bogs within two miles of the town, but their exploitation may have been commercially organised. Anyone with a donkey could have filled panniers for bringing their peat from the mountain, another arduous task. However, Edymore Mountain does not feature in the 1756 Survey. Not until 1777 was there a tenant on Edymore Mountain, Roger McColgan. On the 1777 map Abercorn's agent had pencilled in the names of possible tenants. In the 1787 rental one of these, Patrick Haggarty, was listed as the sole tenant and had two small areas of low quality arable land alongside his house.

A letter to the Earl of Abercorn dated 24 February 1767 records that 'Edymore and Carrigullin mountain [was] let to Houstons for seven years in 1765'. There were four Huston families in Cavanalee at that time, but none in Edymore and

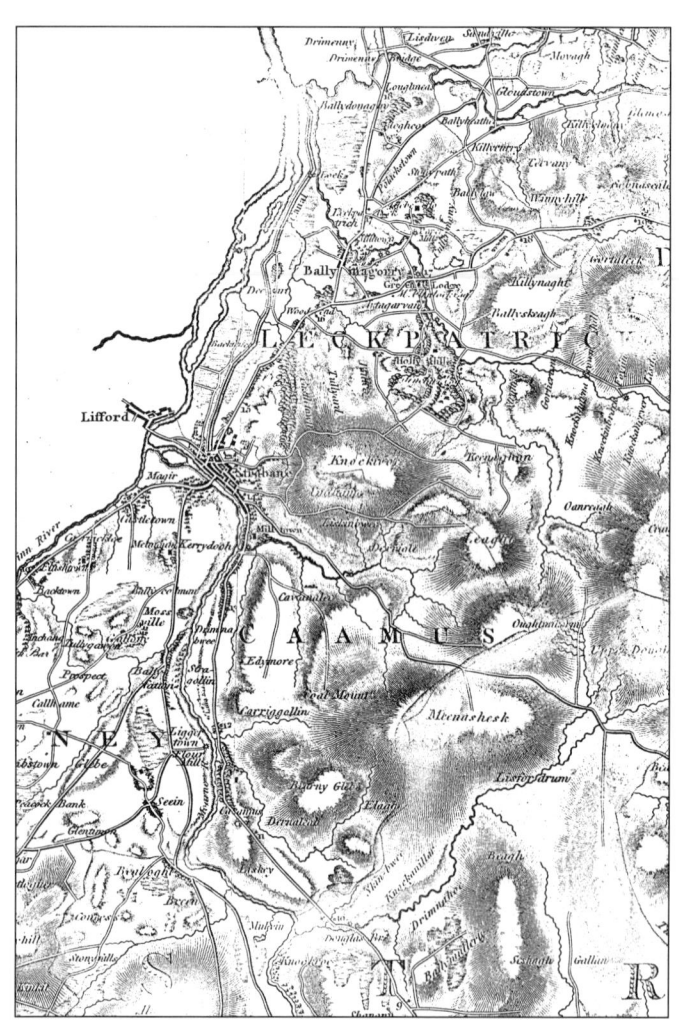

Extract from the County Tyrone map by McCrea and Knox 1813. This map shows a growing Strabane, the Canal and the network of roads in the district at the beginning of the nineteenth century. A star symbol shows the location of mills. The Strabane Mill is on the Milltown side of the Cavanalee River.

Carrigullin. The Huston farm, which abutted Cavanalee Mountain, was that of James (2) Huston. Two years later on 23 June 1769, James Hamilton informed Abercorn: 'I examined the roads to Cavanalee and Edymore mountains, they are convenient enough for tenants to draw turf on slide carrs, which and driving their cattle are the only uses they are to them, if people from this place were to bring their turf from thence, a road for wheel carrs, and pulling down a hill or two would be necessary, but I think it would be best that this bog was first all taken'. Slide cars (slipes) were the usual means by which farmers moved the dried turf (peat) down to their farmhouses. The wheel car (carts) with two solid wheels ideally needed a track that was not beset with ruts that always developed when slide cars were used for any period of time – illustrated on page 11.

Cavanalee Mountain was recorded as extending to 440 acres (180 ha) in 1756. Virtually the whole area was noted as bog and heathy pasture. On higher land overlooking the upper part of the Cavanalee River there was a small five acre (two ha) lough, known as Lough Terrif. Some attempt had been made to drain this lough over the years, resulting in it being shown as a swampy marsh on the 1833 map and fields on the 1854 map – see pages 28 and 29.

The first reference to the tenants on Cavanalee Mountain occurs in October 1765: 'Edward Dooher has that part of Cavanalee Mountain that John Haggerty had … [he] has liberty to get turf'. In March 1767: 'Edward Dooher holds that part with McNamee which John Haggerty had, in Cavanalee'. In 1777 D. McNamee with 157 acres (64 ha) and Mathew and Edward Dooher with 283 acres (115 ha) are named as the tenants. However, a large area of the Mountain was grazed in common with the tenants of the neighbouring landowner. In 1756, this had been Mr McGhee, and at the end of the century, Mr Spotiswood. Reference is made to the 'disputed mountain' on both the 1777 and 1806 maps, with the latter showing the 'New Line of Mearing' (boundary) as well as the precise measurement of the area involved: 60 acres 2 roods 38 perches (98 ha) and 64 acres 0 roods 0 perches (104 ha). The total area for Cavanalee Mountain then became 331 acres (134 ha). The new boundary was agreed with Mr Spotiswood by John James Burgoyne for the Abercorn estate. Various calculations appear on the margins of the original maps – their significance is not evident.

The 1806 map also shows the location of the farms of the then tenants, John McNamee and partners, William Lyon and Patrick Haggarty (also the sole tenant of Edymore Mountain) and Mathew Dooher and partners, with the latter tenants of 70 per cent of the mountain land. There are a few solid lines on the 1806 map, which might suggest that boundaries were being defined by ditches.

The proposed farms pencilled on the 1806 map for Edymore Mountain had not materialised by the 1830s. Patrick Haggarty was still the sole tenant in 1838. We see that only 16 acres (6.5 ha) out of 324 acres (130 ha) were designated as 'reclaimed arable' in 1833, with the rest 'heathy mountain pasture'. By the 1850s there were five farms but each of them only had a few small fields.

There are some small fields shown on the 1833 map near the Cavanalee River. In the valuation survey they are described as being 'moory arable' or 'reclaimed mountain moory arable'. The rest of the mountain land was still 'heathy mountain'. The five farms of the 1830s had become ten farms by 1854, with those alongside the river having a number of small fields near them. The rent of the largest farm (71 acres (29 ha)) on Cavanalee Mountain, tenanted by John and Denis McNamee, was £7.50 in 1806. It had risen to £8.30 in 1838 and to £9.40 in 1846, increasing by another 23p after drainage work was carried out two years later. In fifty years the rent had changed from 10p per acre (25p per ha) to 14p per acre (35p per ha). In 1848 the rent of a similar sized farm in the lower part of Cavanalee was then 85p per acre (£2.13 per ha). No information on the rents of other farms on the Mountain land was found.

Farms in Edymore and Cavanalee during the first half of the nineteenth century

During this period, in both townlands, the Abercorn Papers show that there were very few changes in the sizes of the farms or the continuity of families on them. The farmers noted in 1756, 1777, 1787, 1806 and 1827 are listed in Appendix 10. The rents set in 1787 continued until new and higher rents were set in 1838. These continued at this level until 1858 – see Appendix 11. During this period enclosure (the division of land into individual fields with permanent boundaries) continued apace. Unfortunately the 1833 Ordnance Survey maps did not map all the fields, only those at the margin of townlands – see page 28. 'Ticks' placed alongside roads or townland boundaries indicated the position of the ditches (field boundaries) at that point. By extending these 'ticks' on the map it is seen that a substantial network of fields was then in existence – enclosure was well advanced.

Townland Valuation of 1833

A significant assessment of the natural environment of the townlands resulted from the Townland Valuation of 1833. Surveyors visited both townlands in May, spending five days in Cavanalee and two days in Edymore recording the differing categories of land in great detail. Both the topsoil and subsoil are described for 26 areas in Cavanalee and 15 in Edymore, together with a valuation for each area.

The new Ordnance Survey maps were used to record this information. The descriptions are quite detailed. One example for an area near the lower reaches of the Cavanalee River reads: 'Arable. $1/4$ superior flat soil. $3/4$ moory arable and reclaimed bog, white gravel subsoil'. Another example from an area on the steep Edymore hillside reads: 'Free arable soil. $2/3$ moderately deep $1/3$ shallow cold and wet, half the lot very steep'. The Land Description and Valuation Survey are given in Appendix 3, and the accompanying map in Appendix 4.

The condition of the land in 1833/8 compared with that in 1756

The information contained in the 1833 Townland Valuation can be compared with that given in the 1756 Survey. The surveyors would have assessed the quality of the land in accordance with the normal practice for each period, separated by eighty years. It is possible therefore to obtain some idea of the changes that had taken place during this period.

Four farms, two in each townland, have been considered – two on the higher land and two on the lower land. The lower farm in Cavanalee in 1833–8 had been two farms in 1756. The land description and the rents for each farm have been included, which demonstrate the effect of improvement and inflation during the first quarter of the nineteenth century. The comparisons are shown in Table 3 opposite. They highlight how the land quality had changed as a result of the hard work undertaken over three/four generations. The farms selected had varying types of terrain which is reflected in the wide differences in the levels of rent. The first farm in Edymore did not have any high land, whereas the second was a typical ladder-type farm. The two farms in Cavanalee show the contrast between a farm on high land newly-developed since 1756, and the most fertile of the lower farms located alongside the river which attracted the highest rent of all the farms in the two townlands. The rent for this farm was 85p per acre (£2.10 per ha). At the same time tenants of farms on the Abercorn estate in the parish of Ardstraw, alongside the river Derg, were paying £1 per acre (£2.50 per ha).

The new agent

Another significant event also took place in 1833 when Abercorn's new agent Major John Humphreys came to live in what the Ordnance Survey called Milltown Lodge. The small townland of Milltown (29 acres (12 ha)) lies on the northern bank of the Cavanalee River, where the latter joins the River Mourne. When a new house was built nearby shortly afterwards it was called Milltown House, which is now part of the Strabane Grammar School. After his arrival at Strabane Major Humphreys found a substantial amount of rent payments

Major John Humphreys

EDYMORE

1756 Farm 4 – Samuel Gilliland and William Lowther 37 acres Rent £6.70 (16p per acre)
5a best arable is mostly good land @ 7s 5d
24a coarse arable & best pasture is a little cold & wet in some places, in other light and mossy @ 3s 8d
5a mixt pasture is tolerable good heathy and misky pasture @ 1s 10d
3a stript bog is very barren – no value (Though the whole is improvable)

1833/8 Farm 4 – William Aiken 34 acres Rent £20.12 (59p per acre)
21a moory arable rather light, mod depth, $1/3$ a little exposed, white yellow sandy gravel subsoil @ 12s 6d
3a free light arable part moory, moderate depth @ 14s 0d
7a rocky steep pasture and reclaimed boggy arable @ 6s 0d
2a reclaimed bog and moory arable, rather shallow, yellow and white sandy subsoil @ 7s 6d
3a reclaimed mountain inferior arable, shallow with white sandy gravel subsoil @ 4s 6d

1756 Farm 7 – John Rabb 42 acres Rent £8.04 (19p per acre)
6a best arable and meadow @ 12s 0d
26a coarser arable and best pasture @ 6s 0d
7a mixt pasture @ 4s 0d
3a stript bog – no value

1833/8 Farm 10 – Robert Wilson 41 acres Rent £27.18 (66p per acre)
15a free arable soil $2/3$ moderately deep $1/3$ shallow cold and wet, half the lot very steep @ 12s 6d
12a moory arable moderate depth dry and well situated @ 13s 0d
8a inferior light shallow moory arable @ 9s 0d
7a reclaimed bog and moory arable, rather shallow, yellow and white gravel subsoil @ 7s 6d

CAVANALEE

1756 Farms 1 & 2 – 'The Miller' and Thomas Graham 71 acres Rent £19.06 (27p per acre)
1. 10a best arable is tolerable good land but a little shallow and gravely @ 6s 10d
11a coarse arable/green pasture is very wet and shallow & also rocky & shrubby in some places @ 3s 8d
7a bog & misky pasture very wet & deep of brittle moss & the mill pond prevents improvement @ 1s 3d
2. 41a arable is sharp kindly ground but very steep, shallow, sandy & gravely in many places @ 6s 10d
2a steep oak bank is precipitous and ought to be enclosed – no value

1833 Farm 2 – Galbraith Lowther 71 acres Rent £60.35 (85p per acre)
7a $1/2$ arable, shallow gravely part steep sand and gravel subsoil, $1/2$ a cold wet clay and sandy soil liable to flood @ 14s 0d
18a arable. $1/4$ superior flat soil. $3/4$ moory arable/reclaimed bog, white gravel subsoil @ 18s 0d
9a free arable moderate depth interspersed with some small steep hills @ 22s 0d
7a uneven arable soil, steep and of moderate depth @ 16s 0d
19a free arable soil sound and moderate depth, a little very steep, yellow gravel subsoil @ 21s 0d
3a very steep arable @ 8s 0d plus 3a banks and furzy pasture @ 1s 0d
5a free arable soil of good depth and undulating surface @ 21s 0d

1756 Farm 5 – James Huston 110 acres Rent £8.22 (8p per acre)
18a arable. $3/4$ tolerable, $1/4$ very wet mossy land perishing the seed and not ripening properly @ 4s 0d
46a mixt pasture is wet misky green and heathy @ 1s 10d
46a bog and heathy pasture mostly stript and barren with 7a uncut turf bog @ $1^{1}/4$d

1833 Farm 14 – Andrew and Thomas Huston 111 acres Rent £45.98 (41p per acre)
25a arable. $2/3$ moory of moderate depth gravel subsoil. $1/3$ a free shallow arable @ 14s 0d
18a reclaimed bog @ 7s 6d. Plus 3a free arable @ 13s 0d and 2a of bog and steep banks @ 6d
32a moory arable $1/4$ superior quality, remainder light moderate depth @ 11s 0d
12a moory arable a little steep, moderate depth, white gravel subsoil @ 9s 0d
23a heathy mountain producing some pasture @ 7s 0d

(All areas are given in statute acres)

Table 3. Land descriptions and rents obtained from the 1756 Survey, the 1833 Valuation and the 1838 Estate Rental

outstanding throughout the estate. He would have looked at both the 1833 Valuation of Land data and Ordnance Survey maps, and consulted the estate's surveyors before preparing new leases. In 1835 seven farms in Cavanalee and ten farms in Edymore were given new leases – see Appendix 11. In each case the new rents were virtually the same or fractionally higher than those set in 1806 for farms in the district. In part, the increases in the rents took into account the effect of inflation that had resulted from the Napoleonic Wars.

Tenancy agreements
Tenancy agreements were lengthy documents. The rights reserved to the landlord, including the building of roads through the farm, the planting of timber and the diversion of streams were set out. The term or length of the lease, rent payable and payment of duties were detailed. Primarily, tenants had to maintain the property, but if they built a new cabin their rent would be increased by £5. Tenants had to grind all grain at appointed mills or pay 5s 0d (25p) in lieu. They could not dispose of any manure and had to obtain permission to cut turf (peat), and would have to pay a fine of 10s 0d (50p) if permission had not been obtained in advance. Tenants could not dispose of the farm without permission. The leases, dated 31 January 1835, were to apply from the November 1834 Fair Day.

Only one case of a tenant being unable to pay the rent of the farm came to light in the rentals for Edymore. In both 1848 and 1849 the rent books show that Margaret Porter on farm No. 5 was given notice to quit. It was the estate's policy not to serve the notice to quit until four years' rent was due. This is confirmed as in this case the tenancy did not pass to Robert (1) Davis until 1852. Mrs Porter had been widowed in the early 1840s and possibly did not have any family members to help run the farm. With Major Humphreys living less than half a mile (0.8 km) away at Milltown House he would have had firsthand knowledge of the family circumstances.

Tithes
The tithes set out in the Tithe Applotment Book of 1827 and those shown in the Estate Rentals of 1838 are shown in Appendices 10 and 11. The tithes set for 1838 were, in most cases, slightly higher than those listed for 1827. The compilation of the amount to be paid was based on an assessment of the quality of the land. The same terms as those given in the 1806 assessments were used: ordinary arable, middling arable, moory pasture, etc. Land which had been noticeably improved since 1806 was separately itemised. Three farmers in Edymore and two in Cavanalee who had made some improvements on their farms since 1806 had to pay more than those farmers whose farms had changed little. In 1838, the new Tithe Rentcharge Act converted the tithe into a charge on land which the Abercorn estate passed on to their tenants as an additional charge, payable along with the rent.

The 1827 Tithe Applotment return gives the first indication that the proposed division of the Edymore Common Mountain shown on the 1806 map had started. Owen Conway was the tenant of the northernmost farm of some 20 acres

(8 ha) where his descendants still farmed in 2000. It must have been difficult to find tenants for the three other proposed farms, as they were not tenanted until after 1838.

Progress away from the farms
The 1833 and 1854 Ordnance Survey maps, on pages 28 and 29, show that progress had been made on a number of fronts, including enclosure. There were limestone quarries in the district and small pot limekilns on some farms, four in Cavanalee and ten in Edymore. Nearly all of these were on the higher farms and nearest to the limestone quarries. They had easy access to fuel – turf (peat) banks were probably within yards in many cases. The Cavanalee farms drew their limestone from a small quarry not far from Conthem Hill in Edymore, via a track that descended from the quarry directly to the upper farms of Cavanalee. Most of this track had been pencilled in on the 1806 map. The Edymore farms drew their limestone from a large quarry situated in the highest part of the neighbouring townland of Carrigullin. From that quarry there were tracks leading to the higher farms in Edymore townland. This quarry was referred to in the Abercorn Letters in 1775.

The presence of a corn kiln near the farmyards of the brothers Robert and John Wilson in Edymore is noteworthy as there were only two other corn kilns within three miles. Corn kilns were used to dry grain before grinding and again fuel would have been readily available. Farmers could obtain slates for roofing buildings from a small slate quarry in Edymore. There were two small gravel quarries in Cavanalee and similar quarries were to be found in neighbouring townlands. All these are also shown on the 1833 map. No information has been found to chart progress and change between 1838 and the 1850s other than that provided by the estate rental books. There were no increases in rents during this period other than an increase made to underwrite the cost of drainage schemes on nine farms around 1848. These are noted on the table in Appendix 11. These charges, which in most cases only added about a pound to the rent, continued until the next rent review in 1858. When tracks were being dug for new tiled drains in the 1950s on the farm then tenanted in 1848 by Robert Wilson, the original stone drains were found to be working well.

The Ordnance Survey undertook a revision of the 1833 map in 1854. This showed that every farm had by then a network of fields – the process of enclosure had been completed. The majority of the fields were between five acres (2 ha) and eight acres (3.25 ha) in size. However there were some quite small fields, especially in the upper parts of the Edymore 'ladder farms', some there as small as one acre (0.4 ha). Since 1833 more limekilns had been built. There were fourteen in Edymore and eight in Cavanalee, with a few of them at differing locations compared with 1833. The two limestone quarries were a little larger. The Wilson brothers' corn kiln was still in existence.

Where was the Mill?
The Strabane Mill dates from Plantation times, having been built by 1611. The estate rent books always included the mill as being in Cavanalee until 1876. As a

Ordnance Survey map of Edymore and Cavanalee 1834 edition – surveyed in 1833

Ordnance Survey map of Edymore and Cavanalee 1855 edition – surveyed in 1854

result it could quite easily be assumed that the mill was to be found on the Cavanalee side of the Cavanalee River. No mill is featured on the 1710, 1777 or 1806 maps. The 1710 map shows a defined area of almost 18 acres (7 ha) as mill land and 6½ acres (2.5 ha) of moss, the latter located at the mill-pond. However, the 1777 and 1806 maps do not show a mill on the Cavanalee side of the Cavanalee River – the mill-pond is clearly shown. The area of land, named on the opposite side of the Cavanalee River from the Miller's farm, shown on the 1777 map, was called Drimrallagh – noted earlier as a sessiagh in the ballyboe (townland) of Liskinbwee. This same area of land was called Milltown on the 1806 map. Both the 1833 and 1854 maps show the location of a corn mill on the Milltown side of the Cavanalee River.

The size of the mill-pond was one third of an acre (0.15 ha). The mill-stream feeding the mill-pond ran for almost one and a half miles (2.5 km) parallel to the western boundary of Edymore and within 50 to 250 yards (45 to 225 m) of it in Drumnaboy townland. The mill-stream, using a long length of the Carrigullin Burn, was man-made in parts, displaying quite a feat of engineering for the seventeenth century and it drew on the many small watercourses that came down the hill in both Edymore and Carrigullin. It may have been improved over time.

The only stretch of level land alongside the Cavanalee River between the mill-pond and the road bridge on which a mill could be built is on the northern (Milltown) bank. The water in the mill-pond would have had to be taken across the river by an aqueduct and then in a man-made channel down to the mill about one hundred yards (100m) downstream. This aqueduct is shown on the 1806 map.

The 1756 Survey indicates that the Miller paid a rent of £5.38 for his farm and mill. The table, in Appendix 10, giving details about the farms in 1777 also refers to 'The Miller'. In the 1787 rental, we find 'The Miller' is named as Thomas Lowther, the son of Widow Lowther. The rent for his farm and the mill was £62, taking into account the income the mill generated. In July 1770 Thomas Lowther had discussed the condition of the mill with the agent, James Hamilton. He, in turn, had written to the Earl of Abercorn that in view of 'the dilapidated state of the present mill of Strabane I suggest that it be rebuilt … and that it's very much better that a house in which grain is stored should be built of lime … Thomas Lowther the tenant was pointing out that the rats ran through the thatch and was wishing it slated'. Within three weeks James Hamilton had entered into a contract for rebuilding the mill. It would be '60ft x 20ft (18m x 6m) in the clear' and '8ft (2.5m) at the lowest in the side wall'. The roof was thatched, as the agent felt that it would cost too much to use slates. The total cost was £37 9s 6d (£37.48). A slated roof would have added another £65 – so Thomas Lowther did not get his slate roof. There is no indication of the precise location of this new building.

At the same time as the mill was being rebuilt Thomas Lowther had complained to the agent 'that the brewers which used to grind with him and pay 1s 1d (5p) a sack (of 20 stone, 130kg) for malt are going to Ballymagorry (3 miles, 5 km, north of Strabane) and getting it done for 6½d (2½p)'. James Hamilton told Thomas Lowther that he would have to accept this lower price, but he also told the brewers that they would have to use only the Strabane mill, threatening them with a lawsuit if they went elsewhere.

Ten years later the agent advises Abercorn that 'not so much malt is distilled in this town as used to be, not a fifth part of it, owing to the strictness of the excise officers; … the excise duty is much reduced in this town of late'. To add to this, soldiers were sent to the district in 1782 in an effort to stamp out illicit distilling. Fifty years later a few still-houses are marked and named on the 1833 map in two townlands to the east of Cavanalee, so the making of poteen continued in remote areas for a considerable period of time.

Things had gone from bad to worse where the operation of the mill was concerned as the agent, in 1781, had reported that 'Widow Lowther who holds Strabane mill used to pay her rent very punctually, but she now owes two years' rent, £125. The demand for malt had previously brought her a great deal, but the consumption of that here is very little, none but beer. There is not a still working in this town; the late act silenced them all. There used to be eleven stills in the town. They were reduced to three about three years ago'. Because of this crackdown and even with a new mill, Thomas Lowther, and later his widow, had found life difficult in the late 1770s. However, by 1787, his family had been able to pay off the debt.

In the Abercorn Letters for November 1808 we read that 'David Smyly who holds the Strabane Mill paid up his rent to the hour'. James Hamilton, the agent, commented that 'he is a wealthy industrious man and no favourite of mine'. Apparently David Smyly had promised to transfer his lease of the mill to James Barnhill (farm No. 4 in Cavanalee) when he gave it up. James Hamilton referred to this in two letters. In the first, dated January 1809, he wrote 'Lowther got the Strabane mill for 85 gns [guineas] [£96.69*] instead of Barnhill who had been promised it by Smyly'. In March 1809, he wrote 'Barnhill has given up the quit possession of Strabane Mill to Tom Lowther. To my certain knowledge the Barnhills meant nothing in the slightest degree wrong in the entire transaction. They are an honest industrious family, much respected by their neighbours and they would and could have paid a higher rent for it than anybody else but between hands they have suffered a loss of above £50 and much time and anxiety'. Perhaps James Hamilton's comments of the previous year were right. It is not clear why and when David Smyly became the tenant of the Mill. Unfortunately no further information regarding the mill was found in the Abercorn Letters.

In 1858, the rent for the mill was £20 and the Griffith's Valuation £25. Galbraith Lowther died in the early 1870s and was succeeded by George Doherty in 1876 who is listed as a miller in the 1879 *Slater's Directory*. The mill seems to have closed down shortly afterwards. The 1905 map shows only the outline of the mill buildings – it had become a ruin by then, a sad end to a piece of Plantation history.

---

* The Irish guinea was equivalent to 22s 9d (£1.14) until the currency was amalgamated in 1826

The Miller's farm and Major Humphrey's daughter

Major Humphrey's daughter, Fanny, is better known as Mrs Cecil Frances Alexander (1818–95), the well-known writer of hymns. She lived at Milltown House from 1833 until she married in 1850. She wrote many poems and one of these describes the Miller's farm which she could see (and hear) immediately below the grounds of Milltown House, on the opposite bank of the Cavanalee River. Although this poem, The Farmyard, was published after her marriage when she was living at Derg Lodge, near Killeter, some 5 miles (8 km) southwest of Castlederg, its geographic references fit a Milltown location. From the grounds of Milltown House one sees a ring of hills within a distance of 1¼ – 2 miles (2 – 3.25 km) and all rising above 800ft (250m). Referring to the 1833 and 1854 maps and following a visit to the Killeter district, it is clear that there are no nearby hill tops which fit the scene set in the poem given below – it describes one of the best farms in Cavanalee townland. This poem with its rural setting was one of the many learnt by generations of schoolchildren in County Tyrone.

Cecil Frances Alexander

The Farmyard

Lo, the sun is o'er the hill top,
Lo, the morning breaketh clear;
Merry sounds of mirth and laughter
Waken in the farmyard near.

There the cock sits on the barn door,
Crowing merrily and loud;
While his crimson feathers glitter,
As he shakes his pinions proud.

And the brown hen walks below him,
Picking grains up from the floor;
Bring the fresh egg, bring it quickly,
From her nest behind the door.

There the thresher bids good morrow,
Leaning on his ready flail,
To the milkmaid, as she cometh,
Poising on her head the pail.

By the dun cow meek, and quiet,
She has set her stool so low,
And she sings a gentle measure
As she makes the white milk flow;

Which the sweetly breathing creatures,
Standing patient, love to hear,
Never lift the foot in anger
Never shrink aside in fear.

With his spade across his shoulder,
To the field the workman goes,
While the watchdog, *his* work over,
Seeks the hayloft for repose.

There, I see the horses harnessed
Waiting by the empty cart;
All are cheerful, all are ready,
And a thought thrills through my heart.

'Tis the idle that grow weary,
Gaily rings each busy sound;
'Tis a pleasure to be active;
There's a joy in labour found.

And I feel my blood run freer,
And I own it kind, and good,
That to man the law was given;
He must work to win his food.

Famines – population rise and fall
Whilst the Great Famine of 1845–7 is well recorded there had been periods of poor weather throughout Ireland leading to food shortages, even famine conditions, during the previous hundred years in the Strabane district. There was a three-year period of severe weather 1770–3 leading to famine conditions and an outbreak of fever, with 'the greatest flood on the Mourne ever remembered' in January 1772. There was another poor harvest in 1777 leading to scarcity of food in the following year. In March 1782 there was 'the greatest flood ever remembered', with food shortages the following year. Another poor harvest in 1799 led to food shortages in 1800. In 1808 there was yet another period of food scarcity following the bad harvest in the previous year which had been followed by severe winter weather.

Worse was to come in 1816 following harvest failure, which included the potato crop in many parts, and the inability to save the turf (peat) for winter fuel. A disease epidemic occurred, lasting into 1817. Although there was severe weather in the winter of 1831, with snow and heavy rain in mid-November causing severe flooding in the Strabane district, the harvest had all been saved. Whilst the failure of the potato harvest in much of Ireland in 1845 and 1846 has been extensively chronicled, it appears that the farmers in north Tyrone were affected only to a small degree. No information has come to light to show how the two townlands fared during this period. When comparing the names on the rental records from 1838 with those listed on the Griffith's Valuation of 1858–60, we find that, with two exceptions, there had been no changes in the families in either townland. So were they affected by the famine years, other than the loss or partial loss of two potato crops?

A look at population changes between 1841 and 1851 seems to indicate that Edymore had been affected to some extent during the famine years, Cavanalee less so. Comparing the 1756 Survey with the 1777 and 1806 estate maps indicates that the number of houses had increased during the fifty years. Table 2, on page xiv, covering 1600–2000, shows that there was a greater increase in Edymore when compared with Cavanalee during that time. By 1833, both townlands had about the same number of houses. Not until the 1841 census do we know the precise number of both houses and their inhabitants. At the end of the next decade, after the famine years 1845–7, there had been virtually no change in Cavanalee during the 1840s, whereas in Edymore there was an 18% fall in the number of houses and a 24% fall in the population.

Between 1851 and 1861 there were falls in both the number of houses and people in both townlands. There were 10 fewer houses in both townlands, with a 21% fall in population in Edymore and 24% in Cavanalee, by 1861. The decline in population continued through to 1881 in Edymore and 1871 in Cavanalee when it stabilised until the end of the century.

4

FARMING FAMILIES
from the mid-eighteenth to the mid-nineteenth century

Families below the Edymore and Cavanalee Mountains

The information about families found in the Abercorn Letters covers only those who lived on farms below the estate's designated Edymore and Cavanalee Mountains. After 1800, farmers living on the mountain lands of the two townlands had a new road to take them to and from Strabane. As a result there was subsequently less contact between the farmers on the mountain land and those living in Edymore and the lower land in Cavanalee. Age long co-operation between farmers, as far as seasonal work on the farm was concerned, continued right up to the middle of the twentieth century. Farmers throughout the two townlands also continued to meet on market days and fair days. At the family level another reason for the somewhat limited contact between the two groups was and continued to be a cultural divide between the native Irish and the incomers. The families living on the 'mountainy farms', the native Irish, were Catholics, whilst those on the lower farms, the incomers, were Protestants, with their origins from 'across the water', Scottish, English and Welsh. This divide is reflected in this book as most of the farming families featured will be found living below the mountains, and of Protestant persuasion.

The farmers in 1756 and those who followed them

The first complete list naming the tenant farmers in Edymore is provided by the 1756 Survey. This survey gives the names of eleven men: John Simison, Samuel Gillilan, William Lowther, Alex Todd, Robert Smyly, William Brown, Galbraith Thompson, ? Orr, ? Knox, John Finlay and John Rabb. The Hearth Tax returns of 1666 show that the last two families had been in Edymore for at least the previous 90 years. John Rabb's death in 1782 had been recorded in a letter to Abercorn by his agent (see page 18). How long had the other tenants' families been living in Edymore? The first five surnames do not appear in the 1666 Hearth Tax returns. As the surnames Brown, Thompson, Orr and Knox are found in the 1630 Muster Roll for the Strabane district, these families may have been early settlers. It will be seen that the information obtained from the Abercorn Letters gives only brief glimpses of a few of these families.

In Cavanalee the only names recorded in the 1756 Survey are Thomas Graham and John Barnhill. As both surnames are found in the 1630 Muster Rolls, they also may have been descendants of early settler families. However there was another tenant living in Cavanalee at that time. Jo Colhoun, Abercorn's agent, had written to Abercorn (then staying at his house at Witham in Essex) in

October 1753 regarding a mearing (boundary) dispute at Artigarvan bordering Mr Sinclair's property at Hollyhill. 'I produced one James (1) Huston, tenant in Cavanalee aged 76, who swore he lived many yeares a tenant in Artygarvan, occupied and possessed the land there disputed and walked the mearing before us; that it was all his time peaceably held by the tenants of Artygarvan and without any claiming it or any part of it, until 38 yeares agoe when he sold his tenant right to one Harty and left him and neighbours in full possession as before said, as possitive prooff as ever I heard, and a man of real good character all of which Mr Sinclair owned'. James (1) Huston had been born in 1677 and family folklore contends that he probably came from Ayrshire in his early twenties, around 1700. It is also likely that James (1) had married late in life as his widow, Mary, was the tenant in 1777.

The tables in Appendix 10 list all the tenants and the rents paid by them between 1756 and 1827, and those in Appendix 11 cover the period 1838 to 1900.

Emigration and enlistment

In the Abercorn Letters we find that some farmers got into debt during the latter part of the eighteenth century. Not seeing a future for themselves at home some of them emigrated to America, which posed problems for Abercorn's agents. In 1765, we read that 'John Finlay of Edimore is dead, left his farm to his son who was then in America. On his return gave the mountain part of it [1/3 of the whole] to his brother-in-law for a consideration. As he resolves to go back to America he sold his rights to the remainder to one John McNeilans who I believe a solvent tenant at £95. McNeilans got the crop, 2 cows and a horse and some things belonging to the father'. The 'mountain part' must have been the part marked 'moor' on the 1777 map. In this case the Finlays were not in debt. The son had done well enough in America to wish to return there. America held out good prospects but not everyone could take advantage of them.

John McNeilans tried to 'sell' his farm at the end of 1777. The agent, James Hamilton, wrote to Abercorn in January 1778 informing him that 'John Ward who was to have McNeilans farm in Edimore has given up to McNeilans for £17 10s 0d (£17.50 annual rent). Ward has taken a large house near this farm from Dr Law and much land from the Dr and from Knox who formerly kept the inn here' (Strabane). McNeilans left within ten years, as the tenant, in 1787, was Victor Gordon.

In 1773, James Hamilton reported to Abercorn regarding another case involving emigration. 'Alexander Simison who pays £3 11s 8d [£3.58] in Edimore ran off to America. He has left his wife and children in possession of the ground but of little else. She says, he went in expectation of getting something from a brother he has there, and returning next year, but should he choose to stay, that the holding was to be sold to pay debts. His creditors, who are chiefly his neighbours there, are wanting security for his debts, or that she should now sell it to pay them. Some of them said they would petition your Lordship and I promised to mention it to your Lordship …' Later that year the agent commented that 'Simison's land in Edymore may be sold on paying a fine'.

Alexander Simison, together with his father, John senior, and brother, John junior, appear on the 1777 map's farm descriptions, so it would seem that his father and brother had paid the fine and continued to farm Alex's land as well as their own. When land was sold by a tenant Abercorn insisted on having a year's rent as a fine. No record has been found that would tell us if Alexander Simison stayed in America or if his wife had joined him there.

Another way for a farmer's son to obtain some money was to enlist in the army and to send his pay home. In a letter sent to Abercorn in May 1778, we find that farm 'No. 6 in Edimore [in 1756, No. 10 in 1777] Wm Brown who is joined [joint tenancy] with Isabella Brown [his widowed mother] and was to pay half rent £10 10s 0d [£10.50] came just now to tell me he had enlisted. He brought one of his sisters who is married. Brown's brother-in-law is a John Moor'. It is not known how long he stayed in the army. Did he participate in the American War of Independence between 1776 and 1783? According to the rent books his name continued to be recorded in them until the early nineteenth century. His mother seems to have died about 1782. The rental book then shows that William Brown farmed in partnership with his neighbour Robert Wilson. This might indicate that William Brown only stayed a short time in the army, or, if he had enlisted for a long term, that as long as Robert Wilson paid the full rent the two names remained in the rental book until the tenancy changed. Unfortunately the Abercorn Letters come to an end in 1818 and no other sources of information have been found to tell us about the relations between the estate and the Edymore and Cavanalee farmers.

Major John Humphreys and family

We have already referred to Abercorn's agent, Major John Humphreys, and his daughter Fanny whose poem, 'The Farmyard', described Galbraith Lowther's farm. The farming families in Edymore and the lower part of Cavanalee would have had more than a passing acquaintance with them. Major Humphreys would have visited the farms from time to time and have met the farmers in Strabane on market or fair days, and some of them at church. Fanny would have walked up the roads of the two townlands. On such walks she is reputed to have got inspiration for some of her poems and hymns for children in the 1840s. This piece of folklore was being told to primary school children in 'Miss Young's School' a century later (see page 75). When she walked up the road to Edymore she would have had a lovely view westwards to River Mourne, Raphoe and the Blue Stack mountains and northwards to Knockavoe hill. As the hymn 'All things bright and beautiful' describes, she would have seen 'the river running by' and 'the purple headed mountain'. *Hymns for Little Children* was published in 1848 and some of them are still being sung at the beginning of the twenty-first century. Miss Young's School in Meeting House Street was known as the First Presbyterian School, albeit a national school, when it opened at the end of the nineteenth century – it closed in 1964.

Major Humphreys played a significant role in the administration of Strabane, becoming Provost in 1834 and then chairman of the Strabane Poor Law Guardians in 1838, which oversaw the building of the Strabane Workhouse, opened in 1841. He was also an active member of the Church of Ireland in Strabane, where at least three of the farmers in the two townlands were fellow worshippers. He gave evidence to the Devon Commission whose terms of reference were to inquire into the state of the law and practice in respect of the occupation of land, appearing before the Commission when it visited Strabane in April 1844.

A farmer's will – providing for his widow and family

Information on farming families has come mainly from snippets hidden amongst the Abercorn Letters between 1765 and 1809, but as the nineteenth century progresses more recorded information becomes available. A chance find of an original manuscript document, a will of 1836, has revealed much about the Wilson family in Edymore. Church and estate records add to their story up to the 1870s. The will is that of Robert Wilson whose name first appears in the townland in 1782, when he became the tenant of John Rabb senior's farm after his death in that year. Robert Wilson had been brought up on his father John Wilson's farm at Meenlougher (Meenclogher), a townland noted for its quarries, some 12 miles (19 km) south of Castlederg. We do not know how Robert had been selected to become the tenant of a farm some 35 miles (56 km) from his home and which was far from any Abercorn estate land.

The will is dated 9th November 1836 and is given in full in Appendix 5. The family comprised Robert Wilson, his wife Elenor, two sons, Robert and John, and five daughters, Elizabeth, Mary, Isabella, Margret and Elenor – the last two names as well as their mother's name were spelt that way in the will. The second paragraph states that 'all that farm of Land that I dwell on and now hold and possess under the Most Noble the Marquis of Abercorn … together with all my Chattle and household property, all the cattle, stock, crop, farming utensils etc' were bequeathed to his son Robert, who was also to receive one-fifth of the money left to Robert senior by his father John Wilson. The latter had left £150 to his son Robert senior, which meant that Robert junior would receive £30. Robert junior's annual rent and tithe amounted to £27.18 in 1838.

Robert senior's next concern was for his wife Elenor. Robert junior was to provide his mother with 'Seventy two pecks [720 lbs, 327 kg] of meal, Eight pecks [80 lbs, 36 kg] of meal seeds [oats for sowing], thirty measures of potatoes, One Hundred weight [112 lbs, 51 kg] of clean scutched flax [ready for spinning], a cow of her choice, Summered with sufficient grass and Wintered with sufficient fodder, any end or apartment of the house I live in during her life together with a sufficient portion of household furniture that my executors shall allow of her to have with twenty four wheel car load of turf [peat] Cut win and laid at her door'. Elenor was not to be charged for any of the above which were to be provided 'yearly during her natural life'.

The next and longest paragraph dealt with Robert senior's daughters and son, John. 'I will and bequeath unto my daughter Elizabeth Wilson the sum of Thirty Pounds sterling as a portion in marriage'. Margret, Isabella and Elenor were to receive £20 as marriage portions. This was the usual amount at that time, according to Major Humphreys. The will indicates that although Mary had been promised £20 on her marriage she had not yet received it. If there was still part of her portion to be paid when her father died her brother Robert was to provide the balance. Robert was also charged with giving his other sisters the marriage portion when they reached the age of 45, if they were not then married, and had asked him for it. If any of his sisters died unmarried before the age of 45, Robert would be able to keep the marriage portion.

'And as to my son John Wilson I will and bequeath unto Him the sum of one Shilling Sterling to be paid to him if demanded without him or his Heirs having any more claim against any of my freehold of household property of whatsoever nature or whereinsoever situated that farm I am possessed at my decease'. We do not know why John Wilson was left the 'proverbial shilling'. John had been the sole tenant of his father's joint tenancy neighbouring farm by 1827, so by 1836 he would have been well established. It might be that Robert, being the eldest son, would naturally be expected to look after his mother and unmarried sisters and that he would be ultimately responsible for the payment of the dowries.

Two contemporaries of Robert senior, Thomas Lowther and Nathanial Thompson, had been empowered to act as executors. Thomas Lowther was the tenant of a farm and lessee of the mill at the bottom of the hill in Cavanalee townland. Nathanial Thompson was Robert senior's immediate neighbour. The will was witnessed by Gustavus Lyon, the son-in-law of Nathanial Thompson; Walter Johnston Lowther, possibly the son of Thomas Lowther; and his son-in-law, John (1) Huston (see later).

Daughters and dowries

What happened to Robert Wilson's daughters? The will indicated that Mary was already married. The Strabane Presbyterian Church records show that she had married John (1) Huston on 23 October 1835. John (1) Huston was the second son of Andrew (1) Huston, the tenant of a 65 acre (26 ha) farm in Cavanalee – see abridged family tree on page 78. John and Mary continued to live in Cavanalee for the rest of their lives. They had two sons and three daughters between 1835 and 1847. Margret Wilson married Samuel Huston in the neighbouring townland of Drumnaboy in 1836. They had two children. Although both sisters found their husbands in neighbouring townlands these two Huston families were not related. Social contacts at that time would have been made through the church and *ceilidhing* with neighbours in the vicinity. Later, Isabella married a widower living in Strabane, William Blair, a collector of customs. They were married on 24 August 1853 when Isabella was aged 40 and William 53. No record has been found to show that Elizabeth and Elenor married. As Robert junior and John did not marry, it was probable that Elizabeth and Elenor spent their lives as housekeepers for their brothers. There is no record of Robert junior paying any of 'the marriage portions'.

The size of marriage portions needs to be put in context. For this farming family a marriage portion was almost as large as the annual rent of the farm, so it could have been quite a burden in difficult farming years to find this money. At the other end of the social scale we find that when Fanny Humphreys married Rev. William Alexander in 1850, the marriage settlement was £3,000. The commission paid by the Abercorn estate to their agents enabled Major Humphreys to live the life of a gentleman.

What is missing from the will
The will tells us the size of Robert Wilson's family in 1836 and the provision made for his wife after his death. We do not know if the family had been larger or had experienced earlier deaths during the fever epidemics of the early nineteenth century, especially the cholera epidemic of 1832. It does not tell us the age of the members of the family, or the reason for the differences in the marriage portions between Elizabeth and her sisters. The children might have been born between the turn of the century and 1815 – Isabella was born in 1813. This assumes that the sequence of the names of the daughters in the will started with the eldest Elizabeth – she might have been Robert senior's favourite daughter as she was to get the highest dowry! These girls would have been brought up to use spinning wheels, as we have seen that Robert senior was one of the farmers who had obtained four spinning wheels, in 1796, under the Premium Scheme of the Trustees of Linen Manufacture. The table in Appendix 10 shows all the farmers who received spinning wheels under this scheme.

From the will we find that the basic food requirement for Robert Wilson's wife Elenor was to be 2 lbs (1 kg) of oatmeal a day. She would have a varying quantity of milk for a little over half the year, which would provide her with a little butter and buttermilk to make griddle scones. She was well catered for where potatoes and flax were concerned, but as she got older would she have been able for all the work connected with spinning the flax? Presumably her son Robert would have provided her with the rest of her food requirements. Could she have been in poor health and dependent on her daughters to look after her?

The will also tells us that 1 lb (0.5 kg) of oats used for sowing produced 9 lbs (4 kg) at harvest. Although potatoes and flax were grown and milking cows kept we learn nothing about other crops grown, livestock kept or the farm equipment used. According to John McEvoy in his *Statistical Survey of the County of Tyrone* (1802), twenty-four wheel-car loads of turf equate to twelve tapered clamps of turf measuring 8ft long x 4 ft wide x 6 ft high (2.4 x 1.2 x 1.8 m). This should have provided Elenor senior with more than enough turf to make her 'end' in the house comfortable.

Table 3, on page 25, describes the condition of the land on the Wilson farm in 1833–8 and what it was like in 1756. It would seem that Robert senior had noticeably improved the farm by 1806 as his rent was then raised from £20.31 to £25.31. The rents of his neighbours stayed the same. We have seen that John Wilson had become the tenant of the neighbouring farm by 1827. Robert junior may have become the tenant of the home farm by that time, as it would seem likely that Robert senior, by the time he made his will in 1836, was well into his 70s – he had then been in Edymore for over 50 years. The 1833 and 1854 maps show the farmyards and houses of the two brothers, Robert junior and John, side by side, with nearby corn and lime kilns.

Robert Wilson senior through his will had made formal arrangements for the well-being of his wife in her old age. At the date of his will his two sons and three of his daughters were unmarried. If the sons had married shortly afterwards, would their wives have been prepared to look after his wife, their mother-in-law? The will puts the onus on the eldest son to look after his mother until she dies, with a watching brief by two of Robert senior's friends – the executors. Robert junior died in 1875, two years after his nephew Thomas (3) Huston had taken over the tenancy. John Wilson died in 1879, four years after he had assigned his farm to his neighbour Jane Fulton.

Planning for old age
In Cavanalee, we find that farm No. 8 in 1777, tenanted by Joseph Knox, had passed to his son-in-law William McCrea by 1787. The rental books show that he shared the tenancy with his son James in 1806, continuing until 1838, when James took over the tenancy. However, ten years later, James, by then well into middle age, concluded a deed with James Graham, the son of one of his neighbours, which in effect assigned the farm to James Graham who would become the tenant of the farm and also provide for the 'retirement' of James McCrea and members of his household. This agreement was made with the Abercorn estate agent, James Hamilton junior. This makes fascinating reading and is given in full, minus some of the legal preliminaries and embellishments.

> Indenture 15th June 1848 between James McCrea, Cavanalee and James Graham. Whereas by indenture of the lease of 31st January 1835, Abercorn to McCrea for the life of James Hamilton Junior, or, 21 years from 1st November 1834 with rent of £61 17s $3^{1}/2$d [£61.87] yearly. This indenture witnesseth that the said James McCrea for a consideration of £29 16s 9d [£26.84] to him in hand paid by James Graham, hath made over to James Graham in his possession his farm of 85 acres 35 perches [34 ha]. James Graham to permit James McCrea and his sister Elizabeth McCrea during their lives to have and to hold and enjoy their sitting room or parlour in the dwelling house on said farm and two bedrooms now occupied by them and the use of the kitchen in common with James Graham together with the use of the furniture and bedding therein and also sufficient firing for their use and benefit and also supply with one good milk cow properly grassed and foddered and also supply James and Elizabeth McCrea ten measures of good eating potatoes and three cwt [150 kg] of good oaten meal each year and yearly during their lives and shall pay them yearly annuity of £5 each year to be paid 1st November. James Graham to support and provide Nancy Stewart and her illegitimate daughter by the said James McCrea called Jane McCrea in the manner they have hitherto provided so long and until they shall be paid by James Graham the amount of money due and owed to them by James McCrea.

We find that James McCrea is still named in the rental book until 1860, presumably the year in which he died. He is also listed as the occupier in the Griffith's Valuation of 1858, with the size of the farm is given as 91 acres (37 ha). In the deed it is 85 acres (34 ha). Why is there this discrepancy? Perhaps some land alongside the Cavanalee River had been 'reclaimed'. Did James McCrea continue 'to run the farm' until his death?

Although this is an isolated piece of social history, it does reveal that for a bachelor farmer, having no younger family members such as nephews with wives or unmarried nieces to call upon, it was essential that he could make arrangements for being looked after in his old age. In this case he also included his sister, Elizabeth, and the illegitimate daughter, Jane McCrea, by his servant Nancy Stewart, in the arrangements. It is not stated how much money was to be given to the latter and it would have been most revealing if the dates of birth of all the people concerned were known.

Other farming families

Although little information about other farming families for this period has been found, genealogical information is available for the early part of the nineteenth century for the Huston family in Cavanalee (see family tree on page 78). We see that John (1) (1801–1880) and Mary Huston (c.1810–60) had two sons and three daughters. John's cousin James (5) (c.1802–60) and his wife, John's sister Catherine (1808–94), had two sons and three daughters.

Two new farmers came to Edymore at the beginning of the nineteenth century, Joseph (1) Davis and John (1) Fulton. Joseph Davis was the tenant of half of the original Simison farm (No. 3 in 1756) from 1806, whilst John Fulton had become the tenant of the John Rabb and William Stilly farm (No. 8 in 1806) in 1816. These two families have remained in Edymore up to the present. The Davis family according to family tradition came to Edymore from the Raphoe area of County Donegal, some 7 miles (11 km) northwest of Strabane. Their forebears may have come from Wales at the time of the Plantation (or later), living on the Davis or Bingley estates in that part of Donegal.

Few details about John (1) Fulton's family have survived: he had a brother William (1) who, in 1838, became the tenant of a farm in the next townland of Carrigullin which was later farmed alongside the Edymore farm. From later family records it would seem that the Fulton brothers also came from the Raphoe area. Family tradition holds that the original settler family had come to County Donegal from Yorkshire.

Ministers and rectors

The life of these families away from the farm was closely linked to their place of worship. This relationship has continued for almost all of them right through to the present time. They would all have had good contact with the ministers and rectors of the period, some of whom achieved prominence in Ireland. A distinguished Presbyterian minister in Strabane (1766–98) was Rev. William Crawford, a linguist and literary critic as well as an historian. He wrote a two-volume *History of Ireland* in 1783 and was for a time involved with the Volunteer movement. During Crawford's time John Wesley, the Methodist evangelist, passed through Strabane on four occasions. On his last but one visit, in 1787, he preached to a large congregation in the Town Hall. As there were only a small number of practising Methodists in Strabane at that time, many Presbyterians and Church of Ireland members must have listened to him.

Rev. William Crawford established the Strabane Academy with three teachers in 1786. Initially this school trained potential Presbyterian ministers. Two other schools had been established in the previous decade and by 1821 there were seven schools in the district, most of them providing a classical type of education although mathematics had its place. It is not known if any of the farming families sent their children to any of these schools. There were for a brief period schools in Edymore and Liskinbwee townlands, the former near to the Fulton farm, and the latter a little over half a mile (0.8 km) on the Strabane side of the Cavanalee Bridge. They are both marked on the 1833 map. The Parliamentary Gazetteer notes that the school at Edymore, by the mid-1840s, had 55 boys and 33 girls on its rolls. The teacher had a salary of £5 paid by Lord Abercorn. It had closed by the beginning of the next decade because of the fall in the population after the famine years. The school at Liskinbwee had closed by 1854. By then Edymore children went to schools in Strabane, with Cavanalee children attending schools either in Strabane or the national school in the neighbouring Dergalt townland.

Another outstanding Presbyterian minister at this period was Rev. Alexander Goudy (1833–58). The *Strabane Morning Post*, when reporting his installation, recorded 'he need hardly state that he entered this congregation, free, independent, untrammelled, the pledged of no party, the protégé of no individual'. He is remembered for his active support of tenant right, his stand against Unitarianism, and the Church of Ireland's efforts to nullify the validity of Presbyterian marriages.

The Rev. Alexander Goudy officiated at the marriages of the three daughters of Robert Wilson senior. However, we find that Rev. Goudy couldn't remember the christian names of members of the two families when John (1) Huston married Mary Wilson. In the church records we read that '(x) Huston son of Widow Huston Cavanalee married 23rd October 1835 (y) daughter of Robert Wilson and (z) Edymore'. In 1837, John Wilson was appointed to the Presbyterian Church's congregational committee and session. In 1854, Robert Wilson junior, as well as Robert Gordon of Edymore, and James (4) Huston and Thomas Graham of Cavanalee were members of a committee set up to organise the presentation of a testimonial to Rev. Goudy in recognition of his work for the church and the community. Rev. Goudy was the Moderator of the General Assembly of the Presbyterian Church in Ireland in 1857. After his death the following year in Dublin, his body was brought by train to Strabane and was met by a large crowd. Over one hundred ministers attended his funeral.

Strabane and beyond

During the second half of the eighteenth century Strabane began to grow and become a significant commercial centre, with a strong Presbyterian merchant presence, and attracted eminent clerics and academics to the town. The Lifford bridge was built in 1755, with the bridge at Strabane following at the end of the next decade. Strabane developed as a leading publishing and printing centre, with the first of the local newspapers, the *Strabane Journal*, appearing between 1771 and 1801. This was followed by the *Strabane Newsletter*, 1788–*c*.1810, and the *Strabane Morning Post*, 1811–1840.

No family folklore or tradition came to light regarding the talking points during the period 1750–1850. In the latter part of the eighteenth century these would have included: the agricultural protest movements – the Oakboys and

Steelboys; the rise and fall of the Volunteer movement; the making of poteen, an illicit sideline for some farmers, especially those living in the mountain areas; the problem of emigration; the United Irishmen and the '98 rising. In the first half of the nineteenth century there were: the Act of Union in 1800; the rise of the Orange Order leading to conflicts and fair-day riots; the cholera epidemic of 1832; the Big Wind of 1839; the building of the Workhouse in 1841 and the consequences of the Famine 1845–6. These topics as they affected Strabane district are dealt with in books listed in the bibliography.

A thriving linen market developed during the second half of the eighteenth century in Strabane, which was actively supported by Abercorn. To support this a market house and brown linen hall were built. The Strabane Canal opened in 1796, providing cheap haulage facilities for heavy goods to and from Derry. Traffic on the canal declined after the arrival of the Derry to Strabane railway in 1847. This was extended to Omagh by 1852, with the farming families on the Edymore hillside being able to see the construction of the line as it wound its way parallel to the River Mourne between Strabane and Sion Mills. Earlier, in 1835, they would also have seen the Herdman brothers' flax-spinning mill being built alongside the river Mourne at Sion Mills.

The expansion of the commercial activities is recorded in the *Commercial Directory* 1820, *Pigot's Directory* 1824, the *New Directory of the City of Londonderry and Coleraine with Strabane* 1839 and Slater's *National Commercial Directory of Ireland* 1846. Their coverage shows that farmers were well catered for, with ironmongers and hardware merchants, cart makers, saddlers, tanners, white and black smiths and grain merchants. All these activities had been supported by the improving road network and coach services.

5

A CENTURY OF CHANGE
Farms and farmers from the mid-nineteenth to the mid-twentieth century

Setting the scene
The 1854 OS map and the Griffith's Valuation of 1858 set the scene. The Valuators recorded their work on the OS maps and updated their revisions every four years in (manuscript) books now held in PRONI. However, a comparison of the 1858 Abercorn estate rental documents with the Griffith's Valuation for Cavanalee indicates that some farms and land in the former Cavanalee Mountain area had been omitted or incorrectly allocated by the Valuators. The printed version was incorrect. The Valuators revisited Cavanalee and produced revised figures and maps in 1860. The revision arose from the fact that five farmers in the upper parts of Cavanalee farmed between two and five separate plots of land. One of these farms, tenanted by Anne Haghey, had five pieces of ground spread over half a mile (0.8 km) with some parts not enclosed. In addition, three farms listed on the 1858 printed sheet as being shared by brothers were in fact six separate farms.

The 1858 Griffith's Valuation printed sheet and the revised valuation information for 1860 for Cavanalee as well as the Griffith's Valuation for Edymore are given in full in Appendix 7. The Griffith's map showing the location of the farms in both townlands is featured in Appendix 6. The numbers allocated to farms on this map will be used from here on to show continuity or change of occupiers.

According to the printed Griffith's Valuation for Cavanalee in 1858, the Houston brothers, James senior (4) and John (1) shared farm No. 18. However, the revised Cavanalee valuation for 1860 shows that they had divided the farm into two parts, one with two separate groups of fields and the other having three separate groups of fields. The estate rental records had shown these farms as a single farm with the rent shared by the two brothers.

Extracts from the Griffith's Valuation covering the five families with the longest periods of continuity: Wilson/Houston, Davis and Fulton in Edymore and Houston in Cavanalee, together with the King family later associated with the Houston family through marriage, are given in Table 4 overleaf.

Working the land before the First World War (1914–18)
Towards the end of the nineteenth century and into the early twentieth century farm machinery became a common feature on farms throughout Ireland. No information on how these changes came to the two townlands has been found.

Map No.	Names		Description of Tenement	Area			Rateable Valuation						Total AnnVal		
	Occupiers	Lessors					Land			Buildings					
				A	R	P	£	s	d	£	s	d	£	s	d
	Edymore														
8a	John (2) Fulton	Abercorn	House, offices, land	46	2	20	28	0	0	5	0	0	33	0	0
3 AB	Robert (1) Davis	Same	Same	47	2	10	29	5	0	1	0	0	30	5	0
10	John Wilson	Same	Same	46	2	10	27	0	0	2	0	0	29	0	0
11	Robert Wilson jnr	Same	Same	43	3	20	26	5	0	1	15	0	28	0	0
18	Samuel (1) King	Same	House and land	18	3	10	2	5	0		10	0	2	15	0
	Cavanalee														
17	James (5) Houston	Same	House, offices, land	29	2	15	22	0	0	1	0	0	23	0	0
18AB	John (1) Houston	Same	Same	19	2	10	11	10	0		15	0	12	5	0
19A-C	Jas (4) Houston snr	Same	Same	20	3	30	11	10	0	1	0	0	12	10	0

Table 4. Extracts from Griffith's Valuation of Rateable Property 1858

However an outline of what took place in the west of Ulster shows how horse-powered machines gradually reduced the back-breaking work that had gone on for hundreds of years.

Design improvements saw the introduction of wheel ploughs from the mid-nineteenth century. Disc and zig-zag harrows, and metal rollers appeared towards the end of the century. Seed sowing continued to be done by hand with the seed-sowing fiddle appearing only at the beginning of the twentieth century. By that

Harrowing and sowing

Horse-drawn binder

time machines for sowing grass seed and turnips were in use and also drill ploughs for potato husbandry. Machines for spraying potatoes to counteract potato blight, using a mixture of copper sulphate and washing soda, were used widely.

Cutting grass for hay with scythes continued up to the twentieth century when reapers began to take over. Tedders, to scatter the grass, and rakes, to place the grass in rows, came into use at the same time. Similarly, cereal crops continued to be cut by hand, usually by sickles, sometimes with sythes. The making of

Barn threshing mill – powered by horses outside the barn

Travelling threshing mill powered by a steam engine

STRABANE FOUNDRY.

Having recently erected some additional Workshops, and otherwise improved the Foundry premises, I am now enabled, with increased facility, to execute any order with which I may be entrusted.

FLAX SCUTCHING AND CORN MILL MACHINERY.

On the most approved principles;

FLAX ROLLERS,

Of various kinds, with latest improvements;

Water Wheels, Thrashing Machines,

Suction and Force Pumps, Retorts, &c. for Gas Works.

**PILLARS,
PLAIN AND ORNAMENTAL RAILING,**

WATER AND STOVE PIPES, EAVE GUTTERS,

**SPADE-MAKERS' TOOLS,
FARM BOILERS, PIG TROUGHS,**

Plough Mounting, Sash and Scale Weights,

Window Sashes, for Churches, Cottages, &c.,

FARM YARD BELLS, MILL BRASSES, &c.,

With almost every other description of FOUNDRY WORK, exececuted with despatch, and on Moderate Terms.

Turning, Boring, Mill-Wright, & Smith Work of all kinds.
EXECUTED IN THE BEST MANNER.

Mill Machinery erected and repaired by experienced Workmen.

JOHN STEVENSON.

Strabane, June, 1865.

John Stevenson's Strabane Foundry Advertisement 1865

sheaves, often a job for women and children, and stooks and stacks by the men on the farm continued as before. Only the making of sheaves disappeared when reaper binders appeared after the First World War. Barn threshing machines took over from flails. These were being manufactured at John Stevenson's foundry in Strabane from the 1860s – see advertisement (left). Usually two horses walking round a gear wheel located outside the barn powered them. These were used on a number of farms in the two townlands – the remains of external ring-courses could be seen on two farms after the Second World War. Between the wars they were superseded by travelling steam-powered threshing machines that went from farm to farm.

The flax crop saw virtually no change in its growing or harvesting methods – a hand-only crop right through to its demise at the end of the Second World War. The extent of flax growing can be seen from the number of flax dams found on the Ordnance Survey maps. In 1854 there were four flax dams alongside the Back Burn, whilst in 1905 there were twelve, two of which were in Cavanalee. There were, at that time, ten other flax dams in Cavanalee and two in

A Stevenson flax roller

Edymore, most beside minor waterways, although a few seem to have been in natural hollows in fields for which water was obtained from nearby main drains.

John Young had become the tenant of farm No. 13 in Cavanalee about 1850. He built a flax mill shortly afterwards. As farmers in the two townlands grew flax it is likely that they had supported him. The mill is shown on the 1854 map near the Strabane to Plumbridge road, east of the Cavanalee Bridge. In 1858, John Young's flax mill had an annual valuation of £1 15s 0d (£1.75). The valuation for his farmhouse and buildings was 10s 0d (50p). The flax mill was a very modest building when compared with the corn mill and kiln at Milltown, with their annual valuation of £25. The estate rental records do not record the flax mill and it has not been possible to find any further information about it. After John Young's death in 1877, his widow, Jane, became the tenant, and upon her death in 1889 her son Joseph succeeded her.

Towards the end of the century the flax mill became disused. At that time Joseph Young had installed a threshing mill in an adjoining building. In the 1901 valuation book the threshing mill had an annual valuation of £5. Its location can still be determined one hundred years later. By 1900 Joseph Young had built a substantial new farmhouse, shown as Brook Villa on the 1905 OS map and later known as Brook House. An RAF Officer staying there during the Second World War drew a sketch of it, shown overleaf. The original house with only six

Joseph Young's new farmhouse

Plan of Joseph Young's farm

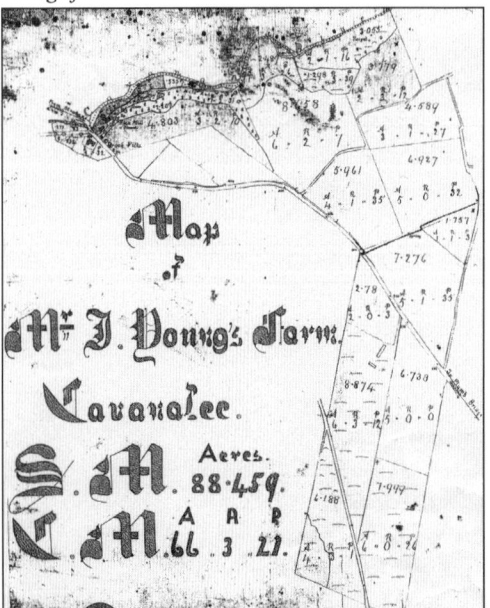

windows to the front was extended shortly afterwards, as shown on the 1905 map and the plan below. The sketch shows the additions to the left-hand side of the house. The map of the farm was probably made in anticipation of its sale in 1916.

Bigger is better – the Fulton farm

In the Griffith's Valuation John (2) Fulton was the tenant of a 46 acre (19 ha) farm in Edymore. At the same time he was also shown to be the tenant of a 52 acres (21 ha) farm in the next townland of Carrigullin, a little over half a mile (0.8 km) from the Edymore farm. The Carrigullin farm was on higher land averaging 200ft (60m) above that of the Edymore farm and was of poorer quality, as reflected in the 1858 rateable valuation which was 30% lower than the Edymore farm.

With almost 100 acres (40 ha) John (2) Fulton was able to keep more cattle than his neighbours. Ten years later he had a profitable dairy herd and much of the milk was made into butter. The chance find of old notebooks in a desk by William (4) Fulton in 1999 included Butter Accounts for 1868, 1870, 1871 and 1872. In 1868, between 63 and 74 lbs (29 and 34 kg) of butter were sold fortnightly from mid-January through to mid-November. Prices varied from 16d per lb in late winter to $10^3/4$d at the end of June, rising to 15d in November, with a much lower amount sold in December. The total income for the year was £103 16s 0d (£103.80). A similar pattern is seen for 1870 but with an increase in the quantity sold in December compared with 1868, giving a higher income of £127 1s 10d (£127.09). In 1871, there was a fall in the quantity sold in January, with only 55 lbs (25 kg) sold each fortnight. The amount sold increased to a peak at the end of March when 77 lbs (35 kg) realised 18d per lb, the highest price over the three years. For the rest of the year the quantity sold and prices achieved matched those of the previous year. The total income from the sale of butter in 1871 was £121 8s 7d (£121.43). This was four times the rent of the Edymore farm – £30 12s 2d (£30.61).

In 1872, even more butter was made and sold as detailed in Table 5 below. The total income for the eleven months amounted to £161 11s 3d (£161.57). The reason for this increase in the amount of milk produced lies in the fact that John (2) Fulton had bought 25 cows between 17 July 1871 and 26 April 1872 from 20 farmers who lived as far away as Castlederg, County Tyrone; Claudy, County Londonderry; and Castlefinn, County Donegal. They were most likely to have been bought at the Strabane market. The prices ranged from £7 to £9 for 14 cows bought up to January and, £10 10s 0d (£10.50) to £12 10s 0d (£12.50) for the 11 bought in March and April. These higher prices would suggest that these cows were in-calf. They would have calved in the summer and were able to provide the extra milk which resulted in the doubling of the amount of butter sold in August and September 1872.

These notebooks show that John (2) Fulton managed his herd in such a way that he had cows calving for much of the year. This was unusual, as most farmers would have had their cows calving in the spring and summer when new grass became available. In 1872, John (2) Fulton also made money through buying calves between February and May and selling them on in June and July after they had been fed on the spring grass. He bought 12 calves for £56 7s 6d (£56.38) and sold them for £95, thereby making a profit of £38 12s 6d (£38.63).

Month	Amount lbs	kg	Ave price d/lb	p/kg
January	135	61	17	15.5
February	143	65	$17^{1}/_{2}$	16
March	209	95	$16^{1}/_{2}$	15
April	280	127	15	14
May	271	123	13	12
June	201	91	$12^{1}/_{2}$	11.5
July	200	91	12	11
August	430	195	$13^{1}/_{2}$	12.5
September	427	194	$13^{1}/_{2}$	12.5
October	206	93	$14^{3}/_{4}$	13.5
November	241	109	$16^{1}/_{2}$	15
December	No entry			

Table 5. Amount and price of butter sold in 1872 by John (2) Fulton recorded in his farm notebooks

The Fulton farm would also have had to produce larger quantities of hay and turnips than most farmers to maintain the milk output to enable the womenfolk on the farm to churn the substantial amounts of butter sent to the market. John (2) and his wife Jane, in 1872, had three daughters aged between 13 and 23, so it could well have been a shared activity between the 'ladies' of the family and their 'general servant(s)'. (See page 71, which refers to the 'general servants' recorded in the 1901 Census.) These three daughters do not feature on the abridged family tree, shown opposite, as no information other than their date of birth has survived.

The notebooks also show that John (2) purchased guano, fertiliser made from bird droppings imported from Peru, and potato manure. On occasions he had surplus potatoes, turnips, corn (oats) and straw for sale. The quantities were small and bought by the same three men each year. These men may well have been farm workers living in cottier houses on the farm. Two neighbouring farmers were also listed. Robert (1) Davis bought six loads of turnips on 1 December 1868. They cost him £3 12s 0d (£3.60). Samuel (1) King bought 32 stone (203 kg) of corn (oats) at 1s $4^1/2$d per stone (1p per kg) on 26 December 1868. In the following November, Samuel King bought 10 measures of potatoes for 7s 6d (38p) and 30 stones (190 kg) of corn (oats) for £1 6s $10^1/2$d (£1.34).

According to the notebooks John (2) Fulton was collecting the rents of 12 farms in townlands lying between Croaghan Hill and Crossy Hill lying just to the west of the road from Lifford to Castlefinn in County Donegal. It is not clear for whom he was acting, possibly the Bishop of Raphoe. However, we find that by 1871, John (2) Fulton's son John (3) had become the tenant of one of these farms in Ardnaglass townland. This farm was some $3^1/2$ miles (5.5 km) from Strabane; its size is not given in the notebooks. His rent was £47, £7 more than that paid by the previous tenant. John (3) continued as tenant of this farm until his death c.1920. Robert (2) Fulton inherited this farm upon the death of his uncle, who had not married. As he was only a schoolboy at that time his father William (1) Fulton sold the farm in 1921 for £800 – Robert (2) was then aged 11. This transaction was the result of political events at that time which meant that County Donegal would become part of Eire with a different economic system.

John (2) Fulton died in 1875. In the following year his widow, Jane, became the tenant of the neighbouring farm through assignment from John Wilson. The size of the combined farms in Edymore and Carrigullin was then 144 acres (58 ha). Jane Fulton continued as the tenant until her death in 1883. As her eldest son, John (3) had been the tenant of the Ardnaglass farm since the death of his father and wished to stay there, the Edymore farm passed to her second son, William (2).

Increasing the size of farms to 1900

Very few changes in the sizes of farms had taken place during the first half of the nineteenth century. However, in the second half of the century, there were a number of amalgamations of farms in both townlands as well as new farms established on the 'mountain land'. Some of this poorer land was also to be found in the upper part of Edymore and named on the 1777 estate map on page 16 as

> ### FULTON FAMILY TREE
>
> **John (1)** b 1785 d 1855 m Elizabeth ? b 1778 d 1833
> **John (2)** b 1824 d 1875 m 1847 Jane Dick b 1828 d 1883
>   John (3) b 1848 d by 1920
>   **William (2)** b 1854 d 1930 m 1898 Mary Jane Stevenson b 1876/7 d 1960
>   Kathleen b 1899 d 1992 m John Baxter b ? d 1974
>   Jane b 1901 d 1986 m Leo O'Connor
>   John (4) b 1903 d 1987 m late 1930s Jane Foster b 1896 d 1980
>   {Their daughter Mary m Leslie Galbraith – three children}
>   Mary b 1904 d 1991
>   **William (3)** b 1906 d 1985
>   Elizabeth b 1908 d 1976
>   Robert (2) b 1910 m late 1940s Molly Stevenson b ? d c.1970
>   Samuel (3) b 1912 d 1962
>   Edward Hall b 1913 d 1996 m 1939 Sadie Laverty b 1913 d 1973
>   {Their children: **William (4)** b 1940 m 1962 Gladys Lockhart b 1939 –
>   Robin   four children
>   Anna b 1914   Elizabeth}
>   Samuel (1) b 1856 d 1907 m ? b ? d 1907
>   {Their children: Samuel (2) b 1903 and William (2) b 1905. Both d Canada}
>   Robert (1) b 1865 d 1950s (Australia)
>   James b 1867 (d USA)
>   Thomas b 1869 (d USA)
>   plus four daughters
>
> **Note:** The names of the tenants/owners of the Edymore farm are highlighted above. It is most likely that John (1) had a brother William (1). A William Fulton was the tenant of a farm in Carrigullin from 1838. No other information about this William Fulton has survived.

Edymore Common Mountain. At the beginning of the nineteenth century the agent was proposing to divide this into four parts, each having about 18 acres (7.25 ha). It is possible that three of these farms were not tenanted until 1827. In the 1850s one of the tenants of these small four farms, Samuel (1) King, would have had three teenage sons to help him improve the farm. However, it seems that he gave up the farm in 1868, when he was aged 64, moving to another small farm in the higher part of Evish townland, neighbouring Cavanalee, where his sons ran the farm.

During the latter part of the nineteenth century some amalgamations of farms took place in Edymore. Robert (1) Davis had purchased the neighbouring farm of Margaret Porter in 1852, increasing his holding to 47 acres (19 ha). We have seen that Jane Fulton acquired the neighbouring farm of John Wilson in 1876, thereby doubling the size of her farm to 92 acres (37 ha). The Fulton family still has a printed copy of John Wilson's lease of 1835, with the 1876 assignment clauses added. In 1884, they purchased the neighbouring farm of Hugh Carland, No. 9 (54 acres (22 ha)). The Fulton family then farmed 146 acres (59 ha) in Edymore plus 52 acres (21 ha) in neighbouring Carrigullin.

Hugh Carland's other farm, Nos. 4/5, was also divided in 1884. George Barnhill purchased farm No. 4 (23 acres (9 ha)). He farmed an almost adjacent farm in Cavanalee, with only two small fields belonging to his neighbour separating the two farms. No doubt the agent felt it better sense to double the amount of George Barnhill's land – he then farmed 44 acres (18 ha). Margaret Aikin acquired farm No. 5 (20 acres (8 ha)) which abutted her farm No. 6 (35 acres (14 ha)). She also farmed another farm in Edymore, No. 7 (45 acres (18 ha)) near the southern boundary of the townland. This meant that the amount of land she now farmed had increased by a quarter.

The three farms, Nos. 11, 12 and 13 were made into two farms when Robert Lowry, the tenant on farm No. 13, moved to a farm in Cavanalee in 1879. This meant that Thomas (3) Huston had increased the size of his farm from 44 to 61 acres (18 to 25 ha), and Alex McCrea's farm increased from 34 to 51 acres (14 to 21 ha).

In Cavanalee two amalgamations took place between 1855 and 1900. In 1873 Joseph (2) Davis, then aged 33, the eldest son of Robert (1) Davis who farmed in Edymore, took over James Graham's farm No. 26 (34 acres (13.75 ha)). In 1882, Joseph (2) Davis acquired the adjacent farm No. 10 (72 acres (29 ha)), formerly tenanted by William Graham. It is possible that these two Grahams were related. This farm had previously been tenanted by Thomas Cuthbertson, from 1868 to 1878. Joseph (2) Davis had married Sarah Cuthbertson, possibly the daughter of Thomas Cuthbertson, about 1874, and would have been quite familiar with the new farm he acquired in 1882.

In the 1890s Joseph Young on farm No. 13 acquired the tenancy of farm No. 23 which abutted his own farm, with both having the Cavanalee River as a boundary. The western boundary of farm No. 23 was the dividing line between Cavanalee and Cavanalee Mountain. Joseph Young's holding then increased from 20 acres (8 ha) to 91 acres (37 ha).

The Griffith's map (Appendix 6) shows the extent of the farms on both the Edymore and Cavanalee Mountains half way through the nineteenth century. In the second half of the century the rough mountain areas were reduced in size as reclamation and improvements in husbandry took place. In Edymore Mountain farms Nos. 20, 21 and 22 remained the same size through to the twentieth century. Around 1880, the Conway family became the tenants of farms Nos. 24 and 25, together with the remaining mountain land.

In Cavanalee Mountain the sequence of events is difficult to map. The valuation books show changes in the sizes of some farms. Towards the end of the century farms Nos. 1 and 2 had increased to over twice the 1860 size. Farms Nos. 24 and 25 remained the same size. It has not been possible to chart the amalgamations of the scattered farms Nos. 3 to 9.

Paying rents – the end in sight

The rents set in 1787 continued virtually unchanged for 50 years until 1838, with many of the farmers having had long leases. However, farmers were paying tithes from 1827, almost certainly earlier. These charges were added to the rent in 1838, with this combined charge usually becoming the new rent that was set in 1858. The rents for the farms in both townlands from 1838 to 1900 are shown on the table in Appendix 11. The rents on some farms were increased further in the period 1860 to 1863, seeming to reflect the Griffith's Valuation of 1858/60. The steepest increases were on farms located in the higher parts of both townlands which had the largest proportion of land that had been improved. Two-thirds of the farmers in Edymore paid their rents half-yearly, but only a quarter of the farmers in Cavanalee. The estate rental books provide no information on this. Further adjustments to the rents by the Abercorn estate, both up and down, occurred in the late 1870s and early 1880s. In the 1880s, four farms in Edymore had their rents increased while six, on the higher land, had their rents reduced. In Cavanalee four farms had their rents increased and four decreased.

The Land Act of 1881 established the Land Commission with authority to adjudicate on fair rents. With the poor seasons of the 1880s and 1890s some of the farmers took advantage of the legislation to have their rents reduced. However, Francis Graham junior's (farm No. 12 in Cavanalee) approach to the Land Commission resulted in an increase in his rent. It had been £14.81 in 1858, £19.70 in 1860, and £20.45 in 1877. The Judicial Review of 1881 resulted in a further increase to £27.50. All but one of these Judicial Reviews were for farms on the higher land in Cavanalee – these are shown on the table in Appendix 11. Two farmers on Cavanalee Mountain went to the Land Commission twice and obtained reductions in rents on both occasions.

Buying their farms

The Land Commission could also make loans of up to 75 per cent of the purchase price to tenants purchasing their farms. The Ashbourne Act (the Land Purchase Act) of 1885 enabled farmers to borrow the total amount of the purchase money for their holdings. William (2) Fulton of Edymore was the only one who took up this offer, approaching the Land Commission in 1888. A letter from the Land Commission to James Fulton, a younger brother of William Fulton, offered an advance of £1,300 to enable them to purchase their holding – see overleaf. William (2) Fulton was then the tenant of three adjacent farms (Nos. 8, 9 and 10), totalling 146 acres (59 ha), with an annual rent of £69.34. The purchase price was almost 19 times the annual rent. This was nearly twice the normal Ulster Custom 'purchase' price of about 10 times the annual rent (see page 15). Repayment of the loan was by annual payments over a period of 49 years with interest at 4 per cent. This scheme was taken up only by larger farmers whose landlords were willing to sell individual farms. Generally, landlords were not satisfied with the conditions of this Act.

The next piece of legislation, the Wyndham Act (the Irish Land Act 1903), enabled landlords and tenants to come to an agreement for the sale of farms

Letter from the Irish Land Commission offering a loan to William (2) Fulton

> **The Irish Land Commission,**
> 24 Upper Merrion Street,
> Dublin, *April 26* 1888
>
> All future correspondence in reference to this matter should be addressed—
> "O.H.M.S.
> JEFFERY BROWNING,
> Solicitor to
> The Irish Land Commission,
> 24 Upper Merrion Street,
> Dublin."
>
> IN THE MATTER OF THE ESTATE OF
>
> *The Duke of Abercorn.*
> An Owner of Land.
>
> Sir,
>
> I am directed to inform you that the Irish Land Commission, have, in accordance with the terms of the agreement and application signed by you, sanctioned the advance of £ *1300* therein applied for to enable you to purchase your holding; and notice is hereby given to you that if you desire to make any application in reference thereto, such application must be made to the Court by Motion on notice to the Owner within one month from the date hereof, at the expiration of which period the Commissioners (if satisfied with the Owner's Title) will, without further notice to you, proceed to make the said advance and to charge your holding with the Annuity payable in respect thereof When such advance has been made a copy of the charging order will be transmitted to you. *Your two applications have been consolidated.*
>
> I am,
> Sir,
> Your obedient Servant,
> DENIS GODLEY,
> Secretary.
>
> To *Mr James Fulton.*

which would be automatically approved by the Land Commission. The government advanced the purchase monies at $3^{1}/_{4}$ per cent interest over $68^{1}/_{2}$ years. With lower interest rates and a longer period in which to pay for the farm, purchase prices would be nearer the Ulster Custom purchase prices.

With the exception of William (2) Fulton, who had already bought his farm, all the farmers in the two townlands took advantage of this scheme between 1903 and 1911, with half of them concluding agreements in 1906. The table in Appendix 12 shows the year when agreements were concluded. One example was recorded in the valuation books: the purchase price paid by Hamilton Aiken for farm No. 7 in Edymore was £480, which was on a par with an Ulster Custom purchase price of 10 to 12 times the annual rent. Thereafter the annual payment was £15.73. The rent paid for this 45 acre (18 ha) farm in 1901 was £18. Farmers had been persuaded to buy the freehold of their farms by the prospect of paying annuities that were lower than the annual rents. Many of the descendants of these farmers found that by the end of the Second World War their annual payments were minimal and the outstanding debts, usually quite small, were paid off.

Markets and traders in Strabane

Slater's Directory of 1846 describes Strabane as 'a thriving market town'. The *Omagh Almanac and County Tyrone Directory* of 1882, claims 'Strabane as a flax, pork, butter and grain market is surpassed by few towns in the northwest of Ireland', with the increased prosperity attributed to its railway links and the canal trade. The principal market day was Tuesday with the most important fair days being 1 February, 12 May, 1 August and 12 November.

From 1851–81 Strabane's population hovered around 4,200/4,300. It then grew in the next decade. By 1891, its population was around 5,000 and it continued at this level up to the Second World War. The directories list a number of merchants who would have served the farmers in the two townlands. Some of these businesses survived for over 100 years. Well known to the farmers were Honeyford & Co, butter and egg merchants; William Harpur, coal merchant, ironmonger and timber merchant; John Duddy, blacksmith; William Stevenson, ironmonger and hardware; and Alex Weir & Co, cattle salesmen – see advertisement below. Other trading families who continued through to the mid-twentieth century included Hill, chemist; Lowry and Rule, grocers; and Stevenson, drapers.

An advertisement by Alex. Weir & Co Ltd featured in a 1913 calendar

Fields and gardens
By 1854 the modern field pattern had developed. The tenants of the small farms on the former Edymore Common Mountain had now enclosed all their land with no rough grazing remaining. Farmers in both the Edymore and Cavanalee Mountain areas had enclosed the better land, but a large area of rough grazing remained into the twentieth century. The 1905 map shows that the farmers in both townlands had joined together most of their original small fields as shown on the 1854 map – compare the maps on pages 60 and 29. By the end of the nineteenth century substantial farm equipment pulled by horses, such as mowers and binders, would not have been able to use the original small fields. Thereafter, there were hardly any changes in the field layout on farms until after the Second World War, when the tractor age took over from the horse age. This is clearly seen when comparing the 1905 and 1951 maps on pages 60 and 61.

On the 1833 map many of the lower farms in both townlands had substantial gardens adjacent to the farmhouse, all surrounded by trees. They all appear on the 1854 map, but had either completely disappeared or were insignificant features by the beginning of the twentieth century.

Lanes and roads
By the beginning of the century all the farmhouses and buildings in the vicinity of the Back Burn had disappeared, as had most of the lanes shown on the 1854 map, which had provided access to them. The exceptions were lanes that gave access to the flax dams. The stones from most of these former buildings had been used in the construction of ditches in nearby fields.

In the third quarter of the nineteenth century the road system was still evolving. The farms developed on the former Edymore Common Mountain were connected to the road that passed through the centre of Cavanalee. This road was later turned along the townland boundary and connected to the Strabane to Plumbridge road. It crossed the track that had allowed farmers in Cavanalee to obtain limestone from a quarry located on Edymore Mountain. This track was also made into a road which continued beyond the quarry to the upper parts of the neighbouring townland of Carrigullin. Another road was built to connect the upper part of Cavanalee with the upper part of its neighbouring townland of Evish. This branched off the Strabane to Plumbridge road, 300 yards (275m) east of Mathew's Bridge. The question 'who was Mathew?' has yet to be answered.

Further increases in the size of farms 1900–45
There were three farm amalgamations between 1912 and 1925 in Edymore. In 1912 Neal Gallagher, who was the tenant of farms Nos. 18 and 19 bought the neighbouring farm No. 17, increasing the size of his holding to 54 acres (22 ha). Robert (2) Huston became the owner of his neighbouring farm No. 13, in 1914. The size of the combined farms was then 112 acres (45 ha). In 1925, the Fulton family purchased farms Nos. 5 and 6 bordering the northern boundary of their farm, which increased the size of their holding to 201 acres (82 ha). (See later).

In Cavanalee the Graham family had run farms Nos. 12 and 15 as one farm since the beginning of the nineteenth century. In 1906, when they purchased the freehold of their farm, they also bought the neighbouring farm No. 14 (18 acres (7 ha)) giving them a total of 72 acres (29 ha). Another branch of the Graham family was the owner of the neighbouring farm No. 11, with 21 acres (8.5 ha). The Grahams had been farming this land since the latter part of the eighteenth century.

In 1934 Thomas (2) Houston bought the farm formerly owned by Joseph Young while retaining the separated 18 acres (7 ha) of his former holding which abutted his new farm. He then farmed 89 acres (36 ha). Later in the century Thomas (2) Houston's son, Roland, purchased most of what had been the Graham farms referred to in the previous paragraph, giving him a total of 153 acres (62 ha).

In 1951 Samuel and William Crumley bought James (7) Houston's farm (farm No. 17), thereby increasing their land holding to 161 acres (65 ha). The two farms were not adjoining and there was a road journey of over half a mile (1 km) between them. James (7) Houston had bought a farm near Omagh.

There was only one major change in the size and shape of farms in the twentieth century. Joseph (1) Davis farmed 47 acres (19 ha) in 1900. By purchasing neighbouring farms we find his grandsons, by 1965, farming 141 acres (57 ha). The table in Appendix 12 shows all the changes in farm ownership during the twentieth century.

The farmhouses and buildings on the farms – 1901 Census

The House and Building townland summary sheets of the 1901 Census provide basic information about the size and construction of houses. One column refers to the construction materials used for the walls, differentiating between substantial and flimsy materials – between stone, brick and concrete and mud, wood or other perishable material. The next column, covering roofs, differentiates between slate, iron or tiles and thatch, wood or other perishable materials. The third column provides an indication of the number of rooms in the house. The fourth column gives only the number of windows on the front of the house. The figures in these four columns are then added together to indicate the class of the house – 1st to 4th. With one exception all the houses in the two townlands were either class 2 or 3. This information is given in Appendix 8.

In Edymore only 3 out of the 13 farmhouses had thatched roofs, whilst in Cavanalee, 12 out of the 17 farmhouses were thatched. Some of the houses were quite large: in Edymore there were 3 houses with 7, 8 or 9 rooms and 3 houses with 10, 11 or 12 rooms; in Cavanalee there were 3 houses with 7, 8 or 9 rooms and only 1 house with 10 or more rooms. The latter was the farmhouse of Andrew Smith, the tenant of the largest farm in the townland, and it had a thatched roof. The house belonging to Joseph Young had been built around 1900. It was the only 1st class house in the townland. A drawing of the house – see page 50 – shows that the house had been extended, as there are 8 windows to the front – there were only 6 in 1901.

The larger farmers needed sufficient rooms to accommodate both their family and the live-in servants. The smallest farmhouses, usually with thatched roofs,

Ordnance Survey map of Edymore and Cavanalee 1907 edition – surveyed in 1905

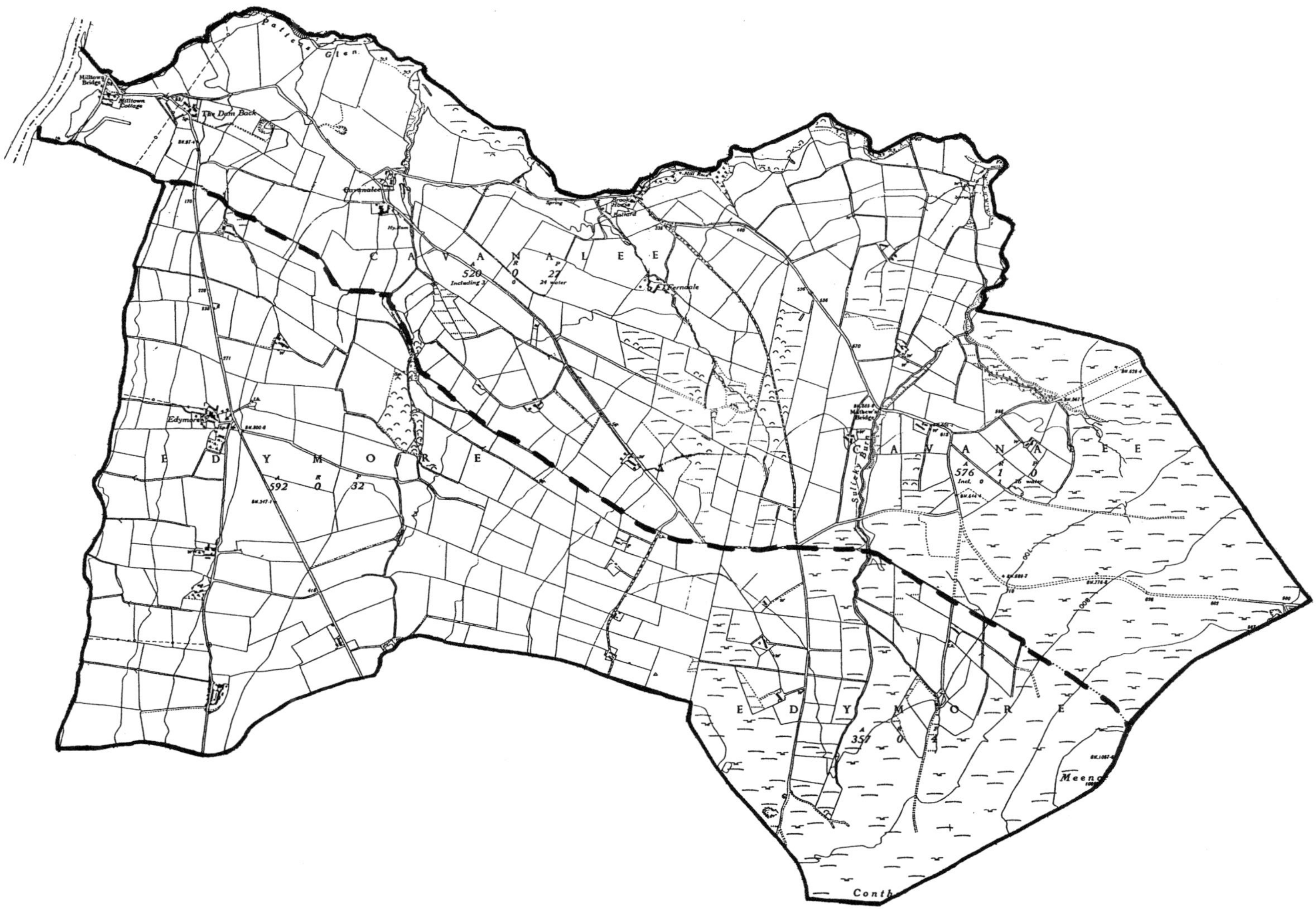

Ordnance Survey map of Edymore and Cavanalee 1951 edition – surveyed in 1951

were to be found on the small farms on the high land. There were a number of new farmhouses built in the two townlands at the turn of the century, but accurate dates are not available. The 1901 Valuation shows a number of increases over the 1880 valuation revisions. In Edymore, William (2) Fulton's rateable valuation had increased from £5 to £8, and Thomas (3) Huston's from £1.75 to £5.80. In 1881, James Aiken had built a new farmhouse and offices: rateable valuation had increased from £2.50 to £5.50. In Cavanalee, Andrew Smith's house had been enlarged, resulting in an increase in valuation from £3 to £5.50. Joseph Young's new house had seen his valuation increase from £2.50 to £15. These farmhouses are still in existence, all showing varying degrees of subsequent modernisation.

Another statistic given in the census returns is the number of out-offices on each farm. Today most farms have only a few large farm buildings. In 1901 the large farms in Edymore had between 10 and 13 farm buildings, whilst the smaller farms had between 3 and 8. The Fulton farm stands out with 21 buildings. A similar pattern is seen for the larger farms in Cavanalee, with one exception: Joseph (2) Davis had the largest farm in Cavanalee, 105 acres (42 ha), but had only 6 farm buildings. The farms on Cavanalee Mountain had between 5 and 7 farm buildings. The range of these buildings, usually built of stone with slated roofs, would have included: byres for both cows and beef cattle; stables; barns for hay, straw and grain and possibly turnips; a 'boiling house' for 'cooking' potatoes for pigs and poultry; pig and poultry houses.

We can see from both the 1901 Census and valuation books that there were, at the beginning of the twentieth century, eight cottages in each townland, owned by the larger farmers. With four exceptions, farm workers occupied all of them. In 1910, the Strabane Rural District Council bought land in Cavanalee on which they subsequently built a house that was continuously tenanted by a farm worker. In some cases farm workers occupied former farmhouses that became vacant after farm amalgamations or when a new farmhouse was built. The valuation books show that although there were frequent changes of farm workers on some farms through to the 1930s, on a few farms the farm workers and their families stayed put for many years.

Working the land from 1918 to 1945

In the 1920s and 1930s farms in the two townlands continued to operate on a mixed farming basis. The layout of fields remained the same throughout the first half of the twentieth century with the exception of the Fulton farm in Edymore. Here the hedges of the small fields in the upper part of the farm were removed to enlarge fields making it easier to use the, now more efficient, horse-drawn binders. Between one and four horses were kept on the farms during this period.

Oats was the main cereal crop, providing food and bedding for horses and cattle and on occasion barley and wheat might be grown. The surplus grain was sold to merchants or to Smyth's Mill in Strabane. Rushes were often used to thatch stacks. A key farm worker, the ploughman, was often the stack thatcher as well. Threshing continued to be carried out in barns on the farms. In the spring of 1944 Robert (2) Huston lost, through a fire, a barn with a threshing mill together with 10 tons of straw and 5 tons of artificial manure. Earlier from the 1930s steam-powered travelling threshing machines appeared in the two townlands. Houston Graham of Strabane operated one of these threshers. During the Second World War the amount of land used for cereal crops increased as a result of a subsidy payable for ploughing up grassland.

Potatoes were grown on all the farms, with acreages varying from 5 to 15 acres (2 to 6 ha). Varieties grown included Arran Banner, Kerr's Pink and King Edward. As the gathering of potatoes was labour intensive, casual labour, usually from the town, supplemented a farmer's own workforce of farm workers and children where available. Potatoes continued to form part of the diet of farming families and were fed to pigs on farms where they were kept. Shallow pits were dug for storage during the winter and the potatoes were placed in heaps, which were then covered with straw held down by soil. Transporting potatoes from the fields to the boiling houses, cooking them and feeding the pigs was a time-consuming and heavy manual task. Any surplus potatoes were sold to various produce merchants, such as Bannigan's in Strabane.

Every farm grew turnips – up to 5 acres (2 ha) was the norm. Lifting turnips in the fields, bringing them to the farmyard, slicing them and then feeding them to the livestock was a regular winter chore.

In the 1920s and 1930s between 2 and 7 acres (0.8 to 2.8 ha) of flax was grown on most farms in the two townlands. Some farmers would have again had to recruit casual labour to help with harvesting the flax crop. During this period flax was taken to Ward's or Maguire's flax mills at Douglas Bridge, some $3^{1}/_{2}$ to 5 miles (5.5 to 8 km) from the two townlands. With only a few exceptions, flax continued to be grown right through to the end of the Second World War. No flax was grown on the Fulton farm during this period or on the Huston farm during the 1930s. Robert (2) Huston was then operating an extensive poultry operation (see later). Growing flax came to an end just after the Second World

Making pits for the storage of potatoes during the winter

War when prices fell, owing to the availability of cheaper imports.

Each farm kept shorthorn cows, which continued to be milked by hand as milking machines only appeared after the Second World War. The exception was the Fultons who bought an Auto Recorder Milking Plant in 1935 (see later). There would only have been a slight increase in the number of cows being milked during this period and rarely would there have been byres catering for more than a dozen cows. The milk was not cooled; after sufficient had been kept back for the house and for making butter, the surplus was put into 10 gallon creamery cans which neighbouring farmers took it in turn to transport by horse and cart to the nearest creamery at Victoria Bridge, 4 to 5$^{1}/_{2}$ miles (6.5 to 9 km) from the two townlands. Nixon Hughey, who farmed in Cavanalee, operated a delivery scheme for a group of farmers. He collected cans at a number of pick-up points, such as Fulton's Corner in Edymore, and took them under contract to Victoria Bridge. Only a few farmers kept a bull, but all farmers raised their own calves. Some farmers bought in young bullocks from the monthly markets, and when these and the farmers' own bullocks had been fattened, they were usually sold to local butchers.

Where pigs were kept farmers had two or three sows and sold their reared and fattened pigs in the markets. Annually, farmers, usually those with large families, killed one or two of the fattened pigs. A butcher from the town who went from farm to farm butchered these on the farms and prepared the meat for use by the farmer's wife. During the Second World War the number of pigs kept declined, mainly due to the government's insistence that more land had to be devoted to the growing of crops.

The keeping of poultry continued to play an important role in the farm economy and poultry flocks increased during the War. As has been noted earlier, the farmer's wife continued to work with the hens, with the sale of eggs providing the money for household provisions and other domestic requirements. The sale of hens at the end of their laying cycle added to this income.

The farming Fulton brothers

By 1925 the Fulton farm, in Edymore, had become the largest farm in the townland with 201 acres (82 ha). However this does not give the whole picture of the Fulton family's farming activities. By that year the farm in Carrigullin had been added to, providing a total of 100 acres (40 ha) of land in that townland. Earlier, in 1923, a 200 acres (81 ha) farm had been bought in Drumenny townland, just off the Strabane to Londonderry road, a little over 5 miles (3.5 km) from Strabane. John (4), the eldest son of William (2) ran this farm as part of the greater Fulton farm enterprise then extending to 500 acres (200 ha), one of the largest in the district. His brother Samuel (3) later joined him. In 1938 the Drumenny farm separated from the Edymore farm, with William (3), the brother of John (4) taking on the Edymore farm – their father had died in 1930. In 1939, Hall Fulton, the youngest brother of William (3), bought Andrew Aiken's farm in Edymore (Nos. 14/15) after the Aiken family had moved to Coshquin, 3 miles (5 km) northwest of Derry city centre, on the County Donegal border. Twelve years later Hall Fulton sold this farm to

Bobby Fulton on his milk round – (above) horsepower in 1938 and (below) engine-power in 1957

Herbert Clarke from the Castlederg district, having bought another farm near Ardstraw.

The prominence given to milk production continued into the twentieth century. In the 1920s the Fultons established a house-to-house milk round in Strabane. Customers had their jugs filled with milk from churns carried around the town on a one-horse milk cart. In 1934, this activity became the responsibility of Robert (2) (Bobby), the third son of William (2) Fulton, after he had returned from Canada (see next chapter). After the Second World War horse power was replaced by motor power.

A number of new developments occurred in the 1930s, possibly as a result of the Northern Ireland 1934 Milk and Milk Products Act, which revitalised the dairy industry. Milk production on the Fulton farm was increased. In 1935 this resulted in the purchase of a Gascoigne four-point Auto Recorder Milking Plant – the first milking parlour in the district. It was the first plant of its kind that the Reading-based Gascoigne company sold in Northern Ireland. Because it was the first, William (3) Fulton received a 10% discount on the purchase price of £175 10s 0d. (£175.50). (See invoice below.) In 1939 the plant broke down and was out of action for two and a half months. No doubt members of the family and the farm workers had quickly to re-learn their hand-milking techniques. The plant was modified and continued working for another twenty years.

These were pioneering days. In the late 1930s William (3) Fulton tried making silage with little success but he did buy a new Fordson tractor in 1940 – another

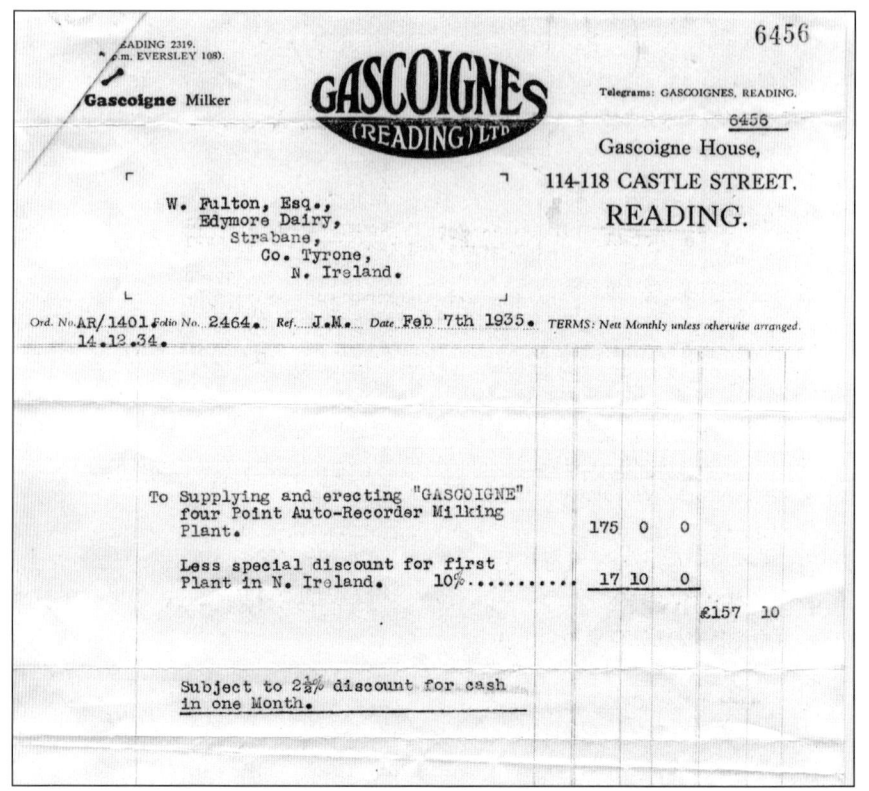

Invoice covering the purchase of the milking plant

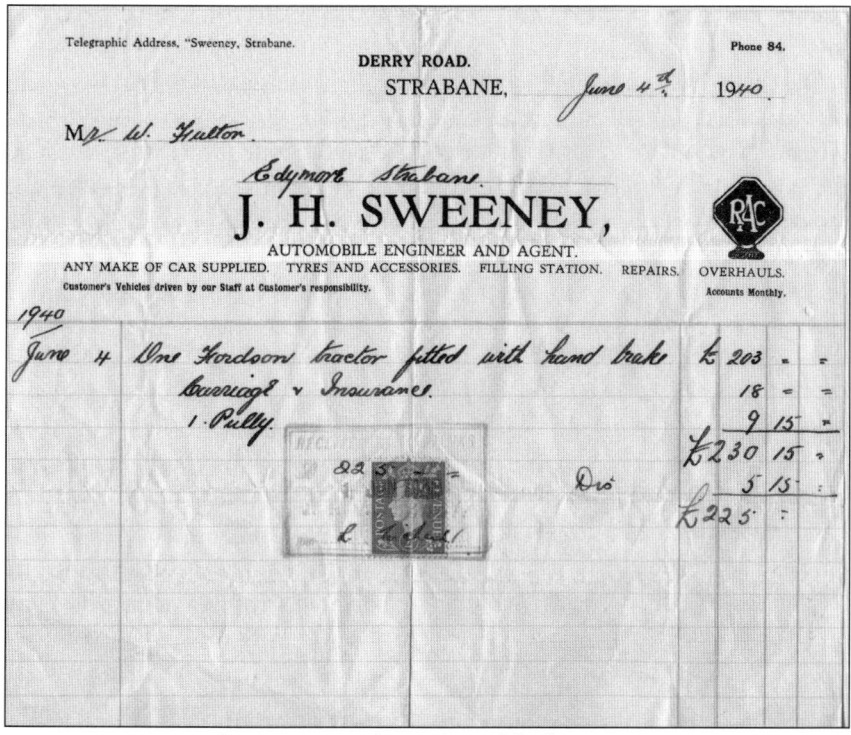

Invoice covering the purchase of the first tractor

first for the two townlands. This was purchased from J.H. Sweeney, Derry Road, Strabane for £203. (See invoice above.) The existing horse-drawn equipment such as ploughs and mowers were adapted so that they could be pulled by the tractor.

Hillside Poultry Farm – a market beyond Strabane

The Huston family, in Edymore, developed a poultry enterprise towards the end of the 1920s – the Hillside Poultry Farm. Advantage was taken of the new pedigree poultry stations from which farmers could obtain hatching eggs and day-old chicks, following the 1924 Marketing of Eggs Act. They increased their flock of laying-hens, with some 400 hens kept in huts and arks. This had been achieved in two ways: firstly through the purchase of day-old chicks, and secondly by hatching batches of 150 eggs in paraffin-oil fuelled incubators. In the late 1920s and through the 1930s consignments of 30 dozen eggs were sent by rail from Strabane to Derry and onwards by the overnight boat from Derry to Glasgow. They were sent to Mrs Huston's brothers who were working at the Singer Sewing Machine Company factory, located on the western side of Glasgow (see next chapter), and who had a ready-made market selling the eggs to their workmates.

A variety of breeds of hen were kept. These included Rhode Island Red, Light Sussex, White Leghorn, Exchequer and Wyandotte. At the ending of their egg laying days, there was a trade in the sale of plucked hens ready for the table. Seven or eight people were hired to pluck the birds so that they could be sold in the local market or direct to butchers, with a small quantity sent to Scotland.

Nothing was wasted – the feathers were sold to mattress manufacturers. The Scottish connection died out in the mid-1930s. If eggs could not be sold in Strabane to Colhoun the grocers, they were sold to an egg merchant, Clayton of Derry. This venture came to an end in 1938.

On this farm turkeys for the local Christmas trade were also reared, one turkey mothering twenty chicks. A few ducks were kept for domestic use. The young children growing up on the farm in the 1930s played their part in this aspect of life on their farm, feeding the hens and gathering the eggs. At the beginning of the twenty-first century diversification is called for; this small-scale example of diversification seventy years ago would only be viable today if a market existed for what are now rare breeds of hens and their eggs.

Declining trades

With the approach of the tractor age the need for the services of both blacksmith/farriers and saddlers declined. In 1896, there were four blacksmiths and four saddlers in Strabane. Ten years later Quinn Brothers had opened a saddlers shop in Abercorn Square. Their advertisement in a 1913 calendar, and a photograph of the last saddler member

Quinn Brothers advertisement 1913

John Quinn

Patrick Duddy

of the family, John Quinn, working in his workshop in the 1950s, are shown opposite. Little seems to have changed in fifty years. By 1970, the last of the saddlers in Strabane, Jack Baxter, retired owing to ill health and died in 1974, having been married to the eldest daughter, Kathleen, of William (2) Fulton of Edymore.

The Duddy family have been blacksmiths in Strabane for upwards of 150 years. The photograph shows Patrick Duddy working in his forge in Townsend Street in the 1950s. In the 1990s Patrick Duddy's son ran his farriery business in the town, his clientele being the owners of leisure horses and ponies.

6

SOCIAL LIFE AND LIVELIHOODS
Farming families from the mid-nineteenth to the mid-twentieth century

A dearth of information
For the last fifty years of the nineteenth century very little has come to light about the life of the farming families. Did life on the farms improve? Tenant right continued to provide a reasonably secure way of life. Would there have been a weekly visit to the town on market days? Would the monthly fair or the twice yearly fairs in May and November have been attended? Without doubt all family members would have attended the services and social activities organised by their churches. The families for which information, both written and oral, has been found from 1850 onwards are Wilson, Huston and Fulton in Edymore, and Houston in Cavanalee, plus Davis in both townlands. Virtually no information came to light about those families that had died out or moved away by 1950; the only exception being the King family who were tenants of one of the small farms on the Edymore Common Mountain from around 1850 to 1868.

A non-farming family – the Humphreys family
The Humphreys family continued to play an important role in the farming life of the district and the civic life of Strabane throughout the latter half of the nineteenth century. Major John Humphreys, Abercorn's agent since 1833, lived at Milltown Lodge and was succeeded by his son Thomas. The 1854 map shows that since 1833 the house at Milltown had been rebuilt. The new Milltown House has survived to the present time, forming part of the Strabane Grammar School, established there in 1956. The Ordnance Survey maps from 1833 to 1907 always called the house Milltown Lodge. Following his marriage in 1854, Thomas and his wife Isabella moved in with his parents – they had seventeen children, with only nine reaching adulthood. Both men held leading positions in the Church of Ireland in Strabane as well as in the commercial and civic affairs of the town, their influence covering a period of over fifty years. Positions held by Major John Humphreys included Provost and magistrate. Thomas (T.W.D.) Humphreys was also a magistrate and a chairman of the Strabane Steamship Company and a land agent. Major Humphreys died, aged 92, in 1872.

Major Humphrey's daughter, Fanny, married the Rev. William Alexander in October 1850, in the parish church in Strabane. This was no doubt the social event of the year and many of the ladies living in the two townlands would have gone to see the wedding. The Rev. Alexander had been appointed the rector of Termonamongan at Killeter, near Castlederg. After five years they went to Fahan near Buncrana in County Donegal, staying there for five years also. In 1860, the

Rev. Alexander became the rector of the parish of Camus-juxta-Mourne – Strabane. The Camus rectory, located just off the Strabane to Victoria Bridge road, was only two miles from Milltown House. This meant that Fanny could see more of her parents and her unmarried sister, Eliza, as well as her brother Thomas and his wife and their family. The Alexanders stayed seven years at the Camus rectory. William was then appointed the Bishop of Derry. He eventually became the Church of Ireland's Archbishop of Armagh and Primate of All Ireland in 1896, the year after Fanny's death. During her life she published eight books of hymns and poems, mostly during a twenty-year period from 1846.

One of the present farmers in Cavanalee was told by his father that Major Humphreys had a reputation for fairness but always endeavoured to maximise the income of the estate. One long-remembered reminiscence confirms this: when Major Humphreys suggested to a farmer living just half a mile (0.8 km) from Milltown House that he should grow trees on some steep land, he was asked: 'who would the trees belong to, Abercorn or me?' 'Abercorn of course' was the reply. 'Then let Abercorn plant them himself' was the rejoinder. The trees were never planted.

Farming families and their servants – the 1901 Census

The 1901 Census provides a unique snapshot of where people lived, their ages and family relationships, including their religious allegiances, plus their employment, at the beginning of the twentieth century. Details of the census covering all the farming families in the two townlands are given in Appendix 8. There were only two large families – Thomas Dooher with eight children and Hugh Devine with seven. However we shall see later that three of the farming families had equally large families in the first half of the century.

A few of the grown-up children of the farmers had occupations other than working on the farm. Alexander Regan's son, William, aged 24, was a clerk. In 1909 he did not take on his father's farms in Edymore and Cavanalee. They passed to James Regan, Alexander Regan's second son. James Regan sold both these farms in 1912. Alexander Regan's daughter Lizzie was a seamstress. Three daughters of Hugh Devine were also seamstresses, with the eldest daughter of Mary Aiken noted as a dressmaker.

Two families had children born in the USA. In Edymore, Hugh and Bridget Conway had three children between the ages of 3 and 7 in 1901. No more information about this family has been found. In Cavanalee, Joseph and Fanny Young had a son aged 15 and a daughter aged 14. Folk memories relate that Joseph Young's wife was a rich American widow and the children were those of her first marriage. This probably explains how Joseph Young became the first man to own a car and build a new substantial house in Cavanalee – perhaps his wife supplied the money for them.

The census also provides information about the men and women, other than family members, who worked on the farms and in the farmhouses. Seven farmers in Edymore and nine in Cavanalee had live-in servants. There were three categories: male farm servants; female domestic; and female general servants. The latter undertook farm work, such as milking cows and working in the harvest fields, as well as domestic work, especially if there were small children in the family. There were three general servants on the Fulton farm, where one of their jobs would have been milking cows.

Eighteen out of the thirty-two servants were born in County Donegal. Only eight of them could speak Irish and five were unable to read. All but two were aged under 40, with eleven of them teenagers. Most of the Donegal-born servants had initially been recruited at the Strabane Hiring Fair. With the increase in the employment of permanent workers as the century progressed, the number of servants recruited at the Strabane Hiring Fair declined although farm and domestic servants continued to be hired up to the Second World War. The numbers depended on the availability of family labour for farm work and the need to have additional help in the house when children were small.

Farming families and their churches
The Wilson family in Edymore were members of the First Strabane Presbyterian Church with brothers Robert junior and John, undertaking church work. However, by 1870, we find that both brothers were elders in the Second Strabane Presbyterian Church, the minister of which in 1859 was the Rev. Andrew Russell (1845–1882), and which at that time drew most of its members from rural areas around Strabane and Lifford. This was an Antiburgher or Seceder church established in 1816. By 1840, the Seceders had come together with the Presbyterians to form the General Assembly. No reason for the Wilson brothers changing churches has been found. Perhaps they had not got on with the new minister of the First Presbyterian Church, the Rev. James Gibson (1859–1873). In a letter written in 1860 to Abercorn by Major Humphreys, Russell was described as 'one of the most excellent and hardworking ministers of the General Assembly'. The Wilson brothers died in the late 1870s.

In the last quarter of the nineteenth century all the farming families in the lower parts of the two townlands were Presbyterians with four exceptions. There was one Catholic family and one Church of Ireland family in each townland, the Regans (Catholic) and Grahams (Church of Ireland) in Cavanalee, and the Conways (Catholic) and Fultons (Church of Ireland) in Edymore.

Before the Rev. William Alexander came to Strabane in 1860, the rector had been the Rev. James Smith (1835–1860). James Smith, an actor before being ordained, stood out in a rural parish in the northwest of Ireland. His wife, Cecilia Mary Grimani, whose forebears were of Italian origin, had also been on the stage. She had met her husband when they were in the same play and they married in London in 1822. According to a later rector, Rev. Smith's congregation benefited from 'his evangelistic enthusiasms and eloquent Calvinistic tinged sermons'. One wonders what the Graham and Fulton families would have made of this unusual duo.

National events – Temperance, Revival and Disestablishment
At the end of the 1850s two major events that evolved from social attitudes at that time brought church people together. In 1858 members of three Presbyterian Churches formed the Strabane Temperance Association. Within

three years the Association had five hundred members. Four years later a similar organisation connected to the Catholic church was established. Both organisations promoted total abstinence. It can be seen that their work influenced later generations.

In 1859 Presbyterians and Methodists in the Strabane district became immersed in the American Revival, news of which had reached Presbyterian congregations in County Antrim in the previous year; the resultant evangelical fervour spread throughout Ulster. The Presbyterian churches and Methodist church in Strabane held joint prayer meetings weekly and it is reputed that over a thousand people from both the town and country areas attended these meetings held in the Butter Market in Strabane.

The next religious event to affect Ireland was the disestablishment of the Church of Ireland in 1869, which meant that the church was largely disendowed, becoming a voluntary body from 1871. This change of status affected the Strabane congregation, which had been planning to build a new church during the previous decade – see below.

Two eminent Presbyterian ministers

Two Presbyterian ministers of the early twentieth century stand out: the Rev. Charles Toland of the Second Presbyterian Church (1886–1916) and the Rev. Edward Clarke of the First Presbyterian Church (1891–1936). They brought about the union of the congregations in 1911. The combined congregation retained the two ministers until the death of Rev. Toland in 1916. The Gordon family in Edymore were members of the Second Presbyterian Church and Robert Gordon served on the committee, which prepared the way for the union of the congregations. Another farmer involved with these events was Thomas (3) Huston, a member of the First Presbyterian Church's Congregational Committee. On his death in 1912, it was reported that 'he had been both an elder from 1894, and Sunday School teacher for many years'.

The Rev. Edward Clarke was highly regarded in the Presbyterian Church and became the Moderator of the General Assembly in 1930. He was very interested in education and encouraged members of his congregation to consider a university education for their sons and daughters – very few girls went to universities during the early part of the twentieth century. In the early 1920s his daughter Jean went to Edinburgh University; as Jean L'Amie, aged 100, she was the oldest member of the Strabane Presbyterian Church in 2005. Two daughters of William (2) Fulton, Jane and Mary, contemporaries of Jean L'Amie and possibly influenced by her father, went to Trinity College Dublin. Jane Fulton became a doctor, eventually living in Yorkshire, whilst Mary became a teacher and later a librarian at the Michigan State University in the USA, returning to Northern Ireland when she retired.

New churches

In 1871 the foundation stone for a new Presbyterian Church was laid and it was opened for worship in the following year. It was built in the Early English Gothic style, overlooking the river Mourne in Meetinghouse Street. Five hundred people

1st Presbyterian Church opened 1872

Presbyterian Church dedicated 1957

attended the ceremony of laying the foundation stone, by which time £3,000 out of the £4,000 required for the project had been raised by the congregation and friends. The church, which could seat 750, was filled when it opened in October 1872. The balance of the money was donated at that time. Two examples of donations were £10 given by John (1) Houston and £2 given by his son Thomas (3). To put this into perspective, John Houston's annual rent for his 20 acre (8 ha) farm at that time was £13. Unfortunately, this church was burnt down on Christmas Day 1938 – the heating system had caught fire. All that was left were the walls, spire and bell. The congregation then moved into what had previously been the Second Presbyterian Church, then used as a hall.

New elders appointed in 1916 included Thomas (5) Houston, who made his mark in local politics later. His son Roland became an elder in 1964. Another example of continuity has been three successive members of the same family who were the organists for over seventy years from 1919 – the three Alfred Forbes. After the Second World War fundraising started in earnest to raise money to build a new church. As the old site was not considered suitable it was decided to build the new church in the Manse grounds on Derry Road. In 1950 test boreholes were dug, with the young farmers of Edymore and Cavanalee to the fore – Roland Houston and William Smyth of Cavanalee, and John (3), Norman and William Davis and Samuel Huston of Edymore. Work on clearing the site started in 1954 and eventually the new church was dedicated on 2 May 1957. Virtually every member of the congregation attended this service. Sadly one Edymore farmer, Robert Gordon, whose generosity provided the new seats, died before the church was completed.

In 1860, the parishioners of the Church of Ireland in Strabane decided to build a new church to replace the original seventeenth century building. When he was the rector, the Rev. William Alexander (1860–67) purchased a site in the Bowling Green and donated it to the Parish. No progress was made during the 1860s and by the time a Committee was formed to organise the project the Church of Ireland had been disestablished. This meant that a possible grant of some £3,000 had been lost. The projected cost was in excess of £6,000. Fundraising started in 1873.

Two farmers in Cavanalee, Robert Hamilton and James Graham, and one in Edymore, Samuel Fulton, a brother of John (2) Fulton, were members of the Church Building Fund Committee, with Samuel Fulton noted as 'a generous subscriber'. The total cost of the church was £7,500; the debt was not finally cleared until 1887. The new church was consecrated on 30th October 1879.

The Catholics of Strabane in the 1890s started to build an impressive new chapel in Barrack Street, designed to rival the new Church of Ireland church. This chapel, dedicated in 1895, replaced the earlier chapel of St John, built in Meetinghouse Street in 1821. Not to be outdone the Methodists built a new church in 1900 in Railway Road at a cost of £1,200. The Smith family, who farmed the second largest farm, was the only Methodist farming family in Cavanalee; another Methodist was Thomas (2) Houston, a retired farmer.

New Church of Ireland Church consecrated 1879

Schools

Most of the children of the farming families attended schools linked to the Presbyterian Church and the Church of Ireland. In 1881, the old Presbyterian Church in Meetinghouse Street was converted into a primary school, mainly for girls. Boys attended for their first two years and then moved to the Academy School on Derry Road. The girls' school was always affectionately know by the names of the head teachers – Miss Black, Miss Young and finally Miss Anderson (Mrs Fleming). It closed in 1964 when the new County Primary School opened. The original Church of Ireland school dated from 1714. The District Inspector of Schools in 1893 reported that the school was 'badly adapted for the purpose'. A new school in the Bowling Green was opened in 1895 on a site donated by Duke of Abercorn.

In the first half of the twentieth century, with the exception of the girls in the Fulton family and two girls in the Huston family, none of the children received any post-primary education. However, the primary education provided was well rounded. Boys certainly received tuition that was of use to them on the farms, and the senior girls in Miss Young's school were introduced to the works of Shakespeare.

New Catholic Church consecrated 1895

Politics

It seems that none of the farming families were involved in serious political activities or events during the last half of the nineteenth century and the first part of the twentieth century. During this period movements were formed to promote a wide range of causes throughout Ireland. The one affecting many Irish farmers was the 'land war' organised by the Land League established in 1879. It organised a campaign against landlordism but was not active in Protestant areas of Ulster. However, the farmers in the two townlands benefited from the subsequent land purchase legislation (see page 55). The Local Government Act of 1898 resulted in the establishment of elected county, urban district and rural district councils. The Home Rule movement from 1870 eventually led to the establishment of Northern Ireland in 1921 and the Irish Free State in 1922, via the 1916 Easter Rising and the Irish War of Independence 1918 to 1921. On the way, in 1912, nearly half a million people in Ulster who did not support home rule signed the Ulster Solemn League and Covenant. Members of at least three of the farming families in the two townlands signed, with one family still having a copy of the document involved. Some of the farming families would have supported the Ulster unionist movement, subsequently becoming members of the Ulster Unionist Party. Thomas (3) Huston's obituary, in 1912, observed that he 'was a strong Unionist and helped forward the cause in his district'.

During interviews, five of the present older generation of farmers said that they had never been told by their parents how the events following the Easter Rising in 1916 and subsequent periods of unrest into the early 1920s had affected their lives and life on their farms. Only one member of a farming family played an active part in public life in the district during the second quarter of twentieth century. This was Thomas (5) Houston (1880–1957), a lifelong and an active member of the Unionist party. He was elected a member of the Strabane Rural District Council in 1922, eventually becoming its Chairman. He was also a member of the Tyrone County Council and its Health and Welfare Committees, as well as serving on the Strabane Board of Guardians until its demise in 1947.

Families after 1850
From the 1850s, genealogical information was found for three of the principal farming families – Fulton in Edymore, H(o)uston and Davis in Edymore and Cavanalee. Genealogical information about another family, King, which spent only a short time in Edymore, showed that members of the family had lived in neighbouring townlands and had connections later with the H(o)uston family. The abridged Fulton family tree is on page 53. Similar family trees for H(o)uston, Davis and King families are featured later in this chapter. The generation sequence of the family names is noted by the number (1), (2), (3) after the first (christian) name and so on.

The Fulton family tree shows that two generations each had ten children. John (2) Fulton (1824–75) and his wife Jane Dick (1828–83) had six boys and four girls between 1848 and 1869. One of the girls died aged 10, all the rest lived well into the next century. We have seen that John Fulton's second son William (1) (1854–1930) had taken over the tenancy of the farm following the death of his mother in 1883.

The 1901 Census confirms a recent change in the religious adherence of this family. The Fulton family had been prominent members of the Church of Ireland for generations. In 1898 William (1) Fulton had married Mary Stevenson. She

Mary Fulton with her adopted nephews Samuel and William and daughter Mary in 1908

had been a member of a Covenanting (Reformed) Presbyterian Church. However it was her husband who 'turned' (changed) from his membership of the Church of Ireland to the Presbyterian Church. This was a rare occurrence, as on marriage it was the usual practice that a wife would join her husband's church, if different from her own. For a young woman of 21 years to persuade a man twice her age to change his religion must be considered most unusual. They both then attended the First Presbyterian Church in Strabane.

The Census also shows that William (1) Fulton's unmarried brother, Samuel (1), also became a Presbyterian. However, their 14-year-old nephew, also Samuel, had not followed his uncles' lead. He continued to live in Strabane working for Honeyford and Company, the egg merchants.

Samuel (1) left the Edymore farm upon his marriage in 1901 or 1902 when he moved to a farm at Larchmount, near Sion Mills. In 1907, Samuel (1) Fulton and his wife both died of typhoid. They left two sons, William (2) and Samuel (2) aged 2 and 4 respectively. Mary Fulton, the wife of William (1), 'adopted' these two orphans. At that time Mary Fulton had five children under 8 years of age. She would certainly have needed the support of her general servants. By 1914, when her youngest daughter, Anna, was born she had a family of 12 children under the age of 15. William (1) died in 1930, his wife Mary surviving him by 30 years.

Thomas (3) Houston became the tenant of the farm of his uncle, Robert Wilson junior, in Edymore in 1873. Some time later, probably around the turn of the century, this family started to spell their surname without the 'o', reverting to the original spelling in estate records. This enables us to differentiate between

> ## H(O)USTON FAMILY TREE
>
> James (1) b 1677 (Scotland) d after 1753 m ?
> James (2) b *c*.1710 d *c*.1775 m Mary ? b *c*.1725 d *c*.1795
>   James (3) b *c*.1756 d *c*.1805
>   Andrew (1) b *c*.1760 d 1834 m Sussanah ?
>   James senior (4) b *c*.1798 d *c*.1860
>   John (1) b 1802 d 1880 m 1835 Mary Wilson b *c*.1810 d before 1864
>   Thomas (3) b 1837 d 1912 m 1877 Annie McCrea b 1843 d 1916
>   Robert (2) b 1878 d 1952 m Mary King b 1897 d 1980
>   Robert (3) b 1927
>   Samuel b 1929 m 1961 Mary Wilson (two daughters)
>   plus six daughters
>   Margaret b 1880 d 1957 (Canada) m 1922 Samuel Burns
>   Robert (1) b 1845 d 1895
>   Plus three daughters
>   Catherine b 1808 d 1894 m James junior (5) her cousin – below
> Thomas (1) b *c*.1764 d m Lucy ?
>   James junior (5) b *c*.1803 d before 1864 m Catherine Houston – above
>   Thomas (2) b 1830 d 1902
>   James (6) b 1841 d 1923 m 1879 Mary Arthur b 1855 d 1905
>   Thomas (5) b 1880 d 1957 m 1929 Elizabeth McKeeman b 1893 d 1972
>   Roland b 1931 m 1962 Kate Jinks (three sons, two daughters)
>   James (7) b 1882 d 1965 m 1928 Isabelle Fulton b 1902 d 1964 (one son)
>   John (2) b 1888 d 1970 m 1939 Isabella King b 1916 (one son, one daughter)
>   Andrew (3) b 1892 d 1924
>   plus two daughters and one son
>   plus three daughters
>   Andrew (2) b 1809 d 1866
>   plus two daughters

the Edymore (Huston) and the Cavanalee (Houston) branches of the family from then on. Thomas (3) (1837–1912) and Annie Huston (1843–1916) had two boys and two girls. In Cavanalee, James (6) (1841–1923) and Mary Jane Houston (1855–1905) had five boys and two girls. In both families one child died in infancy and two in their early twenties. Thomas (3) Huston's eldest son, Robert (2) (1878–1952), and his wife Mary (1897–1980), had two sons and six daughters between 1925 and 1938. Mary Huston was a widow for 28 years.

The Davis family had been tenants of a farm in Edymore since 1795. Robert (1) Davis, the tenant from 1838 until his death in 1877, married Eliza Fulton and they had three sons and two daughters between 1839 and 1848. Their eldest

> *DAVIS FAMILY TREE*
>
> Joseph Davis (1) b ? d ?
> **Robert Davis** (1) b? d 1877 m Eliza Fulton b ? d ?
>   One son and two daughters **plus**
>   *Joseph Davis (2)* b 1841 d 1922 m 1 Sarah Cuthbertson b ? d 1878
>   *Robert (2)* b 1875 d 1958 m *Isabella* Kerrigan b 1905 d 1999
>   Seven sons and two daughters of which the fourth son was
>   John (4) b 1929 (To NZ),   and the fifth son was
>   Samuel (2) b 1930 d 1998 m 1969 Margaret Wallace b 1936
>   *Samuel (3)* b 1969
>   *Trevor* b 1972
>   **John (2)** b 1878 d 1964 m 1921 **Martha** Keys b 1902 d 1994
>   Mary b 1922 m 1944 Nixon Hughey b 1915 d 1986
>   Sarah b 1924 m 1947 Samuel Crumley b 1912 d 1995
>   **John (3)** b 1928 m 1964 Anne Buchanan b 1939 (two girls)
>   **WILLIAM** b 1930
>   Norman b 1932 m 1960 Annie Chambers b 1935 d 1988 (three children)
>   **ROBERT (3)** b 1934 m 1965 Elizabeth Blair b 1929
>   **JOHN (4)** b 1968
>   plus Matilda b 1926 d 1982; Joycelyn b 1941 and Florence b 1945
>
>   *Joseph Davis (2)* b 1841 d 1922 m 2 Matilda Steel b 1843 d ?
>   Samuel (1) b 1880 d ? m (South Africa) ? b ? d ? (two boys)
>   Eliza Jane b 1883 d 1970 m 1908 (NZ) Francis Graham b 1880 d 1944 (5 children)
>   **John (1)** b 1843 d 1915 m Eliza Barnhill b 1862 d 1945
>
> **Note:** Tenants/owners of farms in Edymore in bold, and, tenants/owners of farms in Cavanalee in bold/italics. Owners of land in both Edymore and Cavanalee in uppercase bold.

son, Joseph (2) (1841–1922), married twice. His first wife was Sarah Cuthbertson, the daughter of a farmer in Cavanalee, whom he courted after he became the tenant of the neighbouring farm in 1873. They had two sons: Robert (2) (1875–1958) and John (2) (1878–1964). Sarah died after the birth of her second son in 1878. Joseph (2) married Matilda Steel soon afterwards. They had a son, Samuel (1), born 1880, and a daughter, Eliza Jane, born 1883, who both emigrated in their twenties.

    Robert (2) and John (2) Davis both had large families. Robert (2) married Isabella Kerrigan (1905–1999) and John (2) married Martha Keys (1902–1994). Both brothers married, in the early 1920s, women from the Donemana area who were respectively 30 and 24 years younger than their husbands. Robert (2) farmed in Cavanalee and John (2) inherited the Edymore farm from his uncle, John (1), in 1915; John (1) and his wife Eliza had no family. Robert (2) and Isabella Davis had seven sons and two daughters between 1925 and 1938. Robert (2) died in

1958 with his wife Isabella living until 1999, some 41 years later. John (2) and Martha Davis had four sons and five daughters between 1922 and 1945. John (2) died in 1964 with his wife, Martha, being widowed for 30 years.

We have seen that Mary Fulton, Mary Huston, Isabella Davis and Martha Davis brought up large families. They proved themselves to be very good farm managers, until one or more of their sons were of an age and with sufficient experience to fill that role. It is worth recording that, whereas from the late 1940s the five daughters of John (2) and Martha Davis all married farmers, none of the six daughters of Robert (2) and Mary Huston followed suit.

Other farming family connections

This is exemplified by the King family. Samuel (1) King attempted to break in one of the four small farms on the Edymore Common Mountain between *c.*1850 and 1868. By that date he was aged 64. He then moved to a farm in Evish townland, on the north side of the Cavanalee River, which was run by his sons. Later one of Samuel's sons, Samuel (2), followed by his son, Samuel (3), were the tenants, then owners, of a 32 acre (13 ha) farm in Carrigullin townland (adjoining Edymore) between 1904 and 1934. This farm was then purchased by George Mutch, the owner of two nearby adjacent farms in Edymore and

---

KING FAMILY TREE

Samuel (1) b 1804 d 1884 m Mary Gordon b 1802 d 1875
    John b 1836 d 1922 m Eliza ? b 1842 d 1877
        Mary b 1869 d 1875
        Robert b 1875 d 1877
    Mary Ann b 1838 d c1903   m 1 1860 Hugh Sproule (one son, one daughter)
                              m 2 1865 Robert Williamson b ? d c1899
                                      Robert b c1870 d ? m 1896 Helen ? b 1862 d 1932
                                            Nellie b 1897 d1943 m Robert King – see below
    Samuel (2) b 1842 d 1916 m 1874 Mary Jane Sproule b 1852 d 1921 – see below
        Seven sons and two daughters of whom:
        Samuel (3) b 1877 d 1945 m Agnes Summers b 1876 d 1957, two daughters with eldest
            Isabella b 1916 m 1939 John Houston* b 1888 d 1970 (one son, one daughter)
        Robert b 1884 d 1950 m Nellie Williamson b 1897 d 1943 – see above
            Six sons and four daughters. Their fourth son Frederick b 1927 d 1996 m 1974
                    Margaret Huston b 1931, 2nd daughter of Robert (2) Huston*
        Hugh b 1888 d 1940 m 1921 (NZ) Floriada Rasmussen b 1898 d 1948 (5 children)
        George b 1893 d 1977 m 1921 (NZ) Isabella Rasmussen b 1898 d 1968 (5 children)
        Mary Elizabeth b 1897 d 1980 m 1925 Robert (2) Huston* b 1878 d 1952
    James b 1843 d 1909 m Matilda Sproule b 1847 d ? sister of Mary Jane – see above
        Three sons and three daughters

* Refer H(o)uston Family Tree*

Cavanalee. Samuel (2) King and his brother, James, married two sisters, Mary Jane and Matilda Sproule, whilst their sister, Mary Anne, married Hugh Sproule, a cousin of the two Sproule girls. The Sproule family were also farmers in Evish. Samuel (2) King (1842–1916) and his wife Mary Jane (1852–1921) also had a large family – seven boys and two girls. Their youngest daughter, Mary, became the housekeeper to, and then married, Robert (2) Huston – see the Houston family tree. One of the daughters of Samuel (3) King, Isabella, married John (2) Houston, Cavanalee.

Emigration
Towards the end of the nineteenth century and during the first third of the twentieth century some members of these four families emigrated. In date sequence the earliest examples of sons leaving the farm were members of the Fulton family. The three youngest sons of John (2) and Jane Fulton emigrated. These were Robert (born 1865), James (born 1867) and Thomas (born 1869). No dates for their journeys came to light, but family tradition suggest that they went in their early twenties – the late 1880s or early 1890s. Robert went to Australia where he became a solicitor in Brisbane, living until his 90s. James and Thomas went together to the United States where they developed a successful market gardening business in the Chicago area.

In the next generation another four members of the Fulton family emigrated. The two orphaned sons of Samuel (1) Fulton, William (2) and Samuel (2) emigrated to Calgary, in Canada, in 1926 – they were then in their early 20s. They both became farmers, with Samuel specialising in grain and William in cattle. In 1928, Robert (2) (Bobby) Fulton went to Canada, staying with his cousins until 1934, when he returned home (his father had died in 1930) to develop the retail side of the family's dairying enterprise (see photographs on page 65).

Only one member of the Huston family emigrated. This was Margaret Huston, the daughter of Thomas (3) and Annie Huston. In 1922, she married Samuel Burns, a farmer living near Carrowkeel, off the road from Muff to Moville, in County Donegal. Shortly afterwards they emigrated to Saskatchewan in Canada. However, one member of the Houston family went abroad, eventually returning to Cavanalee. James (7) Houston, when 18, joined the army and found himself in South Africa, becoming a combatant in the Boer War. Upon his discharge and return to Ulster he obtained employment as a chauffeur to a Belfast businessman, Joe Ferguson, whose brother Harry created the renowned Ferguson tractor later in the century. He then returned to Cavanalee in 1911, becoming chauffeur to Joseph Young (farms Nos. 13 & 23) and doing occasional work on the farm. As noted earlier, Joseph Young was the first man to own a car in the two townlands, probably one built by Joe Ferguson. In 1912, James (7) Houston, then aged 30 took up farming when he purchased farm No. 17 from Alex Regan.

Two members of the Davis family emigrated in the early 1900s. They were the two children of Joseph (2) Davis's second marriage to Matilda Steel. Samuel (1) Davis had first worked in Herdman's flax spinning mill at Sion Mills and then went to South Africa, where he worked in the goldmines, settled down and married. His sister Eliza Jane had been courted by a young farmer, Francis Graham, who lived on the adjoining farm. He was the second son of Lowther and Mary Graham. According to the 1901 Census, Mary was a widow with six children aged between 15 and 23. Francis was the second son. In 1904, Francis Graham was aged 24 and Eliza Jane Davis was 21. They went together to New Zealand, not marrying until 1908. This event must have created a topic of conversation in the townland and at both the Presbyterian and Church of Ireland churches, as the Davis family was Presbyterian and the Grahams Church of Ireland. Later, after the Second World War, John (4) Davis, the grandson of Joseph (2) Davis, went to New Zealand where he joined his Aunt Eliza Jane's family at Palmerston North.

In the 1890s, members of the King family left home, although the first to leave got no further than Glasgow. Four of Samuel (2) King's sons, Gordon, Thomas, Samuel (3), and Robert had gone to Glasgow in the late 1890s, having heard of the opportunities for good paid work from their cousin, Robert Williamson, the son of a neighbouring farmer, who had gone there a few years earlier. Later, in 1910, two more of the sons, Hugh and George, emigrated to Canada and obtained work on farms in Saskatchewan. In 1912, they moved on to New Zealand, where, after a spell of farming, they moved on to other careers. They married twin sisters whose parents had emigrated to New Zealand from Denmark. At about the same time, Thomas and Samuel (3), after their marriages, left Glasgow and also went to Canada. However, upon the death of his father,

A typical farm cottage

Samuel (3) returned to run the farm in Carrigullin. In 1934, after selling the farm to George Mutch, he returned to Scotland to rejoin his brothers Gordon and Robert, at the Singer Sewing Machine factory near Clydebank.

Strabane and beyond

Two main interests for the farming families, their churches and the politics of Unionism, have been covered earlier. The families would have gone to Strabane on market and fair days, but their knowledge of the outside world would have come from reading newspapers such as the *Londonderry Sentinel*, as well as hearing about the travels of other people through their social activities. The latter would have been the trigger for the emigration of members of some of the farming families described above. What else would have been talking points for these families?

The weather would, as ever, have been to the fore. The period 1860–64 saw three cold and wet seasons followed by droughts leading to agricultural depression. A similar spell of bad harvests followed in 1877–80. The agricultural depression continued for at least another decade. At the end of June 1871, everyone would have been talking about the murder of a bank official, William Glass, in Newtownstewart, by Thomas Montgomery, a Sub-Inspector in the Royal Irish Constabulary. It was two more years before his execution took place.

At the end of the nineteenth century and up to the First World War Strabane had a wide range of social activities which are noted in the directories of that

Advertising the visit of the circus

time. The 1889 *Omagh Almanac and Co. Tyrone Directory* informed its readers that 'Strabane is renowned far and wide for the excellence and variety of its annual shows held in July. The exhibits last year comprised – Dogs, Poultry, Pigeons, Flowers, Cage Birds, Rabbits, Butter, Bees and Honey, and an exhibition of Home Industries; there were also Horse Jumping competitions on both days of the shows'. This event continued into the Edwardian era. There were also visits from travelling circuses and a Faith Mission Caravan. Some members of the farming families would have contributed to and attended the shows.

The sad news of the sinking of the Titanic, built in Belfast, on her maiden voyage would have been the main non-political news of 1912. The First World War saw many Ulstermen join the forces, but hardly any from the farming community. Many families were devastated following the Battle of the Somme in

Visit of the Faith Mission

1916, when 2,000 men in the 36th (Ulster) Division were killed in action. The events, both peaceful and non-peaceful, following the establishment of Northern Ireland featured widely in the newspapers and on the wireless after the launch of the British Broadcasting Company's Belfast radio station in 1924. These would have included disturbances in Belfast in 1922 and 1935.

The Second World War had only a limited direct effect on the two townlands. Early in 1939 some farmers' sons in the district joined the Territorial Army. One of these was William (2) (Billy) Smyth, the son of William (1) Smyth, Cavanalee. He was called up on the day war broke out on 3 September 1939. He saw service in East and North Africa, Greece, Cyprus, Italy, France and Germany. His first home leave was not until November 1944 and he was eventually demobbed in April 1946.

A radio receiving and tracking unit, installed in a collection of huts, was built on the Gallagher/Hughey farm in upper Edymore. The few men stationed there were billeted on nearby farms. One of these was the officer who drew a picture of Brook House, seen earlier. The deaths of over 700 people in Belfast during the two nights of bombing in April 1941 were mourned by many in the Strabane district. The arrival of American troops in Derry and the development of the naval base there reminded everyone that the war was indeed a world war. On a more local level it was an eerie sight for farmers and their families with a view of County Donegal to see all the lights on there at night, but with blackness over Strabane. Of course, it was not unknown for some people to pop over to Lifford and indulge in a little smuggling to augment meagre wartime rations.

Hiring fair in the 1930s

7

THE TRACTOR AND THE ELECTRONIC AGE
Farms and farmers from 1945 to 2000

The pace of change accelerates with the end of two hundred years of continuity
In the last fifty years there have been massive changes in the lives of people living and working on farms in Ulster. Farming in the two townlands entered the tractor, subsidy and electronic age. Farmers can no longer take for granted that their sons will follow in their footsteps. In the last two decades we have seen the emergence of the electronic age with computers and mobile phones becoming the usual means of communication. This development has fractured the previously traditional ways and continuity of farming family life, a way of life that lasted for over two centuries.

Most of the farming families at the end of the War had young families. Some of their children have continued to live on farms but many of them left both the farms and their home area. It is these children who will need to record the life of farming families during the second half of the twentieth century.

The farmers
To obtain the information about farms and farming during the last 55 years the writer quizzed his farming friends on a number of occasions. He is extremely grateful for their support and the information provided by them: Roland Houston and William (2) (Billy) Smith, Cavanalee, and William (4) Fulton, John (3) (Jackie) Davis, Robert (3) (Bertie) and Samuel (Uel) Huston and Herbert Clarke, Edymore. During this period two and sometimes three generations of the same family have been at the helm. For the lower parts of the two townlands the changes in ownership from 1939 are shown in the table 'Farms and Farmers in the Twentieth Century' in Appendix 12. A complete listing of all the farmers in the two townlands in 2000 is given in Table 7, on page 109. The 1951 map sets the scene, whilst the map on page 108 featuring the Edymore and Cavanalee farms in 2000 shows that there have been many changes in field layouts during the 1950s. The photograph opposite shows a typical farmyard from that period.

The changes in farming, both in the two townlands and throughout Northern Ireland, during the last 50 years have been more far reaching than those that had taken place in the previous 100 years. They have been influenced by government policies, the development of technology, notably the use of electricity and tractors, together with significant improvements in the practice of husbandry, aided by advances in agricultural education. The latter saw three farmers' sons attending courses at Agricultural Colleges. Lowry Smyth attended the Strabane Agricultural College; Norman Houston, Roland Houston's son, went to Enniskillen Agricultural College; and John (4) Davis, Robert (3) (Bobby) Davis'

The Huston farm in Edymore in 1952

son, attended Loughrey Agricultural College at Cookstown.

A few of the farmers have at some time been members of the Strabane Young Farmers Club (YFC), formerly the Glentimon (near Sion Mills) YFC. William (2) (Billy) Smyth was a member before the Second World War. His son, Lowry, was the Club Leader and Treasurer in the 1970s. More recently Norman Houston and John (4) Davis have been active members of the Strabane YFC. Two members of the Smyth family were members of the Ulster Farmers' Union. William (1) Smyth, pre-war, and his son, William (2) (Billy), post-war, were members of the Victoria Bridge branch, Billy becoming the chairman. When the smaller branches were joined together to form a larger North Tyrone branch, Roland Houston became chairman in the 1970s.

Government schemes for agricultural change
At the end of the Second World War it was government policy that farmers should be further encouraged to continue and expand on the excellent production levels attained during the War. In order to bring some order into the marketing of farm produce a number of marketing boards were established in Northern Ireland, the Pigs Marketing Board in 1954, the Milk Marketing Board

in 1955 and the Seed Potato Marketing Board in 1961. The earlier-established United Kingdom (UK) British Egg Marketing Board and the British Wool Marketing Board continued to operate.

Farm Improvement Schemes were introduced with differing aims over time. These resulted in farmers receiving support through advice and grants to help them provide a new infrastructure to accommodate the mechanised farming techniques being developed. Grants were available for the adaptation of existing buildings and/or the erection of new farm buildings, silos and pens for livestock. All the farmers in the two townlands took advantage of these schemes and the results can be seen on their farms today, including silos, byres and milking parlours (Roland Houston, Lowry Smyth, and Bobby Davis), a cattle court (Uel Huston) and pig rearing/fattening units (William (4) Fulton).

Piped water supply installations, from new wells and pumping systems through to water troughs in fields without access to streams, were also developed (see next section). Field drainage schemes were undertaken, with some farmers finding that the nineteenth century drainage systems were often still reasonably effective. Subsidies were also available to encourage the use of fertilisers and the spreading of lime on fields. Great use was made of these from the 1950s through to the 1990s. In the early 1970s, farmers typically would have lime spread at a cost of 5s 0d (25p) per acre (10p per ha) with a coverage of two tons to the acre (0.8 tonnes per ha). In the last few years this had risen to as much as £25 per acre (£10 per ha). During the last decade there has been a trend towards using granulated lime, with 6 cwts (300 kg) being equivalent to 2 ton(ne)s of ground limestone and being more easily spread.

A third area of support was through livestock improvement and animal health schemes. An earlier bull-licensing scheme was overtaken by the introduction of the Artificial Insemination (AI) Scheme, providing access to high quality bulls. The improvement of the cattle stock was reflected in higher milk yields. Sheep and pig quality was also improved. On the animal health front, schemes to eradicate various diseases also proved successful. Bovine tuberculosis was eradicated by 1960 and brucellosis by the early 1970s. During the last decade, however, there has been an occasional case of the latter. Attention paid to annual tasks such as sheep dipping saw a lessening of the effects of sheep scab. The Department of Agriculture, up to the early 1990s, supervised these operations. Since then sheep dipping is only carried out by progressive farmers. The attention given to warble-fly dressing of cattle, after the War, to offset the damage done to the hides, saw its virtual elimination by the late 1980s.

In 1973, the UK joined the European Economic Community (EEC), later the European Union (EU). This led to setting up of the Intervention Board for Agriculture and the winding up of the Marketing Boards, with the exception of the Milk Marketing Board which continued for nearly twenty more years. Eventually there was a return to free trade, with periods of fluctuating farm-gate prices. The edicts coming from the EU increased when the Common Agricultural Policy (CAP) came into play. The overproduction of a range of agricultural products in some EU countries led to the introduction of quota systems. From 1984, the farms engaged in dairy farming were the most affected by quotas (see later). The European Union knows what every farmer is growing through aerial satellite surveillance. All farms have their fields numbered on Ordnance Survey 1:10,000 digital retrievable Integrated Administration and Control System (IACS) maps.

The mid-1980s saw the introduction of a new 'less favoured areas' subsidy scheme, which extended the geographical coverage of the previous scheme. These schemes gave higher rates of subsidy for rearing cattle and sheep. Only the higher land in Edymore and Cavanalee benefited from the earlier scheme. Now virtually all Cavanalee and most of the Edymore farms benefit.

Over the past fifty years farmers have had to develop a wide range of office skills. For many years advice was available from the Department of Agriculture. Perhaps the most useful person helping farmers was, and still is, the auditor/accountant who sorts out the farm accounts for the taxman. In the 1990s one of the farmers, Lowry Smyth, undertook much of this work on his personal computer.

Access to the utilities
Since the end of the Second World War people living in towns have taken for granted the availability of mains water and sewage disposal facilities, mains electricity and, quite often, gas supplies. With the exception of gas (the Strabane production plant closed down in the 1960s) very few people living in Strabane today can remember being without these services. This has not been the experience of people living in Edymore and Cavanalee.

Water
At the end of the War most people in the two townlands obtained their water from wells via hand pumps or in many cases, if the wells were shallow, by dropping buckets attached to ropes into the well and pulling them out when full. A piped water supply had passed through Cavanalee since the latter part of the nineteenth century. This was the main supply pipe for Strabane which drew water from the Cavanalee River almost a mile (1.5 km) upstream from the Cavanalee Bridge at around the 400ft (120m) contour. This cast-iron pipe was duplicated in the 1920s and a third asbestos pipe was added in the 1950s. These pipes took the water by gravity to the reservoir immediately to the east of Strabane at a height of around 200ft (60m).

In the 1950s some farmers also found it possible to make use of gravity to supply water to their farmyards and farmhouses. The Mutch and Smyth farms jointly made use of water coming from a well in a field off 'the Rattleys' (Cavanalee Road) above the Mutch farmyard which is still in use. A gravity supply also operated on Herbert Clarke's farm. In the late 1960s Roland Houston installed a hydraulic ram to take water to a tank in one of the top fields and then by gravity to the other fields on the farm. He tapped into the new mains public supply when it passed the farm in the mid-1980s.

By the mid-1950s all the farmers had installed a piped water supply to their farmhouses and farmyards. This was an essential requirement when a milking machine was purchased. The water pumps were powered by petrol or diesel engines or, in the case of the Hall and William (3) Fulton and Robert (2) Houston farms in Edymore, by electric motors. In the late 1960s a new major mains water pipeline was taken from Castlederg to the Strabane Waterworks reservoir, augmenting the supply from the Cavanalee River. It passed through some of the lower farms in Edymore and Cavanalee. Connections, for which there was a nominal charge, were taken from it to the nearby farmhouses and yards. The supply was metered with a free allowance for the farmhouse of 30,000 gallons (135,000 litres) per year; 100 cubic metres from the mid-1990s. However by the end of the twentieth century everyone living in the two townlands was connected to a mains supply.

One farm, the Fulton farm, needs separate consideration. Four different water supply schemes had been used on the farm for all or part of the last 70 years. First there had been a gravity supply drawing water from the Back Burn, using glazed earthenware pipes, to an open tank (still in existence) in the upper part of the farmyard. More rigorous standards after the War saw William (3) Fulton drawing water, again by gravity, from a spring located on land above the road. He was connected to the mains supply in the 1960s but kept using the spring and Back Burn water around the farm. In 1987 when William (4) Fulton was developing his pig rearing and fattening enterprise he required even more good quality water and installed a new gravity supply using a spring on the upper part of the farm using $^1/_2$ mile (0.8 km) of polythene piping to bring it to the farmyard.

Sewage disposal

In the two townlands there has never been nor will there be a mains sewage disposal facility. Each farm or dwelling has its own septic tank facility. There have been great improvements in the design and effectiveness of septic tanks over the last 50 years. The differences are best seen in Edymore: the tank below a house, formerly a bungalow, built in 1952, has a half-buried concrete tank; a nearby bungalow built in 1998 has a plastic tank system buried completely below ground.

Electricity

The Houston farm in Cavanalee continued to use the water-driven turbine system which had been installed earlier in the century. As this only provided a direct current supply it was used for lighting only, the efficiency depending on the flow of water in the Cavanalee River. The inadequacy of this system meant that petrol or diesel engines were needed to drive the equipment being used on the farm from the late 1940s until a mains supply was provided in 1962. The supply was extended across Cavanalee reaching the mountain area at the same time that the Independent Television (ITV) mast was built a few yards to the east of the townland boundary, just off the Strabane to Plumbridge road in the same year. The Smyth and Mutch farms in Cavanalee were connected to the mains in 1956, at the same time as a supply was taken to the new Strabane Grammar School, which incorporated Milltown House on the opposite side of the Cavanalee River. The rest of Cavanalee was connected to the mains supply by the mid-1960s.

The first mains electricity in Edymore arrived in 1947. In that year two spur lines were taken from the main transmission line between Sion Mills and

Strabane which skirted the western boundary of Edymore townland. One spur went across the fields to the Edymore/Bearney road to serve the Robert (2) Houston and Hall Fulton (later Herbert Clarke) farms. The second spur went direct to the William (3) Fulton farm. The three farmers had to pay the Electricity Board for Northern Ireland (EBNI) for providing this service. Robert Huston paid £50, Hall Fulton £80 and William Fulton £90. These amounts covered a contribution towards the provision of the spur lines and to include all the electricity they used in the next five years! Subsequently the amount of electricity used was metered. The provision of mains electricity to all but one of the farms in Edymore townland was completed by the end of the 1960s.

Gas to oil
Bottled gas was installed by a number of farmers and cottagers during the 1950s and mainly used for lighting and cooking facilities in the farmhouse. As the use of electricity increased the use of bottled gas declined, coming to an end in the last twenty years.

When houses installed their own modern water supply systems or were connected to a mains supply, they usually installed fires with back boilers together with radiators. Coal became expensive, and, even with the increased price of oil in the 1970s, virtually every house in the two townlands had converted to an oil-fired heating system by the 1980s. Any new house or bungalow built since the 1960s installed an oil-fired heating system as a matter of course.

Roads
In 1933 the B72 Strabane to Victoria Bridge road, which passes through Cavanalee at Milltown, was given a tarmacadam surface. The next through road to be tarmacked was the Strabane to Plumbridge road in 1947. The first minor road to be tarmacked was the road to Edymore, going on to Bearney, in 1951. The programme of converting all the dirt tracks to tarmacked roads in the two townlands was completed by the end of the 1950s.

From the time these roads were tarmacked, until the late 1970s, they were regularly maintained, with drainage ditches cleaned out and the verges trimmed by tractor and plough-like attachment at least once each year. There were a number of friendly road-maintenance gangs who carried out this work, which in the spring and summer saw them cutting back the verdant weed growth such as cow parsley. During the last twenty years the Department of the Environment Road Service Section has virtually given up on the minor road maintenance in the two townlands. The original minor roads were wide enough for two cars to pass easily and for some of them even lorries could pass. During the past ten to fifteen years they have all become virtually single-track roads with only the locals knowing where it is safe to pass at the hidden passing places! Car drivers have been known to reverse for upwards of half a mile to the nearest farm lane or farmyard if they meet one of today's heavy goods vehicles.

The only other major road-related project of note was the rebuilding of the Cavanalee Bridge over the Cavanalee River in 1973, after it had been damaged by flood-water. The opportunity was taken to realign the road at the same time.

Strabane on Wednesday 22nd May 1963
The cattle market can be seen in the bottom right hand corner. There was no traffic congestion and there was plenty of parking space on the streets. It would have been much busier two days later – Friday was cattle market day.

Machines and men

The successful running of any farm depends on the efficient use of the equipment to be found on it at any given time. Since the end of the Second World War we have seen the greatest change in the running of farms that has ever taken place. All the farms in the two townlands exemplify this. The success of dealing with such epic changes is governed by the calibre of the men running the farms. Nine of the families farming in the lower parts of the two townlands today have been there for periods of between 120 and 240 years – the farmers know their land and their fields, with many of them unaltered for at least 150 years!

The first tractor, a Fordson, had appeared in 1940 – this had cost William (3) Fulton £225. Postwar, he had a Fordson Major and a Massey Ferguson, and, later a David Brown tractor. However, for the small farmer, it was the Ferguson tractor with its rear-mounted hydraulically-operated equipment that brought him into the modern era. In 1947 Robert (2) Huston bought a petrol-engine Ferguson tractor for £300. This tractor came with a two-furrow plough, a drill plough (for potato planting etc), spring grubber and a linkbox. The latter was used for carrying small loads and even children when they were transported to and from school on wet days! Later a trailer was purchased from John McKinney of Omagh for £50. John (2) Davis' sons persuaded him to buy a similar tractor in 1949. A year earlier Thomas (5) Houston also bought a Ferguson tractor, followed by a TE20 diesel version in 1952. In 1958, his son Roland bought a larger Massey Ferguson tractor.

Over the years new farm equipment appeared every few years. The annual visit in May to the Balmoral Agricultural Show in Belfast and local shows such as the Omagh Show in July let farmers see what was new and enabled them to discuss the pros and cons with fellow farmers before investing in any particular item. There were often fundamental changes in the way tasks were carried out after new equipment was bought. Within a few years, certainly by the mid-1950s, all equipment needing horse-power had gone, as had the horses! Seed drills supplanted the corn fiddle. Farmyard manure spreaders took over from people forking it out over the fields from a horse-drawn cart. Artificial manure spreaders also did away with spreading by hand. Farmers often built new farm buildings employing building workers after hours or at weekends. This saw concrete mixers being purchased, sometimes jointly, as was the case in Cavanalee when Roland Houston and Billy Smyth bought one in 1965.

The new merchants

A new generation of merchants supplied the new equipment and provided services to advance the changing agriculture scene. These included the people who sold and serviced the new machines, those who supplied the feeding stuffs and fertilisers, the people and the firms who bought the output of the farms, crops, cattle, sheep, pigs, milk and eggs, and the proprietors of the markets at which livestock was bought and sold. Outstanding amongst the latter was Jack Boggs. At the end of the War he had been a bus conductor. He started a small auctioneering business and sold hardware/agriculture products in shop premises in Abercorn Square, Strabane. Soon afterwards he took over the running of the market yard in Railway Road. In 1953 Samuel Linton, and the two Robinson brothers, Hill and Ronnie, joined him. These three developed the non-auctioneering side of the business, selling farm equipment, fertilisers, hardware and furniture. Jack Boggs' auctioneering business also expanded. The weekly Friday sales were well supported and buyers for cattle and sheep came from far and wide. However there were a number of local dealers who became familiar faces at the Friday sales. They included George Robinson, Donemana; Samuel Patterson, Lifford; Francis Smyth, Victoria Bridge; and the McDermott brothers of Strabane.

Jack Boggs' business became the largest of its kind in northwest Ulster. After his untimely death at the age of 65 in 1989, his son, Robert, carried on the business on a smaller scale. The cattle market operation came to an end in the 1990s when the Strabane District Council planned a redevelopment of the market yard.

An extensive property and farm sales operation, which included the annual conacre lettings in the late autumn, was also developed by Jack Boggs. A conacre let is for one year less one day. The current system of conacre lettings developed earlier in the century, after the farmers became the owners of their farms. This allowed them to rent land when wishing to expand their farming activities. It also allowed the widows of farmers with a young family to let the farm and obtain an income until a son or sons were old enough to run the farm. Two examples of farmers taking advantage of conacre lettings in Edymore can be given during this period. When George Mutch died in the late 1950s his widow, Annie, let her farm for a number of years until her son Malcolm was old enough to take on its management. At that time Bertie and Uel Huston rented land on which they grew cereal crops to augment those grown on their own farm.

Linton and Robinson Ltd had a number of competitors selling farm equipment. During the early part of the period under review, these included General Trading Services Ltd of Newtownstewart, with a branch in Strabane, together with William McCombe and the Leckpatrick Co-operative Agricultural and Dairy Society Ltd, in Artigarvan. The latter was better known for processing milk and expanded their milk operations considerably in the 1970s. However, trading conditions changed from the end of the 1980s when rationalisation had become a major consideration for milk-processing companies, following the downturn forced on it by the EU. Eventually the Leckpatrick Co-operative Agricultural and Dairy Society Ltd was sold, in 1993, to Golden Vale Co Ltd, a large Irish dairy products group. As a result, the descendants of the original group of farmers who formed the co-operative enterprise in 1901 realised substantial amounts of money. During the last two decades the larger agricultural merchants moved out of the fertiliser business and smaller merchants in the Derg valley took over, including Sydney Jack, Thomas Taylor and Lowry Surplis.

The use of proprietary feeding stuffs increased noticeably during the 1950s and 1960s. The larger, national suppliers included Silcocks, Levers, British Oil and Cake Mills (BOCM), E.T. Green and Thompsons. Regular visitors to farms were the meal company salesmen, many of them being asked in for a cup of tea. However there were two local millers. Robert Smyth and Sons in Strabane and

Cutting oats with tractor and binder on the Fulton farm, 1957

James Miller and Sons in Artigarvan. The Smyths also had a mill at Ballindrait in County Donegal and when this was burnt down, they bought the nearby Patterson's mill. They have continued in business throughout the last fifty years. The James Miller and Sons mill was taken over by the Leckpatrick Co-operative Agricultural and Dairy Society Ltd in 1970. However, in 1998 the subsequent owners, the Golden Vale Co Ltd, closed it down.

Farm crops
Cereals and harvesting
At the end of the Second World War oats and barley were the principal cereal crops which, with hay, were mainly grown to feed the cattle on the farms and were a part of the diet of the horses in use on all farms. The varieties of oats grown in the two townlands were mainly Onward, Stormont Iris and R30, the newer varieties produced increasing yields and shorter straw. Wheat had virtually disappeared as the local climate and soils were not suitable for growing a good quality crop. What little was grown was used on the farm. One of the perennial tasks, the stooking of the sheaves thrown out by the binder, still continued until the introduction of the combine harvester. However, by the end of the 1950s the growing of oats had virtually ceased. Most farmers had grown between 20 and 25 acres (8 and 12 ha), some of which was on land rented in conacre. This released more land for growing grass leading to an increase in the production of silage.

Barley was grown extensively on the lower land in the two townlands. After the War new varieties were introduced including Proctor and later Golden Promise. Farmers found that these varieties also gave larger yields and with shorter straw, which suited the combines that appeared from the 1960s. With the increase in the amount of cattle being kept the acreage under barley increased. The straw was used both for bedding and feeding. Between 20 to 30 acres (8 and 12 ha) were devoted to growing barley on most farms, with some on rented land.

Pitching sheaves up to the stack builder, 1958

Finishing off the last stack in the stack garden, 1959

A little barley was sown in the autumn but most was sown in the spring. The new varieties, together with the increased use of artificial fertilisers, led to an increase in yields, which by the 1990s had reached 2.5 tons per acre (1 tonne per ha) for autumn-sown and 1.5 tons per acre (0.6 tonne per ha) for spring-sown. With most farmers producing more grass for silage, the need for growing barley declined from the 1970s. The Huston brothers ceased to grow barley by the mid-1970s. William (3) Fulton and Herbert Clarke had grown around 30/40 acres (12/16 ha); the former stopped growing this crop in the early 1970s and the latter carried on for another ten years. Virtually no barley has been grown in the two townlands since then. An exception during the last decade was on the Fulton farm, where upwards of 70 acres (28 ha) was let in conacre for the growing of barley which, with potatoes, gave the land a break from producing grass.

After the Second World War saving the harvest continued to be the long-drawn out affair described earlier. Until the late 1940s, early 1950s in some cases, horse-drawn binders cut the cereal crops. With the arrival of tractors, some farmers adapted their horse-drawn binders so that a tractor could pull them along – this took place on the Fulton farm until a combine harvester was purchased. New binders designed for use with tractors appeared in the 1950s – Robert (2) Huston of Edymore buying one in 1951. This did sterling service and was eventually sold to Edward McLaughlin of Ligfordrum in 1985. As not every farmer had a binder, sharing or contracting out the use of the binder quite often took place. Uel Huston cut the cereal crops for Billy Smyth on a shared help basis; the Smyth crop being on lower drier ground in Cavanalee ripened before the higher fields of Edymore. In addition Uel Huston undertook cutting crops on a contract basis for William and Donald Kee in nearby Stragullin townland, which also was an early ripening district, as well as for farmers in Bearney townland, a later ripening area.

The use of steam-engine powered threshing machines ended after the War. Houston Graham of Strabane and Hugh Boyd of Dysart, along with a farmer, Francis Moss of Dernalebe, a townland 3 miles (5 km) south of Edymore, used large Field Marshall tractors in the two townlands. Bill Sayers of Bearney succeeded Francis Moss in the mid-1950s. He used an Oliver tractor, and later, a Fordson Major tractor, continuing up to the end of the 1960s.

By the mid-1960s the use of combine harvesters pulled by tractors had started. William (3) Fulton, Bobby Davis, Uel Huston, Herbert Clarke and Roland Houston all bought trailer combines. However the use of that combination caused problems in the small fields throughout the two townlands. There was always the problem of having barley with a sufficiently low moisture content to please the millers. To overcome this William (3) Fulton manufactured his own grain-drying plant. Self-propelled combine harvesters superseded trailer combine harvesters in the next decade. Bobby Davis purchased one of these machines. By that time he had a second farm of 60 acres (24 ha) at New Buildings, 10 miles (16 km) north of Strabane, near his brother Norman's farm, and so could make good use of such a machine. However most farmers used agricultural contractors. The contractor usually used in Edymore was Roy Russell of Strabane. When using self-driven combines, tractor-drawn trailers had to come alongside periodically to collect the grain. This posed difficulties when cutting barley in the

William (3) Fulton on his first trailer combine harvester, 1971

small fields in the two townlands. In the late 1970s, into the 1980s, some farmers removed hedges to make their fields larger, including Davis in both townlands, Crumley and Houston in Cavanalee and Fulton in Edymore. Ideally combine harvesters are best suited for cutting cereal crops in level, well-drained fields of at least 50 acres (20 ha) in size – these do not exist in either townland!

Grass

At the end of the Second World War the Ministry of Agriculture attempted to persuade farmers in Northern Ireland to grow grass for silage. Initially grass used for silage was the grass that had grown after hay had been harvested. Hay continued to be made in case the subsequent cut of grass converted to silage did not prove to be of good quality. When this grass was cut it was immediately transferred to a pit with a tractor driving up and down the grass to compact it. Molasses was then spread over the compacted grass to keep it moist, as most farmers were unable to keep cutting grass continuously until the pit was full. This practice died out by the 1970s. Farmers still wishing to save a large amount of hay often grew a green fodder crop – oats, barley and peas – to mix with the grass in the silage pits. Corrugated iron or asbestos roofs covered the pits and the space under the roof was used to store bales of straw and/or hay, which in turn helped compact the grass below.

The younger farmers led the way in making silage. In Edymore, Robert (2) Huston's sons, Bertie and Uel, started in 1947 and in Cavanalee, Thomas (5) Houston's son, Roland, two years later. By the mid-1950s all the farmers in the lower parts of the townlands were producing silage. In the beginning a single cut of grass was carried out in July. From the 1950s farmers increased the amount of artificial fertilisers spread on to grassland. Soon two cuts of grass per year became the normal pattern. The first cut was at the end of June, the second mid-August. This increase in the amount of cut grass meant that the early silos were too small and larger ones had to be built. The early ones were in the range 50ft x 15ft (15m x 4.5m) (Robert (2) Huston) to 60ft x 20ft (18m x 6m) (William (3) Fulton). In turn, these were superseded by larger ones such as the one built by Thomas (5) Houston, which measured 60ft x 37ft (18m x 11m), with a second one built in 1988. At that time Bobby Davis built two measuring 100ft x 30ft (30m x 9m). In the 1980s, farmers, especially those specialising in dairying, Roland Houston, Lowry Smyth and Bobby Davis, were making three cuts of grass for silage. Grass was cut in June, mid-July and early September.

At the beginning of the silage era the Ferguson tractor system was used on virtually all the farms in the two townlands, William (3) Fulton preferring to use his David Brown set-up. The Ferguson rear mounted buckrake (a large tined horizontally supported rake) was used exclusively to transport the grass if the fields being cut were near the silos. If not, the grass was raked up and put on low trailers and then taken to the silos where the grass would be transferred to the silo, again by using the buckrake – all very time consuming. The Ferguson system was adapted by other manufacturers, who from the 1960s offered larger tractors (70 – 110 hp) and their own grass-harvesting equipment. At the same time the Danish JF-Fabriken company's forage harvesters appeared and locally made (Johnston) large tipping trailers were being used. With the forage harvester able to blow the cut grass into high-sided trailers two or three tractors were required, especially if two trailers were used to keep a steady flow from the fields to the silos. This meant that neighbours or families with more than one farm shared the costs and labour input. Examples were Roland Houston and Lowry Smyth in Cavanalee and the Davis brothers in Edymore.

Towards the end of the 1980s larger and more expensive equipment came on the market. As such equipment would be uneconomic for the smaller farms in the townlands, some farmers began to use agricultural contractors. Hamiltons of Carrigullin, the next townland to Edymore, offered such a service from 1987, and were able to cut about 20 acres (8 ha) per day. This compares with 5 to 6 acres (2 to 2.5 ha) per day being cut 40 years previously. During the last decade there has been a move to use contractors to produce silage in round bales. This has proved most economic for the smaller upland farmers.

Hay
After the Second World War, the method of producing hay changed when tractor-drawn equipment took over from equipment drawn by horses – mowers and rakes, with trailers taking over from carts. The variable Tyrone weather had always posed a problem for the saving of good quality hay. In order to overcome the problem William (3) Fulton installed a large Lister fan dryer which produced first class hay for his sheep in the winter. Most farmers continued to produce hay as, from time to time, sheep farmers would have bought a load or two, but the amount of grass kept for making hay declined as the amount of grass cut for making silage increased. The majority of farmers had stopped making hay by 1990, with no one engaged in it in 2000.

Haymaking with the Davis brothers in Edymore 1950s

Bringing in the hay on the Fulton farm 1959

Potatoes

Up to the mid-1970s all the farmers in Edymore and Cavanalee grew potatoes. With the advent of tractors, drill ploughs, potato spinners (for uncovering the potatoes in their drills) and powered potato sorters, the work connected with growing potatoes was considerably reduced. However, potatoes had still to be gathered by hand in the fields and 'tatty gatherers' had to be recruited at harvest time, usually October. Their recruitment was often by word of mouth, with the same people coming each year. Needless to say, most, if not all of them, would have been 'on the buroo' – in receipt of state unemployment benefits from the Labour Exchange. If orders had not been received from potato merchants at harvest time, the potatoes would have had to be placed in pits – see illustration on p. 63.

The presence of 'tatty gatherers' caused a great deal of extra work for the farmers' wives as they had to be fed. The ten o'clock and three o'clock teas had to be prepared and taken to the fields. They would be given their mid-day meal in the farmhouse, with fish being provided on Fridays. In the two townlands the farmers' wives were dependent on having the fishman, Tommy Casey of Strabane, call to supply the fish in good time.

With the coming of the Seed Potato Marketing Board in 1961 and the Ministry of Agriculture's campaigns to improve the quality of potatoes, Ministry of Agriculture Inspectors inspected both the growing crops and the potatoes when being sorted and bagged for the potato merchants. The inspectors would then certify them (or otherwise) as being of a suitable quality for the seed trade. Three well-known potato inspectors visiting the two townlands were Messrs McCracken, Williamson and Armstrong. They were regarded with a degree of friendly tolerance.

The Board also set the parameters for the selling price for seed potatoes. In the 1950s and 1960s the varieties grown included the early varieties: Home Guard, British Queen and Arran Pilot. Typical main crop varieties were: Kerrs Pink (for local trade), Gladstone, King Edward and Arran Victory (for UK trade) and Arran Banner (exported to Egypt, Cyprus and the Canaries). During the 1950s the Huston brothers devoted around 20 acres (8 ha) to growing potatoes, whilst Roland Houston had half this acreage. There was a degree of specialisation brought about by location and soil type. Billy Smyth, in the lower part of Cavanalee, had some gravelly well-drained south facing fields and so was able to concentrate on growing early potatoes for the Northern Ireland markets. Nearby, in the next townland of Drumnaboy, the Kee family had similar land and was usually the first to have early potatoes ready to dig by the end of June. However, during the 1960s growing potatoes became less profitable and the export trade declined. As the newer equipment coming in at that time suited large fields, most of the farmers in the two townlands stopped growing potatoes – Roland Houston in 1960, Bobby Davis in 1965, William (3) Fulton in the late 1960s and the Huston brothers in the 1970s.

Potato growing has not died out. With all the farms now devoted to grass, the growing of potatoes provides a break in a minimal rotation system. Since the 1980s a number of potato-only enterprises have been established in the Strabane area. Here farmers specialising in such activities rent land in conacre from the grass farmers. In the last few years Alexander of Ballyheather, Cummings of Woodend, Johnson of Leckpatrick and Kee of Drumnaboy have rented land in both townlands. The machines used by these contractors do all the work, from planting through to digging and gathering and grading/bagging of the crop for sale to the supermarkets.

Turnips

Turnips were an important crop for over 200 years. In the mixed farming era after the Second World War, between three and six acres (1.25–2.5 ha) of turnips were grown on farms. They formed a significant part of the diet of sheep and were fed to cattle to eke out a shortage of home-grown hay. Lifting and snedding (cutting off the tops and roots) turnips on a cold winter's day was not a job eagerly sought after. When they got as far as the farmyard there was still the task of putting them through a hand-turned turnip slicer and feeding them to the cattle. Sheep eating them in the field was the preferred option. As keeping sheep on a regular basis declined so did the growing of turnips – few turnips have been grown in either townland since the 1970s.

Livestock husbandry
Dairy cows

At the end of the Second World War, keeping and milking cows was but one of the many activities taking place on the mixed farms of Edymore and Cavanalee. Eight to twelve cows in milk were typical, the exception being the larger dairy enterprise on the Fulton farm, with its milking parlour in use since 1935. With his brothers Jack (John (4)) and Samuel, and later Hall, running their own farms by the late 1930s, William (3) Fulton continued to run the home farm, producing enough milk to supply all his brother Bobby Fulton's requirements for his door-to-door milk delivery service around Strabane until 1959. After that, and until he ended his delivery service in the 1970s, Bobby obtained his milk from Leckpatrick (Co-operative Agricultural and Dairy Society Ltd). William (3) Fulton reduced his herd, giving up dairying in 1963.

The milking machine era for small farmers was about to commence. Hall Fulton installed a Simplex bucket milking machine in 1947. After Billy Smyth had returned from military service he persuaded his father, William, to buy an Alfa-Laval two-bucket plant for 20 cows which was duly installed in the byre in 1947. Bertie and Uel Huston also persuaded their father Robert to buy a similar plant. The writer, when working for the dairy equipment manufacturer, Alfa-Laval Co Ltd, installed this plant in 1949, and then went on to the next farm of George Moan, later Fred Hamilton, to install a similar plant there. By the mid-1950s most farmers in the two townlands had similar plants – the exceptions were those farms located in the Edymore and Cavanalee Mountain area.

The Shorthorn was the most common breed of cow kept by farmers. The cows gave a reasonable amount of milk, 600/700 gallons (2,700/3,200 litres) per year, and bullocks were suitable for the meat trade. Some of the farmers kept their own bull, others 'borrowed' their neighbours' bulls.

Bringing in the cows on the Davis farm in Edymore, 1950s

After the installation of milking machines the number of milking cows increased and as seen in the photograph above, there had been a move to keeping dairy breeds, mostly Friesians, but some Ayrshires, with Holsteins taking over in the late 1980s. The use made of the Artificial Insemination (AI) Centre at Newtownstewart, from the 1950s, meant that bulls were not needed and that the offspring produced led to cows yielding more milk. Yields were monitored by using the Milk Recording Service. A controlled usage of animal feeding stuffs, when added to the gradually improving quality of silage, led to a gradual increase in the milk yields of all herds. In the 1990s the cows on Roland Houston's farm were producing upwards of 1,200 gallons (5,450 litres) of milk per year, whilst on Lowry Smyth's farm his cows were producing around 1,500 gallons (6,800 litres).

Table 6 (overleaf) shows when farmers installed milking machines and when they changed from bucket milking plants to milking parlours. Initially the latter were the abreast type (cows side-by-side), but in some cases these were superseded by either a tandem or a herringbone (cows in a row) installation.

The number of cows kept by the dairy farmers increased. The typical bucket milking machine catered for 20/30 cows. The milking parlours could cope with twice that number and all the dairy farmers had, by the 1970s, doubled the size of their herds. For example, Billy Smyth, Roland Houston and Bobby Davis were then milking 40/50 and Herbert Clarke upwards of 90 cows. Bobby Davis increased the number of cows to 65 when he purchased more milk quotas (see

Farmer	Bucket Plant	Milking Parlour	Went out of milk
Houston (Cavanalee)	1954	1973 /1978	
Davis	1954	1974/1996	
Crumley	1954	1975	
Mutch	1950		1954
Smyth	1947	1973	
Davis (Edymore)	1954	1970/1995	
W Fulton		1935	1963
Huston	1949		1957
Moan/Hamilton	1949		1990
H Fulton/Clarke	1947	1972	1985

Table 6. Milking machine installations

below) and installed a new parlour in 1995. In all these types of milking plant one man could handle the complete operation from bringing in the cows from the field, or from the cattle court, through to operating the cooling equipment, leaving the creamery cans ready for collection by the Leckpatrick Creamery lorry. However by the mid-1970s bulk collection of milk started which, in turn, meant dairy farmers had to install stainless steel tanks to store the cooled milk as collections only took place on alternate days, although increasing to daily collections at peak periods in the summer.

In 1983 EU quotas came into force. Dairy farmers were told how much milk they could sell each year. Good husbandry had seen outputs rising so it became necessary to reduce the numbers of cows in milk. At the same time the buying power of the supermarkets had seen wholesale milk companies having to reduce their prices, which in turn saw a significant decrease in the price paid to farmers. It has become possible to process milk so that it has a shelf life of upwards of ten days, meaning that supermarket firms can quite easily import cheaper milk which can be sold as fresh milk. Many smaller producers gave up but were able to sell their milk quotas to other farmers, who could then increase their own production. Bobby Davis has already been referred to in this regard. In Cavanalee, Roland Houston saw his original quota of 220,000 litres (48,000 gallons) reduced to 187,000 litres (41,000 gallons) per year. Over a period of two years, in the early 1990s, he was able to buy an additional quota of 40,000 litres (8,750 gallons) per year which enabled him to increase his milking herd to 50 cows, the optimum for his farm. However, milk prices have continued to fall throughout the last ten years. In 1996 milk producers were receiving 23p per litre (13p per pint); in 2000 the price was 19p per litre. Although there has been a slight fall in the cost of feeding stuffs over recent years, overhead costs have risen, so the outlook is bleak for the survival of the smaller specialist dairy farmer. Only five farmers kept dairy herds at the end of the century compared with ten in 1945.

Beef cattle
Shorthorn bull calves were raised and fattened until the 1950s, finding a ready market. However with the concentration on milk production from the 1950s most farmers sold their bull calves in the local market, keeping a few heifers for replacement when the older cows had come to the end of their productive life. However, Bertie and Uel Huston having gone out of milk in the mid-1950s, then bought in beef-breed suckler cows, rearing and fattening the bullocks and selling off the heifer calves, increasing their herds during the 1970s and 1980s. From 1970, for 14 years, Bertie Huston rented the former King, later Mutch, now Sayers, 29 acre (12 ha) farm in Carrigullin. In addition, both brothers rented land in conacre up to 1990. Initially only 15 suckler cows were kept. After giving up milk production these numbers were steadily increased until an average of between 40 and 60 cows was reached. William (3) Fulton, after giving up milk production in 1963, kept around 30 suckler cows up to 1975. He then bought in some stores for fattening, with nearly all his land let mostly to his neighbours as he approached retirement age – he died in 1985, aged 79.

New breeds of beef cattle were introduced to Northern Ireland from Europe and those usually kept by farmers moving into beef production were the Charolais, Limousin and Simental breeds. Other farmers in the two townlands who moved into beef cattle rearing and fattening included, from mid-1980s, Jackie (3) Davis with around 30 suckler cows, and the Davis brothers in Cavanalee with around 70 suckler cows. Herbert Clarke bought in stores and dry cows during this period. In 1988, this branch of farming was devastated following the outbreak of Bovine Spongiform Encephalopathy (BSE) as the market for home-produced beef collapsed. One farmer who was badly affected by this was William (4) Fulton who kept upwards of 200 store cattle for fattening for three years after taking over his uncle's farm. He gave up when prices fell. The market for beef cattle recovered slightly during the 1990s and some of the farmers returned to producing beef cattle on a much smaller scale from the mid-1990s. They have had to live with a price fall of over 30% compared with those obtained before the BSE crisis.

'Getting rid of the muck'
After the Second World War, cattle continued to be kept in byres, large barns, or in earlier traditional outbuildings during the winter. Thus the traditional ways of removing the fouled bedding and dung during the winter continued up to the 1950s. It had been a case of using forks and brushes, loading carts or trailers, and laboriously spreading the dung on to fields by hand. With the advent of the tractor and muckspreader life became a little easier during the 1960s. The 1970s and 1980s saw most of the farmers building cattle courts with slatted floors, their design making the feeding of the cattle and the removal of dung easier. The dung passed through the slats to tanks below ground and the resultant slurry was more quickly disposed of on to the fields by using slurry tankers. These came in different sizes, holding between 1,000 and 2,000 gallons (4,500 to 9,000 litres). Roland Houston and Billy Smyth jointly bought one of 1,000 gallons (4,500 litres) capacity in 1970, replaced by one of 1,500 gallons (6,750 litres) capacity in 1997.

Sheep

In 1945 sheep were to be found on all the farms in the two townlands. As the move to dairying developed, the keeping of sheep declined. Some farmers would buy in store lambs for fattening, others, like Billy Smyth, would over-winter ewes and fatten the lambs in the spring. William (3) Fulton and Herbert Clarke had around 100 breeding ewes selling the lambs in the spring. William (3) Fulton continued this operation until he retired in 1975. Herbert Clarke continued with this size of flock up to the present. From the late 1950s, when the Huston brothers gave up milk production, they started to expand their sheep flock, which had been around 20 ewes, selling the resultant crop of fattened lambs. By the 1950s they had a flock of 40 ewes. In the 1960s this was progressively increased to around 300. After 1985 they reduced their flock by half and continued sheep farming at this level until they retired in the 1990s. William (4) Fulton has had a breeding flock of some 200 sheep since the late 1980s.

Clipping sheep by hand continued up to the 1950s when this annual task was made easier with the increasing availability of electric clippers. Most farmers then took advantage of itinerant professional clippers. One of the problems facing farmers was that the prices they obtained for their wool never matched inflation. Another chore was sheep dipping – another dirty, dangerous and smelly job! Sheep dipping took place twice a year: in June – fly dip; and in October – scab dip. The latter can now be controlled by injections.

Pigs

Keeping sows and rearing and fattening their offspring continued well into the period under review. All farmers kept sows until the 1960s when most of the farmers, who by then were concentrating on milk production, gave up this operation. Billy Smyth was one who gave up pigs in the late 1950s. Herbert Clarke on the other hand kept around 10 sows, fattening their pigs, up to the 1970s. In the 1980s he bought in young pigs for fattening. The Huston brothers, after going out of milk, increased the number of sows so that by the mid-1960s they kept around twenty, fattening their pigs. Jackie (3) Davis kept a similar number of sows. This meant that some traditional farms buildings had to be adapted or new pig rearing units built – a subsidy towards the construction of the latter was available. This form of pig production came to an end in the early 1980s. By that time some farmers, notably Messrs Crumley and Clarke, had started to specialise in pig production and had built larger rearing and fattening units. Subsequently, there was, unfortunately, a downturn in trade due to outbreaks of pig diseases and market prices became erratic. Herbert Clarke gave up this enterprise in the early 1990s.

Another pig enterprise was developed by William (4) Fulton when he took over the Fulton farm in 1986. He built a range of buildings that enabled him to keep upwards of 90 breeding sows and the rearing and fattening of 1800 pigs. As the 1990s progressed the return on fattening pigs declined and he gave up the enterprise in 2000.

Poultry
Even by 1950 it was rare to find poultry roaming freely around farmyards or nearby fields. However, Mary Fulton, wife of William (2) Fulton, continued the long tradition of the farmer's wife keeping the house on the money she made selling eggs to egg merchants by keeping 100 hens in each of her three large henhouses up to the 1950s. Bobby Fulton also kept hens, selling 200/300 eggs weekly on his milkround.

The age of the deep litter house had arrived. Many of the farmers in the two townlands converted, usually the upper floor of traditional farm buildings to cater for their hens. In Edymore the Huston brothers kept upward of 250 hens in existing lofts. It was a dusty environment with the hens enjoying their scratching existence in the 6-inch layer of peat/chopped straw on which they lived. Collecting and cleaning eggs on a regular basis was essential. Pullets were usually bought when at the point of lay – the days of rearing day-old chicks had long since passed.

The Huston brothers and virtually all the other farmers with deep litter units gave up egg production as the return on selling eggs had diminished almost in proportion to the increasing output coming from farmers who had installed battery cage systems. By the 1970s the deep litter era had ended.

Herbert Clarke also kept hens in converted farm buildings, but when the battery system of keeping hens came in during the early 1960s, he had sufficient space available in his farm buildings to keep four thousand rising to five thousand hens in battery cages. He continued with this enterprise until 1980, when increasing costs and low returns made this unprofitable. During this period his eggs had been bought by and delivered to the Leckpatrick Co-operative Agricultural and Dairy Society Ltd at Artigarvan.

The farmers in Edymore and Cavanalee in 2000
The names of the farmers in the two townlands, in 2000, and the map showing the location of their farms, are featured overleaf.

Edymore and Cavanalee farms in 2000

	Farm No.	Farmer
Edymore		
	1	John (3) (Jackie) Davis
	2	Malcolm Mutch (also in Cavanalee)
	3	William (4) Fulton
	4	Robert (3) (Bobby) Davis (also in Cavanalee)
	5	Robert (3) (Bertie) Huston
	6	Samuel (Uel) Huston
	7	Herbert Clarke (part of his farm is in Carrigullin townland)
	8	William Hamilton
	9 & 13	Peter Conway
	10	Sproule Brothers
	12	Peter McFadden
	14	Daniel (Dan) Conway
Cavanalee		
	1	Lowry Smyth
	2	Malcolm Mutch (also in Edymore)
	3	John Crumley, lower farm and George Crumley, upper farm
	4	Robert (3) (Bobby) Davis (also in Edymore)
	5	Samuel and Trevor Davis
	6	Roland Houston
	7	Patrick Dooher
	8	Sean Kelly
	9	Michael Conway
	10	Charles Dooher
	11	Joseph Kelly
	12	Government owned forest land

Table 7. A personal survey of the Edymore and Cavanalee farmers and their farms in 2000

8

CONCLUSION

Four hundred years of change and continuity
We have seen that over the last four hundred years there have been many changes in the way the land in the two townlands has been farmed. The farming families worked hard to convert mostly inhospitable land to productive farmland, with the move from the hand-tool to the horse-machine age taking well over a century and a half, and then from the horse-age through to the tractor and electronic age during the last fifty years.

However, since the Second World War a different model of farming has developed governed by the intervention of government and government agencies. New types of farm buildings appeared. Many farms increased in size, as did many of the fields. Machines have made employed farm workers almost permanently redundant on family-run farms. Most significantly the market structures that had given the farmer the opportunity to negotiate 'his' price have disappeared. Supermarkets, the EU and the Common Agricultural Policy (CAP) have taken over.

Traditional breeds of livestock have been superseded by foreign imports. The production and yields of cereals, potatoes, grass and milk all gained from a more scientific approach to husbandry as the twentieth century progressed. Yes, there has also been continuity, with nine of the families having farmed much of these two thousand acres for between five and eight generations.

The changes in farming have also been mirrored by great social changes, especially during the last fifty years. Key elements for change have included universal education; the widening horizons of communication from newspapers through to television; the impact of changes in power generation from steam (trains and ships) to the internal combustion engine (cars and tractors) and electricity. However, one social activity that has lasted for four centuries in Edymore and Cavanalee, attending one's place of worship, continues but on a slightly reduced scale at the end of the twentieth century.

An end or a new beginning?
What will the future hold, not only for the farmers in Edymore and Cavanalee but also for all farmers in Northern Ireland? In the two townlands only nine sons are likely to continue as farmers during the next twenty-five or so years. On four farms the sons are not involved in farming and on the remaining eight farms there are no sons to inherit. The EU has been enlarged; the stranglehold of the supermarkets will continue and global warming will mean that grass will be the only reliable crop. Could it be that in another fifty years there will be only two 1,000 acre (400 ha) cattle farms, called Edymore and Cavanalee – a return to the days of the O'Neill cattle ranch of 1600?

BIBLIOGRAPHY

Bibliography of books featuring the history of Strabane and district

Jim Bradley et al, *The Fair River Valley: Strabane through the Ages*, John Dooher & Michael Kennedy (eds), Belfast: Ulster Historical Foundation & Strabane History Society, 2000.

William J. Bradley, *Gallon: a History of Three Townlands in County Tyrone*, Derry: Guildhall Press, 2000.

A.A. Campbell, *Notes on the Literary History of Strabane*, Omagh: Tyrone Constitution Office, 1902.

W.J. Carlin, Jim Tinneny & George Haire (eds), *Railway Days in Strabane*, Belfast: WEA People's History Series, c.1993.

Concordia Journal, Nos 2–5, 1993–2003, Strabane: Strabane History Society.

W.H. Crawford, *The Management of a Major Ulster Estate in the Late Eighteenth Century: The Eighth Earl of Abercorn and his Irish Agents*, Dublin: Irish Academic Press, 2001.

Angelique Day & Patrick McWilliams, (eds), *Ordnance Survey Memoirs: Vol 5: Parishes of North, West & South County Tyrone*, Belfast: Institute of Irish Studies, QUB, 1990.

John Dooher & Michael Kennedy (eds), *The Strabane Hiring Fairs,* Strabane: Strabane History Society, 1995.

John H. Gebbie, *Ardstraw (Newtownstewart): Historical Survey of a Parish 1600–1900*, Omagh: Strule Press, 1968.

R.J. Hunter (ed.), *The Plantation in Ulster in the Strabane Barony, Co. Tyrone c. 1600–41*, [Londonderry]: New University of Ulster, 1982.

Robert Hunter & Michael Cox, comps/eds, *The Strabane Barony during the Ulster Plantation 1607–1641*, privately published, 1980.

Michael G. Kennedy, *By the Banks of the Mourne: a History of Strabane*, Strabane: Strabane History Society, 1996.

Michael G. Kennedy, *Strabane Through the Millennium: an Illustrated Chronology 1179–2000*, Strabane: Strabane History Society, 2001.

David Killen, *Through All The Days: a Presbyterian Heritage, Strabane 1659–1994*, Strabane: Strabane Presbyterian Church, 1994.

Rev. Canon Ernest Lovell, *Christchurch Strabane: Centenary 1979*, Strabane: Christchurch, 1979.

Rev. E.E.K. McClelland, *Friendly Strabane*, privately published, 1959.

Mourne Review Journal, No. 1, 1991, Strabane History Society.

William J. Roulston, *The Parishes of Leckpatrick and Dunnalong: their Place in History*, Episcopal Parish of Leckpatrick & Dunnalong, 2000.

Strabane Urban District Council, *Strabane: the Official Guide*, Croyden: Campaign Publicity Ltd, c.1968.

Sheelagh & David Todd, *Register of Gravestone Inscriptions in Leckpatrick Old Burial Ground, Artigarvan, Strabane*, Derry: privately published, 1991.

Valerie Wallace, *Mrs Alexander: a Life of the Hymn Writer Cecil Frances Alexander 1818–1895*, Dublin: Lilliput Press, 1995.

Books in which there is a significant amount of material covering the history of Strabane and district

W.H. Crawford & R.G. Foy (eds), *Townlands in Ulster: Local History Studies*, Belfast: Ulster Historical Foundation & Federation for Ulster Local Studies, 1998.

Charles Dillon & Henry A. Jeffries, *Tyrone: History & Society*, Dublin: Geography Publications, 2000.

George Hill, *An Historical Account of the Plantation in Ulster at the Commencement of the Seventeenth Century, 1608–1620*, Belfast: McCaw, Stevenson & Orr, 1877.

Jack Johnston (ed.) *Workhouses of the North West*, Belfast: WEA People's History Publications, 1996.

Christine Kinealy & Trevor Parkhill, *The Famine in Ulster,* Belfast: Ulster Historical Foundation, 1997.

Peter M'Aleer, *Townland Names of County Tyrone with Their Meanings*, Cookstown: Mid Ulster Printing Co., 1935.

Pat McDonnell, *They Wrought among the Tow: Flax & Linen in County Tyrone 1750–1900*, Belfast: Ulster Historical Foundation, 1990.

John McEvoy, *County of Tyrone: a Statistical Survey 1802*, reprint with an introduction by W.H. Crawford, Belfast: Friar's Bush Press, 1991.

Rosalind Mitchison & Peter Roebuck (eds), *Economy and Society in Scotland and Ireland 1500–1939*, Edinburgh: John Donald, 1988.

Michael O'Hanlon, *Hiring Fairs and Farm Workers in North-West Ireland*, Derry: Guildhall Press, 1992.

E.M. Patterson, *The Castlederg & Victoria Bridge Tramway*, Newtownards: Colourpoint Books, 1998.

M. Perceval-Maxwell, *The Scottish Migration to Ulster in the Reign of James I*, Routledge & Kegan Paul, 1973, Ulster Historical Foundation reprint 1990.

William Roulston, 'The Evolution of the Abercorn Estate in north west Ulster', *Familia: Ulster Genealogical Review* No. 15 1999, pp 54–67.

Alistair Rowan, *North West Ulster*, Harmondsworth: Penguin Books, 1979.

B.M. Walker, *Shadows on Glass*, Belfast: Appletree Press, 1976.

Manuscript material in the Public Record Office of Northern Ireland (PRONI)
Abercorn Papers, including Estate Rentals, maps and the Abercorn Letters; Muster Rolls 1630; Hearth Tax returns 1664/6; Civil Survey of Ireland 1654–67; Down Survey maps 1685; Books of Survey and Distribution; Spinning Wheel Premium Entitlement Lists 1796; Tithe Applotment Books 1824–38; Valuation records 1830–1934; Ordnance Survey maps 1833 onwards; Census 1841–1901; Devon Commission 1845; Cooper photographic archive.

Other manuscript material
Civil Registration records. Fulton farm records – 1835 lease, farm notebooks 1868–72 and 20th century farm documents. 19th century Strabane Presbyterian Church records. Huston family – Wilson will 1836. Houston family – early 20th century farm map and WWII drawing of their farm house. Family tree information covering the Fulton, H(o)uston, Davis and King families.

Journals
Due North (Magazine of the Federation for Ulster Local Studies (FULS)) 1999–present.
Ulster Folklife (Journal of the Ulster Folklife Society) Vols 1–48 (1955–2002).
Ulster Local Studies (Journal of the Federation for Ulster Local Studies) Vols 1–19 (1975-98).

A selection of books providing information about the history of Ulster
J.H. Andrews, *Plantation Acres*, Belfast: Ulster Historical Foundation, 1985.
Jonathan Bardon, *A History of Ulster*, Belfast: Blackstaff Press, 1992.
Jonathan Bell, *People and the Land*, Belfast: Friar's Bush Press, 1992.
Jonathan Bell & Mervyn Watson, *Farming in Ulster*, Belfast: Friar's Bush Press, 1988.
Peter Collins, *Pathways to Ulster's Past*, Belfast: Institute of Irish Studies, QUB, 1998.
L.M. Cullen, *An Economic History of Ireland since 1660*, 2nd ed., London: Batsford, 1987.
T.W. Freeman, *Pre Famine Ireland*, Manchester: Manchester University Press, 1957.
B.J. Graham & L.J. Proudfoot (eds), *An Historical Geography of Ireland*, London: Academic Press, 1993.
Seamus Helferty & Raymond Refaussé, (eds), *Directory of Irish Archives*, 2nd ed., Dublin: Irish Academic Press, 1993.
Liam Kennedy & Philip Ollerenshaw, (eds), *An Economic History of Ulster 1820–1940*, Manchester: Manchester University Press, 1985.
Samuel Lewis, *Topographical Dictionary of Ireland*, London: S. Lewis, 1837.
Peter Roebuck, (ed.), *Plantation to Partition*, Belfast: Blackstaff, 1981.

APPENDIX 1

Finding sources and the search for information

A long period of gestation!
Having lived in Scotland for the past thirty years, I encountered many difficulties when researching this farming history of the two townlands. Much time was spent when on holiday in going to the Public Record Office of Northern Ireland (PRONI) and libraries, not always appreciated by my family. Many of the chapters were originally written as separate essays and linking these into a coherent narrative proved difficult and time consuming. In this section I describe how I went about the task of finding out about the rural history of Ulster and the Strabane district. I certainly spent a great deal of time at all the usual places frequented by local historians in Ulster and spent many a delightful hour quizzing my friends and former neighbours about what happened on their farms since the Second World War. Above all, I benefited by having known some of Ulster's most knowledgeable local historians. What follows is how I went about obtaining the information featured in the book.

Finding out about local history
My interest in local history developed in the mid-1960s, when I undertook a survey of the farriery industry of Northern Ireland for the Rural Industries Development Committee of the Northern Ireland Council of Social Service. I found that many of the farrier families had been engaged in their skilled trade of shoeing horses for generations. The Duddy family of Strabane is a classic example. From these men I learned how their trade had been affected by the changes in farming during the first half of the twentieth century.

Where does one start? I started by reading three books written by the late Professor Estyn Evans (1905–1989), the pioneering social geographer of Queen's University Belfast (see illustrations on page 11). In his books he endeavoured to link habitat, heritage and history and on many occasions stressed the need to address 'the continuities of culture and landscape'. A contemporary of Evans, the late Professor J.C. Beckett, in a lecture given in 1963, remarked that 'the history of Ireland must be based on a study of the relationship between the land and the people ... the physical conditions inspired by life in this country and the effect on those who have lived there'. I have endeavoured to keep these thoughts in mind when trying to find out what happened to the farming families and their farms during the last four centuries.

In the 1960s, I 'discovered' PRONI, then under the direction of Kenneth Darwin and later Brian Trainor. I became aware that a vast amount of information about the past, in and around Strabane, was to be found in the Abercorn Papers. I obtained copies of the maps of the two townlands for 1777 and 1806. When looking at the latter map I saw that Abercorn's agent had pencilled in a proposed road which is the straight portion of the present Carrigullin Road. After this road was built some of the roads shown on the 1806 map did not survive into the mid-twentieth century. Walking through some fields of barley in Edymore I was able to determine the line of the earlier road which had connected three farms – the height of the barley was shorter along the line of the old road which had been abandoned a century and a half earlier. What else would the landscape reveal about the past? I would need to find out how to research my local history, the history of the Strabane area.

The opportunity to do this occurred two years later when I attended an evening class at Newtownstewart. The leader of the class, Bill Crawford, then a stalwart of PRONI, showed the participants how they could research the development of the townlands in the parish of Ardstraw during the nineteenth and early twentieth centuries. The next year I attended another class, held in Strabane, when Bob Hunter, then of the former Magee University College, guided a class through the period of the Plantation of the Strabane Barony (1607-1641), and provided material which allowed the participants to undertake research tasks. The results of the participants' labours finally appeared in print in 1982. Both Bill Crawford and Bob Hunter encouraged me to delve further into and write up the history of 'my' two townlands.

Much of the information was obtained through visits to PRONI and the local history collections held by the Western Education and Library Board in Omagh and Derry and by the North Eastern Education and Library Board in Coleraine. I also looked through the records still held by the Presbyterian Church in Strabane. Living in Scotland I had to rely on the inter-library loan scheme to obtain books which widened my knowledge of the history of Ulster and the Strabane district. At some time or other I consulted all the books in the bibliography. It lists over thirty publications that deal with many aspects of the history of the Strabane area – over twenty of them were published in the last fifteen years, mostly by local people actively engaged in studying and researching a wide range of their local history topics. In addition I was helped and supplied with information by Bill Crawford, Bob Hunter and John Dooher, secretary of the Strabane History Society.

The dearth of information about the Strabane district

Finding the information, which would provide an insight into the life of farming families in this rural area, has taken a great deal of time. Anyone undertaking a local history project in the Strabane area is at a disadvantage because of the lack of certain types of information available for other parts of Ulster. The 1659 census of County Tyrone has not survived. This would have told us who was living in the Strabane area in the mid-seventeenth century. The Hearth Tax returns of 1664/6 only provide the names of some of the better-off people. The Ordnance Survey Memoirs (OSM) of the 1830s for the Parish of Camus-juxta-Mourne (Strabane and the area immediately to the southeast) have been lost. These would have contained information on life in Strabane and the townlands lying between the neighbouring parishes of Leckpatrick and Ardstraw. The latter are included in volume five of the *Ordnance Survey Memoirs of Ireland* published in 1990. The parishes featured in that book enable us to find out what was happening elsewhere in North Tyrone and, by inference, in the townlands in the immediate area of Strabane.

The investigations into and the surveys of the historical social life of the past undertaken by the late Estyn Evans and his cohort of students over the years bypassed North Tyrone. The Mourne country, County Down and counties Derry and Donegal were their preferred exploration areas. Rarely does one see even a reference to the 'folklife' of the Strabane district in any of the *Ulster Folklife* journals. The staff of the Ulster Folk and Transport Museum have over the years made many trips to the Glenelly Valley and the Sperrins but have not explored westwards from Plumbridge. Even John McEvoy in his *Statistical Survey of the County of Tyrone*, published in 1802, provides little information about Strabane and its immediate neighbourhood.

The Abercorn Papers

All local historians, past, present and future, in the Strabane area have been, are, or, will be, grateful to the forebears of the Duke of Abercorn in that they employed extremely able agents whose records have been kept for hundreds of years. These records were transferred to the care of PRONI in the 1960s. The Earldom of Abercorn was awarded in 1606, the Marquessate in 1790 and the Dukedom in 1868. The family had owned substantial areas of land in the Strabane and east Donegal area since the seventeenth century until the beginning of the twentieth century. They have played important roles in Ulster political life throughout much of the last four hundred years.

The extensive Abercorn papers include the Irish Estate Papers with rentals and household accounts covering nearly two hundred years, and maps, surveys and plans that cover two hundred and fifty years. The highlight of the archive is the extensive collection of the Abercorn Letters. These include the correspondence that passed between the Earls/Marquesses and their agents and other estate officials in Ireland and Scotland between 1736 and 1818. As the Estate Records provide information down to townland level, I was able to obtain much valuable information about the farms and farmers in the two townlands. Looking through the Abercorn Letters I found letters referring to people living in the two townlands during the latter part of the eighteenth century and early part of the nineteenth century.

The 1756 Abercorn Rent Assessment and Land Valuation Survey lists the tenants and number of houses and provides information on the type and quality of land found in the two townlands. Subsequent surveys of 1777 and 1806 also include maps, which cartographically are to a high standard. For the most part they are as accurate as the later Ordnance Survey (OS) maps. The Estate Rental books cover the period 1787 to *c.*1900.

Other sources of information

The payment of tithes by farmers who were not members of the established Church of Ireland was resented. This led to occasional protests in various parts of Ireland during the latter part of the eighteenth century, which continued into the early 1830s. Tithe Applotment Books were compiled between 1823 and 1837 in order to determine the amount of the tithe which occupiers of farms should pay directly to the Church of Ireland.

The 1833 Valuation was primarily a valuation of land. The field books and the maps recording this information are to be found in PRONI. For the Strabane area the first Ordnance Survey (OS) maps surveyed in 1833 were used. The Griffith's Valuation of 1858 tells us where families lived, who was the landlord of their house or land, including its area, plus the rateable annual valuation of both houses and land. The 1854 map shows their location. As valuation records have been amended and added to right through to the twentieth century, it has proved possible to account for all the farming families in the two townlands from 1756 up to the present time.

Census records from 1841 provide information on the number of people living in the townlands plus the number of houses. This information for the two townlands is shown in the table on page viii. For some years it has been possible, in Northern Ireland, to look at the Census Enumerators' records for 1901. Information on the farming families provided by the 1901 Census is given in Appendix 8. The Census also provides information about the types and quality of buildings on the farms.

Although a number of newspapers were published in Strabane between 1771 and 1837, the copies that have survived provide little news about local events. Later, this information was published in newspapers in Omagh and Derry, with Strabane editions of the Omagh papers available throughout the twentieth century. Information about some members of the farming families has been obtained from newspapers.

Some original documents came to light during the researches. These have provided unique information about aspects of life in the two townlands. In addition a few examples of folklore passed down through two or three generations have also been included

Maps
Most important was the information gleaned from maps. The earliest map showing the two townlands is the 1609 Bodley's Plantation Survey Map. After the flight of the Earls of Tyrone and Tyrconnell, in 1607, a scheme for the plantation (colonisation) of six of the nine counties of Ulster was mooted. Commissioners visited the county towns and organised juries of Irishmen who provided them with the location of the townlands and described the area in which they themselves lived. The map for the Strabane district is little better than a rough sketch, but it shows Cavanalee surrounded by hills.

The 1685 map of the Strabane area by Sir William Petty, Ireland's first geographer, is a more accurate map, but shows very few townlands. One feature clearly shown was the extensive bog in low-lying land immediately west of Edymore. An estate map *c.*1710 shows the two townlands in outline form. Their shapes approximate to the actual boundaries that are to be seen on later maps, both those of the estate surveyors and the Ordnance Survey. It shows that 'Meansesk' (Meenashesk) was located at the eastern end of the two townlands.

The Abercorn estate maps of 1777 and 1806 provided a wealth of information. There were separate maps of Edymore, Cavanalee and the Edymore and Cavanalee Mountains, each on sheets measuring 16 x 12 inches approximately (40 x 30 cm). The accuracy of the surveyors' work on both series of maps is reflected in that these maps have been reduced and joined together and they are shown on pages 16 and 17. They were the agents' and surveyors' working documents.

The first six inch to the mile (1/10256) Ordnance Survey map of the Strabane district which was surveyed in 1833 was published in 1834. This series of maps was prepared to delineate townlands. They show built-up areas in detail, but only feature roads, houses and watercourses in rural areas. Fields are only shown at the margins of the townlands. Elsewhere on the maps ticks are to be seen alongside roads where field boundaries were located. Unfortunately it is not possible to determine field patterns at that time. However all the fields can be seen, some twenty years later, on the maps surveyed in 1854 and engraved in 1855, the first to show contours. Later OS six inch maps are the revisions of 1905 (1907 edition) and 1951. The revision of 1972 is to a scale of 1:10000. Another map consulted was the one inch to one mile (1:63360) Land Utilisation Survey Map of 1948. The original large scale survey maps for north Tyrone have not survived.

APPENDIX 2

1756 Rent Assessment and Land Valuation Survey

The areas of the farms in this survey are given in Plantation acres. Multiply by 1.62 to give statute acres and by 0.66 to give hectares (ha).

CAVANALEE

I. Mill Tenement	A	R	P		£	s	d	
Best arable	5	2	00	@ 11/0	3	00	6	The first distinction is tolerable good land, but a little
Coarse do. & green pasture	6	2	00	@ 6	1	19	0	shallow & gravelly. The 2nd is very wet & shallow
Bogg and Misky pastr	4	0	00	@ 2	0	8	0	and also mossy, rocky & shrubby in some places.
Road		1	24		-	-	-	The last is very wet & deep of brittle moss & the
Content	16	1	24		5	07	06	mill pond prevents its improvement. Houses 6.

II. Thos Graham's Holding								
Arable	24	3	24	@ 11/0	13	13	10	The first distinction is a sharp kindly ground but
Steep oak bank	1	1	08		-	-	-	very steep, shallow, sandy & gravelly in many
By road		2	32		-	-	-	places. The second is a precipitous & ought to be
Content	26	3	24		13	13	10	inclosed as it occasions the loss of some cattle
								to Tenants. Houses 4.

III. Held by John Barnhill								
Arable	26	1	00	@ 10/8	14	00	00	The arable here is also a little steep, shallow &
By road		1	20		-	-	-	gravelly in some places & in others light cold &
Content	26	2	20		14	00	00	mossy, about an acre of it would be good Meadow,
								but that the Mill pond keeps it a little wet & misky
								& consequently coarse & sour. Houses 2.

IV. Upper South Cavanalee now divided into 3 parts

To wit Lower Division

Arable & Meadow	18	0	00	@ 8/6	7	13	00
Mixt pasture	3	1	00	@ 2/6	0	08	01
Content	21	1	00		8	01	01

The first distinction is a middling good ground, but a little light, cold & mossy in some places. The second is now very coarse & stript, but reclaimable. This is a compact farm & may be further improved. Houses in this and the two following 4.

V. Upper South Division

Arable	11	1	00	@ 6/6	3	13	01
Mixt pasture	28	1	00	@ 3	4	04	9
Bogg & heathy pasture	29	0	00	@ /2	0	04	10
Content	68	2	0		8	2	8

About three quarters of this is tolerable, the rest a very wet mossy indifferent sort of land, perishing the seed & not ripening properly. The second is wet misky green & heathy, seven acres of the last is uncut Turf bog, the rest is mostly stript & barren. But the whole farm is very Improvable.

VI. Upper North Division

Arable	12	0	00	@ 7/0	4	04	00
Mixt pasture	24	1	08	@ 3/2	3	16	10
Bogg & heathy pasture	9	0	00	@ /2		1	6
Content	45	1	08		8	2	4

About half the first distinction is Tolerable, the next very wet & deep of moss. The second is Tolerable good misky and Heathy feeding & some spots of it reclaimable. Two acres of the last is uncut Bog and the rest yields little pasture.

VII. Upper North Cavanalee

Best arable	20	0	00	@ 12/0	12	0	00
Coarse do. & best pasture	43	0	00	@ 7	15	1	00
Mixt Bogg & Mtn pastr	40	0	00	@ 2/6	5	0	00
Road	1	1	20		-	-	-
Content	104	1	20		32	1	00

The first distinction is good land. The second is very shallow steep & gravelly in many places, in other light and mossy. Twelve acres of the last is a little stript & barren, the next is Tolerable good misky & heathy feeding, and the 2nd & 3rd Articles may be much Improved. Note that three Acres of the above is claimed by the Tenants of this town, but at present it lies beyond the Brook, which annually changes its course and Sometimes every new Flood. Houses 6.

APPENDIX 2

VIII. New Mountain Division

Best Arable & green pasture	5	0	00	@ 6/0	1	10	0
Misky Mtn pasture	9	1	00	@ 2/6	1	03	01
Coarse Strip'd Mountain	11	2	00	@ /3		2	10
	25	3	00		2	15	11

Half the first is Middling ground, the rest light & mossy and wet & spring. Part of the second is very wet, but misky & some spots of it perhaps may yet be reclaim'd, the last Article is very much stript & nearly barren. But the whole is Improvable. House 1.

IX. Mountain Division

Arable and green pasture	7	0	00	@ 5/0	1	15	0
Bogg & Heathy pasture	258	3	00	@ /6	6	09	4
Lough	3	1	10		-	-	-
Content	269	0	10		8	4	4

Above half the first distinction has been labour'd, the next is green & misky but a little steep. Very little of the second Distinction is Misky being Generally wet & course but mostly pasturable. Note That there is a large Tract of Mountain exclusive of the above which is Grazed in Common between this & Mr McGhee's Tenants. Houses 2.

EADANMORE

I. John Finlays

Best Arable & Meadow	6	0	00	@ 12/0	3	12	0
Coarser Do. & green pasture	24	2	00	@ 6	7	17	0
Mixt pasture	9	0	20	@ 3	1	7	4
Stript or old cut Bog	12	1	20		-	-	-
Road		1	13		-	-	-
Content	52	1	13		12	16	4

The first Distinction is mostly good Land. The Second is of the middle kind, being cold wet shrubby & springy in many places. The Third is Misky heathy & Bogy. The Fourth is nearly Barren. Houses 1.

II. Alexander Todd's Holding

Arable & green pasture	4	3	13	@ 10/0	2	8	3
Mixt pasture	6	2	37	@ 4	1	6	10
Stript Bogg	3	2	16		-	-	-
Content	15	0	26		3	15	1

The first distinction is mostly good land. The Second is Tolerable of its kind, which is Misky wet & heathy. The 3rd yields but little pasture. But the Severale Articles are improvable. Houses 2.

III. John Simison's Division

Best Arable	5	0	00	@ 12/0	3	0	00
Coarser do & mixt pasture	24	0	00	@ 5	6	0	00
Road		1	02		-	-	-
Content	29	1	02		9	0	00

The first distinction is mostly good land. The Second very wet cold & springy, Two acres of it Shrubby & a like quantity a little mossy and not yet Throughly reclaimed. But the whole is very Improvable. Houses 3.

IV. Saml Gillilan & Wm Lowther's

Best Arable	3	0	00	@ 12/0	1	16	0
Coarser do. & Best pasture	14	2	00	@ 6	4	7	0
Mixt pasture	3	2	25	@ 3		11	0
Stript Bogg	1	3	00		-	-	-
Road	0	0	25		-	-	-
Content	23	0	10		6	14	0

The first distinction is mostly good land. The Second is a little cold & wet in some places, in other light & Mossy. The third is Tolerable good heathy & misky pasture. But the 4th is very Barren. Tho the whole is improvable. Houses 2.

V. Robt Smyly's Division

Best Arable & Meadow	8	1	30	@ 12/0	5	1	3
Coarser Do. & best pasture	38	3	20	@ 6/6	12	12	8
Mixt pasture	10	0	20	@ 3/	1	10	4
Old cut or Stript Bogg	6	1	04		-	-	-
Road	0	0	25		-	-	-
Content	63	3	19		19	4	3

The first Distinction is mostly good land. The Second is mostly wet cold & springy, & in Some places is Shrubby and mossy. The Second (third) is misky, wet & heathy. The 4th is almost Barren, but each distinction may be improved and Note that what is Said of this Farm will be nearly Applicable to the three following Ones. Houses 4.

VI. William Brown's Division

Best Arable & meadow	4	2	00	@ 12/0	2	14	0
Coarser Do. & best pasture	16	0	00	@ 6	4	16	0
Mixt pasture	5	3	30	@ 3		17	9
Coarse Stript Bogg	2	1	00		-	-	-
Road	0	0	31		-	-	-
Content	28	3	21		8	07	9

Houses in this and the next following 6.

APPENDIX 2

VII. John Rabb's Divison

Best arable & Meadow	4	0	00	@ 12/0	2	8	0
Coarser Do. & Best pasture	16	0	00	@ 6	4	16	0
Mixt pasture	4	0	30	@ 4		16	9
Stript Bogg	1	3	09		-	-	-
Road	0	0	13		-	-	-
Content	26	0	12		8	00	9

VIII. Gabriel Thompson's Division

Best Arable & Meadow	4	0	00	@ 12/0	2	8	0	Houses 2.
Coarser Do. & best pasture	16	2	20	@ 6	4	19	9	
Mixt pasture	4	1	22	@ 3		13	2	
Stript Bogg	1	1	20		-	-	-	
Road	0	0	18		-	-	-	
Content	26	2	00		8	0	11	

IX. Orr's part

Arable & green pasture	25	0	24	@ 6/0	7	10	10	The first Distinction in general is bad and
Mixt pasture	7	1	20	@ 3	1	2	1	indifferent sort of land, being very shallow, cold,
Stript Bogg	1	3	00		-	-	-	wet & springy, and in some places shrubby, & also
Road	0	0	28		-	-	-	light & mossy. The Second is wet misky & Boggy.
Content	34	1	32		8	12	11	The 3d very Barren, But all of it will admit of great improvement. Houses in this & the next 4.

X. Knox's Division

Best Arable & Meadow	9	2	20	@ 12/0	5	15	6	The first distinction is mostly good land. The
Coarser Do. & best pasture	29	2	16	@ 6	8	17	7	Second is a little cold wet & springy & in some
Mixt pasture	8	1	00	@ 3	1	0	9	places light & mossy. The third is partly wet,
Stript Bogg	4	2	20		-	-	-	Shrubby, Misky & Heathy. The Fourth is Barren.
Road	0	0	34		-	-	-	But all of it may be much Improved.
Content	52	1	10		5	13	10	

Bogg Held in Common	41	0	00		This is all uncut.

Note: In the 'Farms and farmers from 1756 to 1827 with rents and tithes' table in Appendix 10, and the 'Land descriptions/rents in 1756 and 1833/1838 for four farms', on page 25, the areas have been converted to statute acres.

APPENDIX 3

Land Description and Valuation Survey 1833

The publication of the first Ordnance Survey 6 inch to 1 mile maps in 1833 enabled surveyors to record the differing categories and condition of land for purposes of valuation. The map on page 126 (Appendix 4) records the land description areas numbered below, which exclude areas under five acres. Areas are given to the nearest statute acre, with the valuation per acre in shillings and pence, and the total valuation in £.s.d. based on the precise measured area.

Land in Cavanalee surveyed 6–9 May 1833

No.	Description	Area acres	Valuation s. d.	Total £. s. d.
1	¹/₂ arable, shallow gravelly part steep yellow sand & gravel subsoil ¹/₂ a cold wet clay and sandy soil liable to flood	7	14.0	4.19.11
2	Arable. ¹/₄ superior flat soil. ³/₄ moory arable and reclaimed bog, white gravel subsoil	18	18.0	16. 1. 3
3	Free arable moderate depth interspersed with some small steep hills	19	22.0	20.10. 3
4	⁵/₆ arable moory soil, ¹/₆ a superior arable part steep	37	14.0	15.15. 4
5	Uneven arable soil, steep and of moderate depth	34	16.0	27. 5. 4
6	Free arable soil sound and moderate depth, yellow gravel subsoil	19	21.0	19.11. 3
	Also banks, furzy pasture and very steep arable	5	av 5.0	1. 6. 0
7	Free arable soil of good depth and undulating surface	36	1.0	37.11. 6
	Also banks, furzy pasture and steep arable	5	av 2.9	14. 3. 8
8	Sound shallow arable soil part steep, yellow sand/gravel subsoil	15	15.6	11.15. 0
9	Moory arable of moderate depth, yellow sand subsoil	20	12.0	12. 3. 9
10	Moory arable of moderate depth, yellow subsoil	22	12.6	13.15. 0
11	Free arable soil a little steep of moderate depth, part light moory arable, white subsoil	21	13.6	13.19. 3
12	Light moory arable moderate depth part reclaimed bog white subsoil	18	11.6	9.12. 6
	Also wet reclaimed bog	6	5.6	1.13. 0
13	Arable ²/₃ moory ¹/₃ a free arable of good depth	12	10.6	6. 4. 6
14	Moory arable moderate depth, a little exposed, white/yellow subsoil	34	11.0	18. 9. 7
	Also reclaimed bog and steep pasture	6	av 3.6	1. 0. 0
15	Moory arable soil shallow and steep, white/yellow subsoil	21	8.6	9. 0. 9
16	Rough mountain pasture, part inferior heath & part with good grass	41	1.5	2.17. 3
	Also moory arable	5	6.0	1. 7. 0
17	Arable. ²/₃ moory of moderate depth whitish gravel subsoil ¹/₃ a free shallow arable	28	14.0	19.17.10
18	Reclaimed bog	18	7.6	6.18. 4
19	Moory arable, ¹/₄ superior quality, remainder light moderate depth	32	11.0	17.14. 4

APPENDIX 3

No.	Description	Area	Valuation	Total
20	Moory arable, a little steep, moderate depth, white gravel subsoil	17	9.0	7.16. 9
21	Free arable of moderate depth a little moory, steep and exposed	17	12.0	10. 4. 4
22	Reclaimed mountain, part arable and part pasture, white sandy gravel subsoil	22	6.0	6.13. 8
23	Heathy mountain producing some pasture	132	1.2	7.14. 0
24	Moory arable or reclaimed mountain white sandy gravel subsoil	15	7.0	5. 7.11
25	Reclaimed mountain moory arable white gravel subsoil	32	8.0	12.17. 6
	Also mountain pasture and steep banks	5	1.0	5. 3
26	Heathy steep mountain pasture	325	$3^{1}/_{2}$d	4.14. 8
	Also reclaimed mountain	7	3.6	1. 5. 4
		1097		

Land in Edymore surveyed 13 and 14 May 1833

No.	Description	Area	Valuation	Total
		acres	s.d.	£. s. d.
1	Light shallow arable very steep, white/yellow sandy gravel subsoil	23	12.0	13.17. 3
2	Free arable soil moderately steep	57	15.0	42. 9. 2
3	Free arable soil $^2/_3$ moderately deep $^1/_3$ shallow cold and wet, half the lot very steep	104	12.6	64.16. 3
	also shrubby pasture	5	1.6	7. 6
4	Moory arable $^2/_3$ moderate depth $^1/_3$ shallow, light mixed with gravel	52	13.0	33.10. 3
5	Moory arable moderate depth dry and well situated	29	13.0	18.11. 7
6	Moory arable rather light, moderate depth, $^1/_3$ a little exposed, white yellow sandy gravel subsoil	62	12.6	38.16.10
7	$^1/_3$ superior deep moory $^2/_3$ of a lighter quality and moderate depth, part a little exposed	28	13.6	19. 0. 9
8	Inferior light shallow moory arable	36	9.0	16. 2. 0
	also rough pasture	7	1.9	11. 4
9	Moory boggy uneven shallow arable with broken wet pasture	15	6.6	4.15.10
10	Reclaimed bog & moory arable, rather shallow, yellow and white sandy subsoil	46	7.6	17. 3. 3
11	Reclaimed mountain inferior arable, shallow with white sandy gravel subsoil	37	4.6	8. 6. 0
	Also heathy pasture	38	9	1. 8. 3
12	Rocky steep pasture and reclaimed boggy arable	24	6.0	7. 3. 1
13	Free light arable part moory, moderate depth	40	14.0	28.4.10
14	Reclaimed boggy arable	16	6.0	4.16. 1
15	Heathy mountain pasture	330	5d	6.17.10
		951		

(The manuscript document was signed by Robert Innes, Baronial Valuator)

APPENDIX 4

Land Assessment and Valuation map 1833

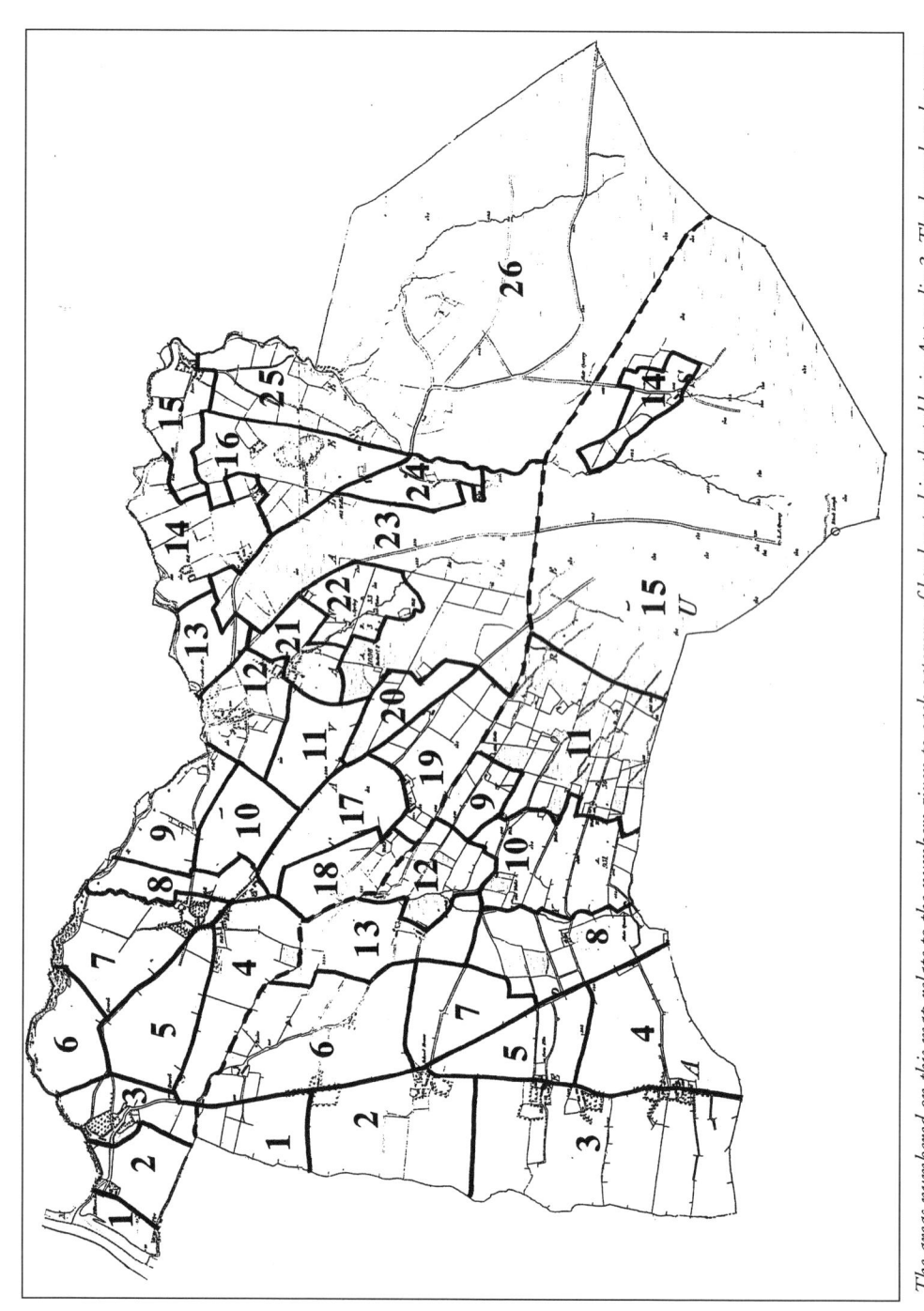

The areas numbered on this map relate to the numbers given to each category of land noted in the table in Appendix 3. The boundary between Cavanalee and Edymore is shown by a dotted line.

APPENDIX 5

Robert Wilson's will 1836

In the Name of God Amen, Robert Wilson of Edymore do make and publish this my last will and testament as follows, I give devise and bequeath unto Thomas Lowther and Nathanial Thompson and the Survivor and Survivors of them and to the Heirs and Assigns of such Survivor all my Freehold property of farm and Dwelling house together with all chattle and Household property of Whatsoever Nature and Whereinsoever Situated that Farm possesed at my Decease In Trust.

First I give and beqeath unto my son Robert Wilson all that farm of Land that I dwell on and now hold and possess under the Most Noble the Marquis of Abercorn situated in the townland of Edymore Parish of Camus & County of Tyrone, together with all my Chattle and house hold property all the cattle stock crop farming utensils &c all that I now possess at my decease of whatsoever nature or whereinsoever situated, and also to my son Robert Wilson I will and bequeath the one fifth part of one Hundred and fifty pounds bequeathed and willed unto me by my late father John Wilson of Meenlougher,

I will and bequeath unto my dear wife Elenor Wilson two Barrels of Shilling or Seventy two pecks of meal and Eight pecks of meal seeds thirty measures of potatoes One Hundred weight of clean scutched flax a milk cow Summered with sufficient grass and Wintered with sufficient fodder and she is to have her choice of any one of the milk cows that posses at my decease and she is to have any end or apartment of the house I live in during her life together with a sufficent portion of household furniture that my executors shall allow of her to have with twenty four Wheel car load of turf Cut win and laid at her door all the above Heirs free of all charges she my dear wife Elenor is to posses year and yearly during her natural life.

I will and Bequeath unto my daughter Elizabeth Wilson the sum of Thirty Pounds Sterling as a portion in marriage, I will and Bequeath unto my daughter Margret Wilson the Sum of Twenty Pounds Sterling as a portion in Marriage I will and bequeath unto my daughter Isabella the Sum of Twenty Pounds Sterling as a Portion in Marriage I will and Bequeath unto my daughter Elenor the Sum of Twenty Pounds Sterling as a portion in Marriage my Daughter Marys portion which I promised to pay at her Marriage If any of said portion or sum remains unpaid at my decease I allow my son Robert Wilson to pay the same after my decease, And If any of above named daughters die before her marriage It is my will that her above named portion shall die with her, and also in case any of my above named daughters does live to arrive at the period of fourty five years of age without having been married It is my will that said daughter or daughters shall at such period (of) age without being married have a right if she choose to demand of my son Robert Wilson their above named portion and it is my will that my said Robert Wilson shall pay each of them the same at such period of their age without being married and as to my son John Wilson I will and bequeath unto Him the sum of one Shilling Sterling to be paid unto him if demanded without him or his Heirs having any more claim against any of my freehold of household property of whatsoever nature or whereinsoever situated that farm I am possesed at my decease.

And I do hereby utterly disallow evoke and disanul all and every other former testaments wills legacies bequests and executors by me in anywise before named willed and bequeathed Ratifying and confirming this and no other to be my last will and testament In witness whereof I have hereunto set my hand and seal this Ninth day of November anno Domini One Thousand Eight hundred and thirty six.

Signed Sealed Published
and delivered by the said
Robert Wilson the testator
as and for his last will
and testament in presence
of us who have hereunto   (Signed) Robert Wilson (his seal)
Set and subscribed our
Names as Witness at
the desire and in the
presence of Robert Wilson
the Testator and in the
presence of each other
    Witness present
    Gustavus Lyon
    John Huston
    Walter Johnston Lowther

APPENDIX 6

Griffith's Valuation map 1858/1860

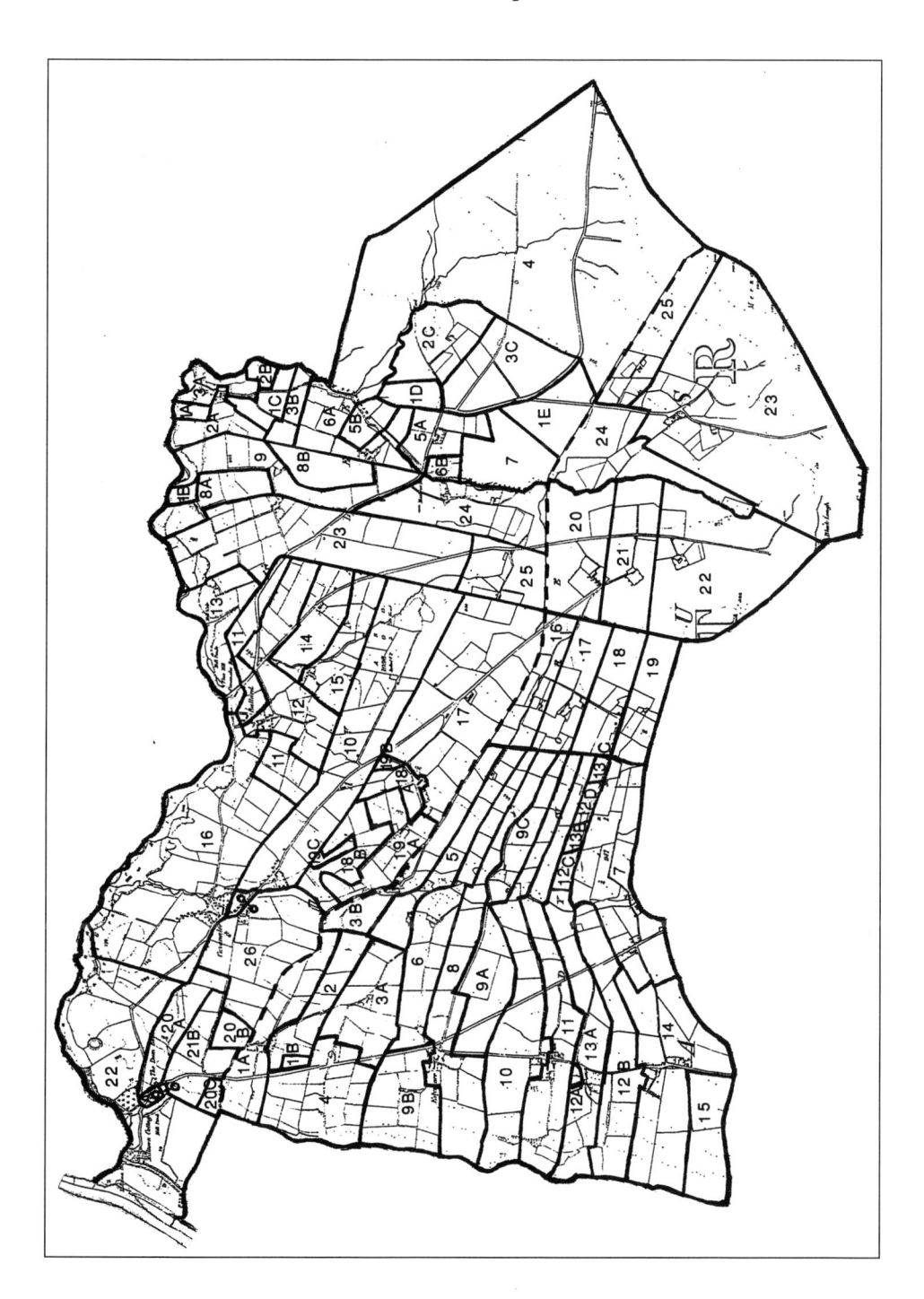

APPENDIX 7

Griffith's Valuation: Printed Version 1858

EDYMORE

PARISH OF CAMUS.

No. and Letters of Reference to Map.		Names.		Description of Tenement.	Area.			Rateable Annual Valuation.						Total Annual Valuation of Rateable Property		
		Townlands and Occupiers.	Immediate Lessors.					Land.			Buildings.					
					A.	R.	P.	£	s.	d.	£	s.	d.	£	s.	d.
		CAVANALEE— *continued.*														
	c	James Hobson,	Galbraith Lowther,	House,	—	—	—	—	—	—	0	15	0	0	15	0
23				Water,	2	3	30	—			—					
				Total,	1098	1	24	384	15	0	44	5	0	434	0	0
		EDY MORE. (Ord. S. 5 & 10.)														
1 A		William Gordon,	Marquis of Abercorn,	Herd's ho., offs., & ld.	25	2	10	19	5	0	0	15	0	21	5	0
— B					1	3	0	1	5	0	—					
2		Robert Gordon,	Same,	House, offices, and land,	25	0	30	18	0	0	1	10	0	19	10	0
3 A		Robert Davis,	Same,	House, offices, & land,	24	1	30	18	5	0	1	0	0	30	5	0
— B					23	0	20	11	0	0	—					
4		William Sawyers,	Same,	House, offices, and land,	23	0	20	17	10	0	1	0	0	18	10	0
5					20	2	30	11	0	0	—			11	0	0
6	a	William Aiken,	Same,	House, offices, & land,	35	3	5	22	0	0	2	0	0	24	0	0
7					45	1	20	23	10	0	—			23	10	0
	6 b	Robert Porter,	William Aiken,	House,	—			—			0	5	0	0	5	0
	7 a	Unoccupied,	Same,	House and office,	—			—			1	5	0	1	5	0
	— b	Unoccupied,	Same,	House,	—			—			0	5	0	0	5	0
8	a	John Fulton,	Marquis of Abercorn,	House, offices, and land,	46	2	20	28	0	0	5	0	0	33	0	0
—	b	George Devin,	John Fulton,	House,	—			—			0	10	0	0	10	0
—	c	Unoccupied,	Same,	House,	—			—			1	0	0	1	0	0
9 A					21	3	10	14	0	0	2	5	0			
— B		Hugh Carolan,	Marquis of Abercorn,	House, offices, & land,	20	0	30	15	0	0	—			36	10	0
— C					12	0	15	5	5	0	—					
	o a	James Gallagher,	Hugh Carolan,	House,	—			—			0	5	0	0	5	0
10		John Wilson,	Marquis of Abercorn,	House, offices, and land,	46	2	10	27	0	0	2	0	0	29	0	0
11		Robert Wilson,	Same,	House, offices, and land,	43	3	20	26	5	0	1	15	0	28	0	0
12 A					0	2	5	0	10	0	1	10	0			
— B		Robert Lowry,	Same,	House, offices, & land,	31	0	25	20	15	0	—			24	10	0
— C					2	1	15	1	5	0	—					
— D					1	2	0	0	10	0	—					
	B a	Neal Quinn,	Robert Lowry,	House,	—			—			0	5	0	0	5	0
	— b	Mary M'Loughlin,	Same,	House,	—			—			0	5	0	0	5	0
13 A	a				30	3	5	20	15	0	1	10	0			
— B		Gustavus Lyan,	Marquis of Abercorn,	House, offices, & land,	2	1	10	1	5	0	—			24	0	0
— C					1	0	20	0	10	0	—					
14		James Aiken,	Same,	House, offices, & land,	51	2	30	36	10	0	2	10	0	39	0	0
15					19	2	20	15	0	0	—			15	0	0
16		Michael M'Conway,	Same,	House, office, and land,	10	3	35	3	10	0	0	5	0	3	15	0
17	a	William Regan,	Same,	House, office, and land,	18	1	30	3	10	0	0	10	0	4	0	0
	b	Eleanor Regan,	William Regan,	House,	—			—			0	5	0	0	5	0
18		Samuel King,	Marquis of Abercorn,	House and land,	18	3	10	2	5	0	0	10	0	2	15	0
19		Neal Gallagher,	Same,	House, office, and land,	19	0	20	3	5	0	0	10	0	3	15	0
20		Bernard Beirne,	Same,	House, office, and land,	30	1	25	2	5	0	0	10	0	2	15	0
21		James Young,	Same,	House and land,	28	0	10	3	0	0	0	10	0	3	10	0
22		James Kerr,	Same,	House and land,	65	3	20	3	5	0	0	10	0	3	15	0
23	a	Patrick Hegarty,	Same,	House, offices, and land,	134	3	0	7	5	0	1	10	0	8	15	0
—	b	Joseph Lucas,	Patrick Hegarty,	House and office,	—			—			0	10	0	0	10	0
24		Edward Hegarty,	Marquis of Abercorn,	Land,	30	0	30	4	0	0	—			4	0	0
25		William Hegarty,	Same,	House and land,	27	2	16	1	15	0	0	5	0	2	0	0
		Marquis of Abercorn,	In fee,	Turbary,	—			—			—			6	5	0
				Total,	947	1	36	388	5	0	32	10	0	427	0	0
		STRAGULLIN. (Ord. S. 5 & 10.)														
1	a	Aaron Gordon,	Marquis of Abercorn and Captain Murray,	House, offices, and land,	56	2	25	39	5	0	10	5	0	49	10	0
—	b	Thomas M'Loughlin,	Aaron Gordon,	House,	—			—			0	10	0	0	10	0
—	c	John Fleming,	Same,	House,	—			—			0	10	0	0	10	0
2		Hugh Houston,	James Parker,	House, offices, and land,	29	1	20	22	0	0	0	15	0	22	15	0
3		James Parker,	Marquis of Abercorn and Captain Murray,	House, offices, and land,	31	2	10	21	10	0	1	0	0	22	10	0
4	a	John Boake,	Same,	House, offices, and land,	36	3	20	26	15	0	4	15	0	31	10	0
—	b	Robert Ferguson,	John Boake,	House,	—			—			0	5	0	0	5	0
5				Water,	20	2	0	—			—			—		
				Total,	174	3	35	109	10	0	18	0	0	127	10	0

Griffith's Valuation: Printed Version 1858

CAVANALEE

PARISH OF CAMUS.

No. and Letters of Reference to Map.		Names.		Description of Tenement.	Area.	Rateable Annual Valuation.		Total Annual Valuation of Rateable Property.
		Townlands and Occupiers.	Immediate Lessors.			Land.	Buildings.	
					A. R. P.	£ s. d.	£ s. d.	£ s. d.
—	e	MILLTOWN—*continued.* Galbraith Lowther,	Marquis of Abercorn,	Corn-mill and kiln,	—	—	25 0 0	25 0 0
2	a	John Humphreys,	Col. Skipton,	House, offices, and land,	10 3 10	20 0 0	36 0 0	56 0 0
—	b	Thomas Hart,	John Humphreys,	House,	—	—	1 5 0	1 5 0
—	c	John Snodgrass,	Same,	Ho., offs., & sm. garden,	—	—	1 0 0	1 0 0
3		. . .	. . .	Water,	0 2 35	—	—	—
				Total,	14 3 37	24 15 0	69 5 0	94 0 0
1 A		CAVANALEE. (Ord. S. 5 & 10.) Anne Haghey,		House, offices, & land,	34 0 30	15 15 0	—	6 5 0
— A	a	Anne Haghey,		House, offices, & land,	—	—	0 15 0	6 5 0
—	b	Edward Dooghan,	Marquis of Abercorn,	House, offices, & land,	—	—	0 15 0	6 5 0
—	c	Patk. Dooghan, sen.,		House, offices, & land,	—	—	0 15 0	6 5 0
— B					2 1 10	0 15 0	—	
2		Patrick Dooghan, sen.,	Same,	Herd's house and land,	9 3 5	1 10 0	0 5 0	1 15 0
3		Edward Dooghan,	Same,	Land,	8 1 25	0 15 0	—	0 15 0
4		Anne Harkey, Patk. Dooghan, sen., Edward Dooghan, Anne Dooghan, Patk. Dooghan, jun.,	Same,	Mountain,	295 0 0	3 5 0	—	0 15 0 / 0 15 0 / 0 15 0 / 0 10 0 / 0 10 0
—	a	John Smith,		House (*part of*),	—	—	0 5 0	0 5 0
		Marquis of Abercorn,	In fee,	Turbary,	—	5 0 0	—	5 0 0
5	a	Anne Dooghan,	Marquis of Abercorn,	House, offices, & land,	42 1 10	7 0 0	1 0 0	8 0 0
	b	Patk. Dooghan, jun.,		House, offices, & land,		7 0 0	1 0 0	8 0 0
6	a	Cormack M'Namee,	Same,	House, offices, & land,	48 2 15	6 10 0	0 15 0	7 5 0
	b	Bernard M'Namee,		House, offices, & land,		6 10 0	0 15 0	7 5 0
7	a	Denis M'Namee,	Same,	House, offices, and land,	71 0 35	18 0 0	1 10 0	19 10 0
—	b	John Robb,	Denis M'Namee,	House and office,	—	—	0 15 0	0 15 0
—	c	James Hagarty,	Same,	House,	—	—	0 5 0	0 5 0
8	a	Edward Hagarty,	Same,	House, offices, and land,	30 0 15	8 15 0	1 0 0	9 15 0
—	b	William M'Gillin,	Edward Hagarty,	House,	—	—	0 5 0	0 5 0
—		Patrick Hagarty,	Same,	House,	—	—	0 5 0	0 5 0
9		John Coyle,	Marquis of Abercorn,	House and land,	17 2 25	2 5 0	0 10 0	2 15 0
10	a	William Culberston,	Same,	House, offices, and land,	72 1 34	31 0 0	1 0 0	32 0 0
—	b	Thomas Culberston,	William Culberston,	House and office,	—	—	1 0 0	1 0 0
—	c	John Burke,	Same,	House,	—	—	0 5 0	0 5 0
11 A	a	Thomas Graham,	Marquis of Abercorn,	House, offices, & land,	10 3 0	3 5 0	0 10 0	8 15 0
— B	a				10 1 5	5 0 0		
12	a	Francis Graham, sen.,	Same,	House, offices, & land,	35 0 0	14 10 0	1 0 0	15 5 0
—	b	Robert Mayne,	Francis Graham, sen.,	House,	—	—	0 5 0	0 5 0
—	c	John Mullen,	Same,	House and office,	—	—	0 15 0	0 15 0
13	a	John Young,	Marquis of Abercorn,	House, office, and land,	19 2 10	8 10 0	0 10 0	10 15 0
	b			Flax-mill,			1 15 0	
—	c	Unoccupied,	John Young,	House,	—	—	0 5 0	0 5 0
—	d	James Young,	Same,	House,	—	—	0 5 0	0 5 0
14		Andrew M'Shea,	Marquis of Abercorn,	House, offices, and land,	18 1 30	7 5 0	1 0 0	8 5 0
15		Francis Graham, jun.,	Same,	House, offices, and land,	18 2 0	8 5 0	1 0 0	9 5 0
16	a	James M'Crea,	Same,	House, offices, and land,	91 0 0	60 10 0	3 0 0	63 10 0
—	b	Stephen M'Brierty,	James M'Crea,	House,	—	—	0 5 0	0 5 0
—	c	Michael Walsh,	Same,	House,	—	—	0 5 0	0 5 0
—	d	Anne Parker,	Same,	House and office,	—	—	0 15 0	0 15 0
17	a	James Houston,	Marquis of Abercorn,	House, offices, and land,	69 2 15	22 0 0	1 0 0	23 0 0
—	b	Rebecca Houston,	James Houston,	House,	—	—	0 5 0	0 5 0
—	c	Robin Hamilton,	Same,	House,	—	—	0 5 0	0 5 0
—	d	Susanna Houston,	Same,	House,	—	—	0 10 0	0 10 0
18	a	John Houston,	Marquis of Abercorn,	House, offices, & land,	40 2 0	12 0 0	0 15 0	12 15 0
	b	James Houston, sen.,		House, offices, & land,		12 0 0	1 0 0	13 0 0
—	c	Mary Houston,	John Houston,	House,	—	—	0 5 0	0 5 0
19		Robert Hamilton,	Marquis of Abercorn,	House, offices, and land,	34 0 20	24 0 0	2 10 0	26 10 0
20 A	a	William Hunter,	Same,	House, offices, & land,	13 3 25 / 4 2 25 / 2 2 30	11 5 0 / 3 5 0 / 2 0 0	2 5 0 / — / —	18 15 0
— B								
— C								
21 A		James Barnhill,	Same,	House, offices, & land,	1 0 0 / 21 3 0	1 5 0 / 17 5 0	1 5 0 / —	19 15 0
— B								
22	a	Galbraith Lowther,	Same,	House, offices, and land,	71 2 30	63 10 0	8 10 0	72 0 0
—	b	James Kelly,	Galbraith Lowther,	House,	—	—	0 15 0	0 15 0

Griffith's Valuation Amendments 1860

CAVANALEE

Map. No	Names Occupiers	Immediate Lessors	Description of Tenement	Area A R P	Rateable Valuation Land £ s d	Building £ s d	Total AnnVal £ s d
1 A	Anne Haghey	Marquis Abercorn	Land	2 0 20	1 0 0		
B			Land	2 1 10	15 0		
C			Land	7 1 30	2 15 0		
D			Land	6 1 0	5 0		
E			Land	18 3 0	10 0		
3Ab			House, offices & land	0 2 0	10 0	15 0	6 10 0
2 A	Patk Dooghan sr	Same	House, offices & land	8 3 20	3 15 0	15 0	
B			Land	2 2 0	1 5 0		
C			Land	27 3 25	2 5 0		8 0 0
3 Aa	Edwd Dooghan	Same	House & offices	6 1 20	3 0 0	15 0	
B			Land	6 1 20	2 5 0		
C			Land	21 2 5	1 5 0		7 5 0
4	Anne Haghey				15 0		
	Patk Dooghan sr				15 0		
	Edwd Dooghan	Same	Land	220 2 0	15 0		3 5 0
	Anne Dooghan				10 0		
	Patk Dooghan jr				10 0		
5 A	Anne Dooghan	Same	House, offices & land	14 2 0	4 10 0	1 0 0	
B			Land	6 0 30	1 10 0		7 0 0
6 A	Patk Dooghan jr	Same	House, offices & land	17 3 20	5 5 0	1 0 0	
B			Land	3 3 0	15 0		7 0 0
7	Cormk McNamee				5 0		

APPENDIX 7

	Bernd McNamee	Same	Land	18 1 0	5 0		10 0
8 A	Cormk McNamee	Same	House, offices & land	13 1 20	5 0 0	15 0	
B			Land	9 3 25	1 0 0		6 15 0
9	Bernd McNamee	Same	House, offices & land	25 1 10	6 15 0	15 0	7 10 0
Nos 10 to 17 as on the printed Griffiths Valuation for the Parish of Camus page 75.							
18A	John Houston	Same	House, offices & land	5 0 30	2 15 0	15 0	
B			Land	14 1 20	8 15 0		12 5 0
b	Mary Houston	John Houston	House			5 0	5 0
19A	James Houston sr	Marquis Abercorn	House, offices & land	18 0 20	9 15 0	1 0 0	
B			Land	1 0 0	10 0		
C			Land	1 3 10	1 5 0		12 10 0
Nos 20 and 21 as on the printed Griffith's Valuation – NOTE in No 20 William Hunter replaced by Wm Barnhill							
22 a	Galbraith Lowther	Marquis Abercorn	House, offices & land	71 2 30	60 10 0	8 10 0	69 0 0
b	James Kelly	Galbraith Lowther	House			15 0	15 0
c	James Hobson	Same	House			15 0	15 0
23 a	Denis McNamee	Marquis Abercorn	House, offices & land	71 0 35	18 0 0	1 10 0	9 10 0
b	John Robb	Denis McNamee	House			15 0	15 0
c	James Hagarty	Same	House			15 0	15 0
24 a	Edward Hagarty	Marquis Abercorn	House, offices & land	30 0 15	8 15 0	1 0 0	9 15 0
b	William McGillin	Edward Hagarty	House			5 0	5 0
c	Patrick Hagarty	Same	House			5 0	5 0
25	John Coyle	Marquis Abercorn	House & land	17 2 25	2 5 0	10 0	2 15 0
26	Robert Hamilton	Same	House, offices & land	34 0 20	24 0 0	2 10 0	26 10 0

Abbreviated first names: Patk = Patrick; Edwd = Edward; Bernd = Bernard; Cormk = Cormack; Wm = William.
Note: sr = senior and jr = junior
The main tenements (holdings) in Cavanalee are shown on the 1854 map, in Appendix 6, using the numbers and upper case letters given above, and on the printed Griffith's Valuation tables.

APPENDIX 8

1901 Census – farming families only

EDYMORE

Names	Relation	Religion +	Read/ Write	Age	Occupation/(House Type etc) See footnotes on p 137	M/NM/ W +
William Gordon	Head	Pres	W	80	Farmer (W/R1/Rm4/F5/B13)	M
Matilda	Wife	Pres	R/W	75		M
Robert	Son	Pres	R/W	38	Farmer	M
Annie	D-in-law	Pres	R/W	28		M
William J	Son	Pres	R/W	34	Farmer	NM
Cicily Scanlan	Servant	RC	W	40	Domestic servant (b Donegal)	NM
Michael McGilloway	Servant	RC	R/W	20	Farm servant (b Donegal)	NM
John Davis	Head	Pres	R/W	62	Farmer (W/R1/Rm4/F4/B6)	M
Eliza	Wife	Pres	R/W	39		M
William McHugh	Servant	RC	R/W	23	Farm servant	NM
Annie Flin	Servant	CoI	W	31	Domestic servant	W
John Aiken	Head	Pres		70	Farmer (W/R1/Rm5/F5/B8)	M
Annie	Wife	Pres	R/W	63		M
Joseph Lucas	Servant	CoI	R/W	21	Farm servant	NM
David Aiken	Head	Pres	R/W	30	Farmer (W/R1/Rm3/F2/B12)	NM
Robert	Brother	Pres	R/W	28	Farmer	NM
Martha	Sister	Pres	R/W	26	Farmer's daughter	NM
William Gallagher	Servant	Pres	R/W	20	Farm servant	NM
William Fulton	Head	Pres	R/W	46	Farmer (W/R1/Rm5/F4/B21)	M
Mary Jane	Wife	Pres	R/W	24		M
Kathleen	Daughter	Pres		1		
Jane	Daughter	Pres		1m		
Samuel	Brother	Pres	R/W	44	Farmer	NM
Samuel	Nephew	CoI	R/W	14	Egg Store assistant (b Louth)	
Mary Bonar	Servant	RC	W	35	General servant (b Donegal I/E)	NM
Annie Harkin	Servant	RC	R/W	19	General servant (b Donegal I/E)	NM
Maggie Harkin	Servant	RC	R/W	18	General servant (b Donegal I/E)	NM
Thomas Houston	Head	Pres	R/W	50	Farmer (W/R1/Rm5/F5/B13)	M
Annie	Wife	Pres	R/W	57		M
Robert	Son	Pres	R/W	23	Farmer's son	NM
Margaret	Daughter	Pres	R/W	21	Farmer's daughter	NM
Thomas	Son	Pres	R/W	19	Farmer's son	NM
John McNamee	Servant	RC	R/W	48	Farm servant (b Donegal I/E)	NM
Anne Quinn	Servant	RC	R/W	18	General servant (b Donegal I/E)	NM
John McCrea	Head	Pres	R/W	50	Farmer (W/R2/Rm3/F4/B10)	M
Lizzie	Wife	Pres	R/W	45		M
Annie	Daughter	Pres	R/W	18	Farmer's daughter	NM
Thomas	Son	Pres	R/W	16	Scholar	
James	Son	Pres	R/W	13	Scholar	
Martha	Daughter	Pres	R/W	12	Scholar	
Patrick Hill	Servant	RC	R/W	20	Farm servant (b Donegal)	NM
Bridget McMonagle	Servant	RC	R	25	Domestic servant (b Donegal I/E)	NM

APPENDIX 8

James Aiken	Head	Pres	R/W	50	Farmer (W/R1/Rm4/F5/B13)	NM
Hamilton	Brother	Pres	R/W	46	Farmer	M
Isabella ?	Aunt	Pres	R/W	85		W
?	Servant	RC	W	34	Domestic servant (b Donegal)	NM
?	Servant	RC	W	20	Domestic servant (b Donegal)	NM
?	Servant	RC	W	22	Farm servant (b Donegal)	NM
?	Servant	RC	?	17	Farm servant	
Joseph Conway	Head	RC	R/W	30	Farmer (W/R1/Rm2/F2/B3)	M
Rose Ann	Wife	RC	W	22		M
Cassie	Daughter	RC		4		
Isabella	Daughter	RC		3		
Michael J	Son	RC		1		
Hugh Conway	Head	RC	R/W	30	Farmer (W/R1/Rm2/F2/B2)	M
Bridget	Wife	RC	W	29		M
Sarah Ann	Daughter	RC		7	(b USA)	
Mackel J	Son	RC		5	(b USA)	
Barnett S	Son	RC		3	(b USA)	
Hugh	Son	RC		9m		
Alexander Regan	Head	RC	R/W	55	Farmer (W/R2/Rm2/F2/B4)	M
Annie	Wife	RC	R/W	50		M
William	Son	RC	R/W	24	Clerk	NM
Lizzie	Daughter	RC	R/W	21	Seamstress	NM
James	Son	RC	R/W	16	Farmer's son	
Annie	Daughter	RC	R/W	11	Scholar	
Jessie Sayers	Niece	RC		3		
Neil Gallagher	Head	RC	R/W	53	Farmer (W/R1/Rm2/F3/B8)	M
Eliza	Wife	RC	R/W	49		M
Neil	Son	RC	R/W	21	Farmer	NM
Lizzie	Daughter	RC	R/W	19	Housekeeper	NM
Sarah	Daughter	RC	R/W	14	Scholar	
Bernard	Son	RC	R/W	10	Scholar	
Joseph	Son	RC	R/W	8	Scholar	
Margaret Aiken	Head	Pres	R/W	52	(W/R1/Rm2/F2/B6)	W
Mary	Daughter	Pres	R/W	21	Dressmaker	NM
Sarah	Daughter	Pres	R/W	15	Scholar	
Eliza	Daughter	Pres	R/W	15	Scholar	

CAVANALEE

James Lowry	Head	Pres	R/W	50	Farmer (W/R2/Rm4/F4/B12)	NM
Fanny McKelvey	Servant	RC	R/W	29	General Servant	NM
George Barnhill	Head	Pres	R/W	70	Farmer (W/R1/Rm4/F4/B12)	NM
Eliza Jane	Wife	Pres	R/W	71		NM
Robert	Son	Pres	R/W	30	Farmer	NM
John Richmond	Servant	RC	R/W	30	Farm servant	NM
Sarah O'Donnell	Servant	RC	R/W	17	General servant (b Donegal)	NM
Joseph Davis	Head	Pres	R/W	59	Farmer (W/R2/Rm3/F3/B6)	M
Matilda	Wife	Pres	R/W	58		M
Robert	Son	Pres	R/W	22	Farmer's son	NM
John	Son	Pres	R/W	21	Farmer's son	NM
Eliza Jane	Daughter	Pres	R/W	17	Farmer's daughter	
Patrick George	Servant	RC	R/W	16	Farm servant	

Andrew Smith	Head	Meth	R/W	37	Farmer (W/R2/Rm5/F5/B13)	M
Maggie	Wife	Meth	R/W	35		M
Robert Joseph	Son	Meth		4		
Clarence D	Son	Meth		3		
Isabella M	Daughter	Meth		1		
Kathleen V	Daughter	Meth		2m		
John McGillon	Servant	RC		37	Farm servant (I/E)	NM
Cassie Campbell	Servant	RC	R/W	34	Domestic servant (b Donegal I/E)	NM
Mary Graham	Head	CoI	R	47	(Farmer) (W/R2/Rm2/F2/B7)	W
Thomas	Son	CoI	R/W	23	Farmer	NM
Francis	Son	CoI	R	21	Farmer	NM
Cassie	Daughter	CoI	R/W	19		NM
Lowther	Son	CoI	R/W	18	Farm labourer	NM
William	Son	CoI	R	17	Farm labourer	
John	Son	CoI	R/W	15	Scholar	
William T Graham	Head	CoI	R/W	40	Farmer (W/R2/Rm2/F4/B8)	NM
Matilda	Mother	CoI	R/W	67		W
Mary A	Sister	CoI	R/W	38	Farmer's daughter	NM
Rebecca E	Sister	CoI	R/W	27	Farmer's daughter	NM
William Elliot	Servant	Pres	R/W	18	Farm servant	NM
William Lyons	Servant	RC	W	15	Yard boy	
Joseph Young	Head	Pres	R/W	42	Farmer (W/R1/Rm4/F6/B13)	M
Fanny	Wife	Pres	R/W	40		M
Jack F	Son	Pres	R/W	15	Scholar (b USA)	
Fannie F	Daughter	Pres	R/W	14	Scholar (b USA)	
George Finlay	Servant	CoI	R/W	20	Farm servant	NM
Andrew McNab	Servant	CoI	R/W	18	Farm servant	NM
Annie Hegarty	Servant	RC	R/W	27	General servant (b Donegal)	NM
James Houston	Head	Pres	R/W	60	Farmer (W/R2/Rm2/F2/B5)	M
Mary J	Wife	Pres	R/W	48		M
Thomas	Son	Pres	R/W	20	Farm worker	NM
Cassie	Daughter	Pres	R/W	17	Scholar	
Mary Ann	Daughter	Pres	R/W	16	Scholar	
John	Son	Pres	R/W	12	Scholar	
Andrew	Son	Pres	R/W	8	Scholar	
Thomas Houston	Head	Meth	R/W	70	Farmer (W/R2/Rm2/F2/B5)	NM
James McGurk	Head	RC	R/W	36	Farmer (W/R2/Rm2/F2/B5)	NM
Kate	Sister	RC	R/W	39	Housekeeper	NM
Francis O'Donnell	Servant	RC	R/W	15	Farm servant	
Charles Dooher	Head	RC	R/W	37	Farmer (W/R2/Rm2/F2/B5)	M
Bridget	Wife	RC	R/W	29		M
Patrick Joe	Son	RC	R/W	10	Scholar	
Mary M	Daughter	RC	R/W	7	Scholar	
Daniel	Son	RC	R	5	Scholar	
Bridget A	Daughter	RC		2		
Charles	Son	RC		6m		
Patrick O'Donnell	Servant	RC	R/W	20	Farm servant	NM
William Dooher	Head	RC	R	61	Farmer (W/R2/Rm2/F2/B5)	M
Madge	Wife	RC	R/W	35		M
Thomas Dolan	Servant	RC	R	26	Farm labourer (b Donegal)	M

APPENDIX 8

Name	Relation	Religion	R/W	Age	Occupation	M/NM/W
Patrick Dooher	Head	RC	W	60	Farmer (W/R2/Rm2/F2/B6)	M
Mary	Wife	RC	R/W	50		M
Sarah Ann Casey	Niece	RC	R/W	20		NM
Michael Conway	Head	RC	R/W	70	Farmer (W/R1/Rm4/F5/B7)	W
Michael	Son	RC	R/W	35	Farmer	NM
William	Son	RC	R/W	31	Farmer	NM
Bernard	Son	RC	R/W	20	Farmer	NM
Hannah Boal ?	Servant	RC		35	Farm servant (b Donegal I/E)	NM
Edward McColgan	Servant	RC		16	Farm servant	
Thomas Dooher	Head	RC	R	63	Farmer (W/R1/Rm2/F2/B7)	W
Mary Anne	Daughter	RC	R/W	26	Farmer's daughter	NM
Patrick	Son	RC	R/W	24	Farmer's son	NM
Elizabeth	Daughter	RC	R/W	22	Farmer's daughter	NM
Maggie	Daughter	RC	R/W	20	Farmer's daughter	NM
Thomas	Son	RC	R/W	19	Farmer's son	NM
Charles	Son	RC	R/W	16	Farmer's son	
Sarah	Daughter	RC	R/W	14	Scholar	
John James	Son	RC	R/W	12	Scholar	
Hugh Devine	Head	RC	R/W	56	Farmer (W/R2/Rm2/F2/B5)	M
Bridget	Wife	RC	R/W	46		M
Ellen	Daughter	RC	R/W	18	Seamstress	NM
Bridget	Daughter	RC	R/W	16	Seamstress	NM
Margery	Daughter	RC	R/W	14	Seamstress	
Sarah	Daughter	RC	R/W	11	Scholar	
Catherine	Daughter	RC		7		
Patrick	Son	RC		3		
Annie May	Daughter	RC		1		
Bernard McNulty	Servant	RC	W	27	Farm labourer	NM
John O'Donnell	Head	RC	W	47	Farmer (W/R2/Rm2/F3/B5)	M
Ann	Wife	RC	W	45		M
Patrick	Son	RC	R/W	21	Farmer's son	NM
John	Son	RC	R/W	18	Farmer's son	NM
Francis	Son	RC	R/W	16	Farmer's son	
Mary	Daughter	RC	R/W	14	Scholar	

+ ABBREVIATIONS

Religion: Pres = Presbyterian; RC = Roman Catholic; CoI = Church of Ireland; Meth = Methodist
Read/Write: R/W = can read and write; R = read only; W = write only; Blank = cannot read or write
M/NM/W: M= married; NM = not married (not entered those under 18); W = widow or widower
b = born in county or country indicated, otherwise born on County Tyrone; m = months; I/E = can speak Irish and English

FOOTNOTES

Occupations:	'Farmer's son or daughter' indicates that they worked on the farm
	'General servant' worked both on the farm and in the farmhouse
	'Domestic servant' worked only in the farmhouse including the dairy
(House Type etc):	W = **Walls** of 'stone brick or concrete'
	R1 = **Roof** of 'slate, iron or tiles'
	R2 = **Roof** of 'thatch, wood or other perishable material'
	Rm2 = **Rooms:** Houses with 2, 3 or 4 rooms
	Rm3 = Houses with 5 or 6 rooms
	Rm4 = Houses with 7, 8 or 9 rooms
	Rm5 = Houses with 10, 11 or 12 rooms
	F = **Windows in front of house:** Exact number
	B = **No of buildings on farm:** Includes the farmhouse and all outbuildings

APPENDIX 9

Brief extracts from original documents

1756 Rent Assessment and Land Valuation Survey (see Appendix 2)

Robert Wilson's Will 1836 (see page 127)

APPENDIX 9

This Indenture MADE the thirty first Day of January in the Year of our Lord One Thousand Eight Hundred and thirty five.

BETWEEN the Most Noble JAMES, Marquis of ABERCORN, of the One Part, and John Fulton of Edymore in the County of Tyrone, Farmer, of the other Part, **Witnesseth**, That for and in consideration of the Rent hereby reserved, and of the Covenants, Conditions, and Agreements, herein after contained, which on the part and behalf of the said John Fulton his Heirs, Executors, Administrators, and Assigns, are to be paid, kept, observed, and performed, he the said Most Noble James, Marquis of Abercorn, HATH granted, released, and confirmed, and by these Presents DOTH grant, release, and confirm unto the said John Fulton (in his actual possession now being, by virtue of a Bargain and Sale to him thereof made by the said Most Noble James, Marquis of Abercorn, for one whole Year, by Indenture, bearing Date the Day next before the Day of the Date of these Presents, in consideration of Five Shillings, Sterling, and by force of the Statute for transferring Uses into possession,) and to his Heirs and Assigns, ALL THAT AND THOSE

That Farm of Land in the townland of Edymore aforesaid as at present in the use and occupation of the said John Fulton, Containing forty four Acres three Roods and fifteen Perches, be the same more or less Statute Measure, with all the Rights, Members, Privileges, and appurtenances thereunto in any wise belonging or appertaining

1835 Lease Agreement between the Marquis of Abercorn & John Fulton (see page 26)

10. What is the condition of the farming population generally; is it improving or otherwise?—The condition of the large farmers is comfortable and respectable. The small tenantry are a struggling industrious people, with little or no capital; they consequently depend very much upon the produce of the season for the means of paying their rents, and for their own subsistence. Labourers are a mixed class, consisting of cottiers, who give two days work in the week for a cottage, to which sometimes a small garden is attached. The hired labourers live with the farmers, are fed by them, and get from five to six guineas a year. Farmers in comfortable circumstances frequently educate one of their sons as a surgeon, or for the Presbyterian ministry; the other male members of the family work on the farm, until farms are purchased for them, as circumstances permit. The daughters get portions on marriage, from £20 upwards. When the tenant dies and leaves a widow with young children, she generally keeps on the farm, and supports them by it. When children are left without parents, some relation or friend manages the farm till the eldest son is of an age to take care of it. The labourers hold their cottages under the farmers, who build and ought to keep them in repair; but this, in many instances, is sadly neglected. I hardly know any subject beset with greater difficulties, than the condition of the cottier and labourer of the country; nor do I see how any improvement in the present system can be effected, except by the landlords taking them out of their present position, by making them their tenants.

Extract from the 1845 Devon Commission Report – Part of the comments made to the Commission by Major Humphreys in April 1844 (see page 38)

This Indenture made the fifteenth day of June in the year of our Lord one thousand eight hundred and forty eight Between James McCrea of Cavanalee in the County of Tyrone farmer of the one part and James Graham of Cavanalee aforesaid farmer of the other part Whereas by Indenture of Lease bearing date the thirty first day of January one thousand eight hundred and thirty five the Most Noble James Marquis of Abercorn did grant release and confirm unto the said James McCrea All that and those that farm of Land in the townland of Cavanalee aforesaid as then and now in the use and occupation of the said James McCrea To hold the same to the said James McCrea his heirs and assigns for the life of James Hamilton Junior Esquire or twenty one years from the first day of November then last at the yearly Rent of forty one pounds nineteen Shillings and three pence halfpenny Sterling

Deed between James McCrea and James Graham 1848 (see page 41)

APPENDIX 10

Farms and farmers from 1756 to 1827 showing rents and tithes

EDYMORE 1756 Rental/Land Val	1777 Map	1787 Rental	1806 Map/Rental	Tithes 1827	
1 55 £12.82 John Finlay	1 52 John McNeelans	£22.50 Victor Gordon *4*	1 51 £22.50 Robt Gordon 1A 1B	Victor Robert	£2.62 £2.42
	2 15 John Simison jnr	12 £7.50 Thomas Sawyer	2 24 £12.66 William Sawyer	Same	£4.17
3 47 £9.02 John Simison	3 17 Alex Simpson 4 15 John Simison snr	36 £15.32 John Simison *1*	3 24 £12.66 Joseph (1) Davis	Same	£2.54
4 37 £6.70 Samuel Gillilan and William Lowther	5 34 Samuel Gillilan and William Lowther	£15.63 William Lowther	4 34 £15.63 William Lowther and James Porter	William Aikin	£3.02
2 24 £3.76 Alex Todd	6 22 James Porter	£9.06 James Porter	5 22 £9.06 James Porter	Thomas	£1.95
	7 18 Thomas Sawyer	£7.50 Thomas Sawyer	6 18 £7.50 Thomas Sa(w)yer	William (with 2)	
5 103 £19.21 Robert Smyly	8 53 William Paterson	£24.38 John Paterson to widow Anne 1795	7 53 £24.37 Anne Paterson	Brian Carland	£5.05
	9 43 John Rabb junior	£20.60 John Rabb junior	8 43 £20.60 John Rabb junior and William Stilly	John (1) Fulton (from 1816)	£4.04
6 47 £8.38 William Brown	10 46 Widow and William Brown	£10.31 each William Brown/Robert Wilson	9 46 £20.62 William Brown and Robert Wilson	John Wilson	£2.10
7 42 £8.04 John Rabb	11 41 John Rabb senior	£20.31 Robt Wilson *4*	10 41 £25.31 Robert Wilson	Same	£5.64
8 43 £8.05 Gabriel Thompson	12 43 Galbraith (?) Thompson	£20.01 Galbraith Thompson (d 1795) *4*	11 and 12 34 £15.06 Nathanial Thompson	Nathaniel with James	£3.21
9 56 £8.65 John Orr	13 56 George Orr	£8.13 each Galbraith Thompson/George Orr	13 36 £15.06 Jos Thompson 14 28 £8.13 James Hamilton	Same	£5.63
10 85 £15.65 ? Knox	14 85 Widow and William Knox	£22.50 William Knox £15.00 Alex Knox *4*	15 85 £37.50 Ezekial, Alex and George Knox	Ezekial and Alex junior	£5.04
68 Common Mountain			16 76 4 parts (not let)	O Conway	34p
Edymore mountain Not in the Survey	324 Roger McColgan	£7.50 Patrick Haggerty	324 £7.50 Patrick Haggerty and partners	Patrick, William and Edward	£2.06

Numbers not in bold represent the size of farms in statute acres. **Bold numbers** are the numbers given to the farms in the 1756 Survey and the 1777 and 1806 estate maps

The numbers *1*, *2*, or *4* in the third column indicate the number of spinning wheels awarded by the Trustees of Linen Manufacture under their 1796 Premium Scheme

The **Tithes 1827** column shows the amount assessed and the name of the farmer if different from 1806

APPENDIX 10

CAVANALEE 1756 Rental/Land Val	1777 Map	1787 Rental	1806 Map/Rental	Tithes 1827	
1 27 £5.38 'TheMiller'	**1** 27 'The Miller'	£62.00 Thomas Lowther	**1** 27 £62.00 Thomas Lowther	Galbraith	
2 44 £13.68 Thomas Graham	**2** 44 Thomas Graham *4*	£37.50 Thomas Graham	**2** 44 £37.50 Thomas Graham	With *1*	£8.06
	3 14 James Barnhill	£15.75 James Weir and James Hunter	**3** 21 £15.75 James Hunter	Same	£2.64
3 43 £14.00 John Barnhill	**4** 15 John Barnhill				
	5 14 Joseph Barnhill	£15.75 John Barnhill *2*	**4** 21 £15.75 James Barnhill	Same	£2.80
4 34 £8.05 Upper S Cav Lower	**6** 34 Thomas Huston	£16.75 Wm Huston jr	**5** 34 £16.25 Alex Kerr – James	Same	£3.65
	7 34 Francis Graham	£9.81 Lowther Graham *2*		Same	£1.54
	8 60 Joseph Knox	£51.25 William McCrea *4*	**6** 84 £51.75 William/James McCrea	James	£8.72
7 173 £32.05 Upper North Cavanalee	**9** 52 Thomas Graham	£10.94 Thomas Graham	**7** 23 £7.31 Lowther Graham **8** 34 £10.53 Thomas Graham	Thomas Graham	£2.29
	10 10 James Dougherty	£3.44 James Dougherty	**9** 10 £3.44 James Dougherty	Samuel	77p
	11 17 Owen McCrossan	£4.03 John McCrossan	**10** 17 £4.08 James McNamee and James Gillion	John McNamee and James Gillion	63p
8 42 £2.80 New Mountain Div	**12** 42 John Huston	£8.12 John Huston	**11** 19 £8.12 Francis Graham	Same	£1.34
			11a 17 £7.57 John McPhee	Same	98p
6 72 £8.12 Upper N Divison	**13** 73 William Huston	£18.75 William Huston (Son) *2*	**12** 73 £18.75 William Huston	Robert Hamilton	£4.93
5 110 £8.12 Up S Division James (1) Huston	**14** 110 (Widow) Mary Huston	£18.75 Mary Huston to her sons in 1795 *4*	**13** 112 £18.75 Andrew and Thomas (1) Huston	Same	£6.57
Cavanalee mountain 430 £8.22	**1** 157 Denis McNamee	£8.75 Denis and John McNamee	**1** 78 £7.50 John McNamee and partners	Denis McNamee 40ac	£1.30
Boundaries disputed in 1777, but agreed by 1806	**2** 283 Mathew and Edward Dooher	£8.75 Mathew and Edward Dooher	**2** 19 £1.50 William Lyon and Patrick Haggarty	30a William and Edward Hegarty	96p
1777 - 440 acres 1806 - 331 acres	**3** Disputed with other landowners		**3/4** 234 £4.38 Mathew Dooher and partners	Dooher family 260ac	£4.83

Numbers not in bold represent the size of farms in statute acres. **Bold numbers** are the numbers given to the farms in the 1756 Survey and the 1777 and 1806 estate maps

The numbers *1*, *2*, or *4* in the third column indicate the number of spinning wheels awarded by the Trustees of Linen Manufacture under their 1796 Premium Scheme

The **Tithes 1827** column shows the amount assessed and the name of the farmer if different from 1806

APPENDIX 11

Farms and farmers from 1838 to 1900 showing rents and tithes

EDYMORE

1838 Acreage/Rents/Tithes/Tenants	1858 Acreage/Rents/Tenants	Rent/Tenant changes after 1860
1A 27 £17.30+£3.36=£20.66 Victor Gordon	1 27 £19.66 (¹/₂ yr) William Gordon 1857	From 1863 £38.66 for both *1* and *2* run as one farm
1B 25 £16.50+£2.36=£18.86 Robert Gordon	2 25 £18.72 William Gordon 1859	
2 + 6 42 £27.83+£3.75=£31.58 William Sayer	4/5 43 £31.57 (¹/₂ yr) William Sawyers*	1861 £36.70 1876 Hugh Carland 1884 farm *4* 23 ac to John Barnhill, Cavanalee and farm *5* 21 ac to Margaret Aikin
3 24 £15.40+£2.18=£17.58 Robert (1) Davis	3 47 £30.60 (¹/₂ yr) Robert (1) Davis	1861 £38.80 1877 John (1) Davis **1881 JR £34.00**
4 34 £17.40+£2.72=£20.12 William Aikin	6 35 £20.14 (¹/₂ yr) William Aiken*	1865 (yearly) John Aikin 1875 Margaret Aikin
5 22 £11.16+£1.67=£12.83 Thomas Porter to Margaret Porter - given notice 1848 & 1849	Then to Robert (1) Davis 1852 (*see 3 above*)	
7 53 £34.17+£4.53=£38.70 Brian Carland	9 54 £38.73 (¹/₂ yr) Hugh Carolan*	1865 (yearly) Hugh Carland 1884 William (2) Fulton farmed with *8*
8 43 £26.97+£3.64=£30.61 John (1) Fulton 1816	8 46 £30.61 John (1) Fulton	1875 Jane Fulton 1883 William (2) Fulton
9 46 £24.98+£3.80 =£28.78 John Wilson **Dr**	10 46 £29.27 (¹/₂ yr) John Wilson	1876 Jane Fulton - then farmed with *8*
10 41 £24.00+£3.18=£27.18 Robert Wilson jnr **Dr**	11 44 £27.98 (¹/₂ yr) Robert Wilson jnr	1873 Thomas (3) Huston 1879 now 61 acres
11/12 34 £19.94+£2.87=£22.81 Nat Thompson **Dr**	13 34 £24.24 (¹/₂ yr) Gustavus Lyan	1865 Alex McCrea 1879 now 51ac 1885 John McCrea 1887 £38.46
13 36 £21.80+£3.40=£25.20 John Thompson **Dr**	12 35 £26.25 Robert Lowry	1867 (yearly) 1879 divided between *11* and *13* Lowry to Cavanalee
	7 45 £24.67 (¹/₂ yr) William Aiken see *6*	1861 £29.05 1865 John Aikin 1883 £26.00 1901 £18.00
14 19 £14.35+£2.66=£17.01 Alex Knox 1836 **Dr**	14 52 £29.65 (¹/₂ yr) James Aiken*	1862 (yearly) 1885 Andrew (1887 *Rent combined* 1890 James Aiken
15 45 £20.36+£2.81=£23.17 Robert Johnston	15 20 £12.33 Hamilton Aikin 1860	1879 Margaret Aiken *for 14/15* £51.50) 1890 Hamilton Aiken

APPENDIX 11

16A 20 £2.54+0.26=£2.80 Owen McConomy	*16* 17 £2.82 (½ yr) Michael (1) Conway*	1861 £5.15	1863 (yearly)	1887 £4.50
B 18 Not yet tenanted	*17* 18 £2.42 William Regan	1860 £5.05	1881 £4.50	1887 Alex Regan 1900 £3.60
C 19 ditto	*18* 19 £4.10 Samuel King		1868 £5.50 Patrick Hegarty 1877 £11.00 1881 £14.00 1899 £6.00	
D 19 ditto	*19* 19 £5.00 (½ yr) Neal Gallagher	1868 £9.10	1887 £7.00 Neal Gallagher	1900 £5.60
Edymore mountain	*20* 30 £5.00 Bernard Beirne (Burns)	1863 (yearly) James Burns	1877 £7.50	1881 £14.00 1890 Margaret Aikin *see15*
	21 28 £5.00 James Young	Hamilton Aikin 1890 (*see15*)		
324 £7.50 Patrick Heggarty & partners	*22* 66 £5.00 (½ yr) James Kerr	William Johnston 1879		
	23 135 £6.38 Patrick Hegarty*	Michael McConomy 1878		
	24 30 Edward Hegarty* **Land see Cav24**			
	25 28 £1.82 William Hegarty*			

Numbers in bold are those given to farms on the **1806** map

Numbers in bold/italics are those in the **1858/1860 Grffith's Valuation** and associated map (see text)

* Note surname spelling change. Areas in statute acres. Rents paid yearly except where shown. In columns 1 and 2 **dates in bold** show the year the tenancy was acquired. **JR** = Judicial Review – see text.

Dr – Rent increased to that shown in the next column as a result of drainage work having been carried out c1848 – see text.

CAVANALEE

1838 Acreage/Rents/Tithes/Tenants	1858 Acreage/Rents/Tenants	Rent/Tenant changes after 1860
1 Corn Mill £10 Galbraith Lowther	Noted in Milltown Townland	1876 £10.00 George Doherty
2 71 £60.35+ ? Galbraith Lowther	22 71 £60.35 Galbraith Lowther	1864 paid 3 years 1879 £61.21 Robert Lowry 1884 James Lowry
3 21 £20.02+ ? William Hunter	20 21 £21.45 (½ yr) William Hunter	1868 George Barnhill
4 21 £17.23+£2.53=£19.76 James Barnhill	21 23 £19.76 (½ yr) James Barnhill	1861 £20.35 (½ yr) 1864 John Barnhill 1877 £18.50
5 34 £23.27+£3.28=£26.55 Robert Hamilton	26 34 £26.56 (½ yr) Robert Hamilton	1862 James Graham 1873 £25 32 Joseph (2) Davis 1877 £27.23
6 84 £53.15+£1.84=£54.99 James/Wm McCrea **Dr**	16 91 £61.00 (½ yr) Jas McCrea (**see p.44**)	1860 £63.14 (½ yr) James Graham 1876 £61 23 Robert Wilson
7 23 £9.52+£1.39=£10.91 Thomas Graham	11 21 £10.91 Thomas Graham	1863 £13.65 Lowther Graham 1877 £11.25 **1881 joined with *12***
8 34 £12.75+£2.06=£14.81 Francis Graham	12 35 £14.81 Francis Graham senior	1862 £19.70 1865 Francis Graham junior 1877 £20.45 **1881 joined with 11** with a **JR** £27.50 1889 Francis & William T Graham
9 10 £5.20+0.69=£5.89 James Dougherty	13 20 £11.43 John Young + Flax Mill	1862 £12.05 1877 Jane Young **1882 JR** £10.00 1889 Joseph Young
10 17 £4.97+0.50=£5.47 John McNamee	(10 to *13* and 7 to *23*)	
11 19 £8.30+£1.31=£9.61 Francis Graham junior	15 19 £9.52 Francis Graham junior	1860 £11.65 1865 Denis McNamee
12 17 £5.71+0.88=£6.59 Andrew McPhee	14 18 £7.09 Andrew M'Shea*	1863 £10.15 1884 £9.25 Alex Regan
13 73 £27.97+£4.50=£32.47 Wm Cuthbertson **Dr**	10 72 £33.47 William Culbertson*	1868 Thomas Cuthbertson 1878 £35.00 1882 Joseph (2) Davis
14A 65 £17.83+£3=£20.83 Andrew Huston	17 70 £21.72 (½ yr) Jas (5) Houston jnr*	1880 Robert Houston 1895 Reps of Robert Houston **1899 JR** £19.00
14B 46 £23.15+£2.00=£24.15 James (4) Huston snr	18 20 £26.12 for John (1) Houston 19 21 both farms James (4) Houston snr	1880 James (6) Houston (See *25* below) 1876 Thomas (2) Houston

APPENDIX 11

Farm	Griffith's Valuation	History
Cavanalee Mountain	25 18 £2.28 John Coyle	1868 £3.70 Wm Coyle 1870 £6.00 James (6) Houston **1881 JR** £3.70
1 £8.30 - £9.40 in 1846 John & Denis McNamee and Bernard & Cormack McNamee **Dr**	23 71 £9.73 Denis McNamee	1861 £13.02 1880 Wm McNamee 1885 £22.00 Jas McNamee 1901
	9 25 £4.77 Bernard McNamee	**1860 9 joined with 8** 1862 combined rent £17.00
	8 23 £14.53 Cormack McNamee	1880 Bernard McNamee 1893 Arthur McGurk
	7 8 £15.60 Bernard/Cormack McNamee	1880 Catherine O'Brien **1881 JR** £14.00 **1899 JR** £11.20
2 Edward Haggerty	24 30 £12.71 Edward Hagerty*	1861 £15.86
	6 22 £11.47 Patrick Dooghan junior*	1860 £10.10 1895 Charles Dooher
	5 20 £10.00 Anne Dooghan*	**1883 JR** £7.00 1893 William Dooher
	4 220 Dooghan*/Haghey families	1893 Next generation family
4 Edward Dooher	3 34 £22.52 (½ yr) Edward Dooghan*	1861 £15.86 1893 Patrick Dooher
3 Patrick Dooher	2 39 £11.50 Patrick Dooghan senior *	**1881 JR** £8.75 1893 Thomas Dooher
	1 38 £9.10 Anne Haghey	**1881 JR** £8.00 B Gallagher **1893 JR** 6.40 1899 Hugh Devine

Numbers in bold are those given to farms on the 1806 map

Numbers in bold/italics are those in the **1858/1860 Grffith's Valuation** and associated map (see text)

* Note surname spelling change. Areas in statute acres. Rents paid yearly except where shown. In columns 1 and 2 **dates in bold** show the year the tenancy was acquired

Dr – Rent increased to that shown in the next column as a result of drainage work having been carried out c1848 – see text. **JR** = Judicial Review – see text.

APPENDIX 12

Farms and farmers in the twentieth century excluding the mountains

EDYMORE

G M No	Area	Occupier in 1901	YoP	Changes up to 1919	Changes 1920-1937	Changes from 1939
1 & 2	52	William Gordon	1904	1904 Robert Gordon		1957 Martha Davis; 1964 John (3) Davis
3	47	John (1) Davis	1915	John (2) Davis		1964 Martha Davis; 1965 Robert (3) and William Davis; 1994 Robert (3) Davis
4	23	George Barnhill	1911	1913 Matilda Mutch	1935 George Mutch	1957 Annie Mutch 1970 Malcolm Mutch
5 & 6	20/35	John Aiken	1906	1906 David Aiken	1925 William (2) Fulton	1938 William (3) Fulton 1986 William (4) Fulton
8, 9 & 10	46/54/46	William (2) Fulton	8 & 10 1888; 9 1906		1930 Mary Fulton	
11	61	Thomas (3) Huston	1908	1913 Robert (2) Huston	11 & 13 run as one farm	1952 Mary Huston. Farm divided in 1960: Robert (3) Huston farm 11; Samuel Huston farm 13
13	51	John McCrea	1907	1908 Thomas McCrea	from 1914 Robert (2) Huston	
7	45	Hamilton Aiken	1903		c1920 Robert Aiken	1942 George Moan; 1951 Frederick Hamilton; 1993 William Hamilton
14/15 (*)	71 + 100	James Aiken	1906		1930 Andrew Aiken	1939 Hall Fulton; 1951 Herbert Clarke
16	17	Michael (2) Conway	1907	1907 Michael (3) Conway		1947 Thomas Conway; 1988 Peter Conway
17	18	Alex Regan	1909	1909 James Regan; 1912 Neal Gallagher; 1919 Bernard Gallagher	17, 18 & 19 run as one farm from 1912	1943 Nixon Hughey 1968 William and Robert (3) Davis 1987 John (4) Davis
18 & 19	18/18	Neal Gallagher	1909	1919 Bernard Gallagher		

KEY: G M No = Farm number shown on the Griffiths Valuation Map (see Appendix 6); **Areas** in statute acres; **YoP**: Year of purchase following Wyndham Act 1903

(*) This 171 acre farm lies within Edymore and the adjoining Carrigullin townland - 71 acres in Edymore and 100 acres in Carrigullin.

APPENDIX 12

CAVANALEE G M No	Area	Occupier in 1901	YoP	Changes up to 1919	Changes 1920-1937	Changes from 1939
22	71	James Lowry	1906	1915 William (1) Smyth		1958 William (2) Smyth; 1985 Lowry Smyth
20	21	George Barnhill	1906	1913 Matilda Mutch	1934 George Mutch	1957 Annie Mutch 1970 Malcolm Mutch
21	22	Robert Gordon	1904		20 & 21 now one farm	
26 & 10	33/72	Joseph (2) Davis	1906	1905 Joseph (2)/John (2)/Robert(2)	1958 Isabella Davis	1999 Trevor and Samuel Davis
16	91	Andrew Smith	1906		1937 Saml/Wm Crumley	1983 John Crumley
11	21	Reps of Lowther Graham	1906	1906 Mary Graham 1907; Reps of Mary 1910; Thomas Graham		1952 Lowther Wilson; 1982 10ac to Roland Houston 10ac to Saml/Wm Crumley
12 & 15	35/19	William T Graham	1906	1906 12 & 15 joined with 14		1947 John Lindsay; 1956 Thomas Boyd;
14	18	Alex Regan	1906	William T Graham		1964 Roland Houston
13 & 23	71	Joseph Young	1906	1916 William Miller	1923 Harry Sherrard 1934 Thomas (5) Houston	1957 Roland Houston. From 1964 he farmed a single farm comprising 12, 13, 14, 15, 23, 25
17	70	Alex Regan	1909	1910 James and Alex Regan 1912 James (7) Houston		1951 Samuel and William Crumley 1983 George Crumley
18 & 25	20/18	James (6) Houston	1907		1923 Thomas(5)Houston	1934 25 to 13/23 and 18 to 19
19	21	Thomas (2) Houston	1906	1902 James (6) Houston	1923 Thomas(5)Houston	1934 William & Nixon Hughey; 1947 William and Robert (3) Davis; 1987 John (4) Davis

KEY: **G M No** = Farm number on Griffiths Valuation Map (see Appendix 9); **Areas** in statute acres; **YoP**: Year of purchase following Wyndham Act 1903

(*) This 171 acre farm lies within Edymore and the adjoining Carrigullin townland - 71 acres in Edymore and 100 acres in Carrigullin.

INDEX

Abercorn, Earls of (Hamilton family), 6, 10
    Claud, Lord Hamilton (Second Baron of Strabane), 6
    Duke of, 75
Abercorn Estate, 6, 9, 15–16, 45, 55
    Agents, 7, 8, 9, 10, 18, 20, 24, 35, 36, 54
        Burgoyne, John James, 23
        Colhoun, Jo, 35–6
        McClintock, John, 8
        Hamilton, James, 15, 18, 19, 22, 30–31, 36, 41
        Humphreys, Major John, 24, 26, 32, 37–8, 40, 70, 72
    Surveyor
        Starrat, William, 21
    tenancy agreements & leases, 8, 15, 18, 19, 26, 37, 41, 53–7
        notice to quit, 26
        purchase of farms, 55–7, 94
Abercorn Letters, 8, 9, 18–9, 21, 27, 31, 35–8
Act of Union, 44
agrarian revolt
    Oakboys, 43
    Steelboys, 44
agricultural colleges
    Enniskillen, 86
    Loughrey (Cookstown), 87
    Strabane, 86
agricultural labourers *see* cottiers
Agriculture
    Department of, 88, 89
    development of, 10, 15, 46–8, 58, 62, 86–9, 93, 99
    drainage & irrigation, 10, 22, 23, 27, 88
    equipment
        binders, 47, 58, 62, 95, 97
        carts, 11, 22, 93, 105
        combine harvesters, 95, 97, 99
        drills, 93, 101
        fiddle, 46, 93
        flails, 48
        forks, 10, 105
        harrows, 10, 46
        hooks, 10
        mowers, 58, 67, 99
        muckspreader, 105
        ploughs, 10, 47, 67, 91, 93, 101
        rakes, 47, 99
        reapers & reaper binders, 47, 48
        scythes, 10, 47
        shovels, 10
        sickles, 10, 47
        slide cars, 11, 22
        slipes, 11, 22
        spades, 10
        tedders, 47
        threshing, 47, 48, 49, 62–3, 97
        tractors, 58, 66, 68, 81, 86, 91, 93, 97–9, 101, 105, 110
        wheel cars, 11, 22
    fertilisers & manure, 52, 63, 88, 93, 94, 97, 98, 105
        lime, 88
        slurry, 105
    Government Grants schemes, 88, 89
    Mechanisation, 45–6, 48, 58, 63, 64, 66, 86, 88–90, 93, 95, 97, 99, 110
    Ministry of, 98, 101
    womenfolk & children, role of, 12, 48, 52, 68, 71–2, 101, 107
Alexander
    Mrs Frances Cecil (née Humphreys), 32, 37, 39–40, 70, 71
    Rev. William, 39–40, 70–71, 74
Alexander (Ballyheather), 102
Ardnaglass (townland), 52
Argyll, Earl of, 1
    McDonnell, Lady Agnes (daughter), 1
Artigarvan, 9, 36, 94, 95, 107

Ballindrait (Co. Donegal), 95
ballyboes
    definition, 2
    Liskinbwee, 30
    Teadanmore, 3
    Cauaneley, 3
Balmoral Show, Belfast, 93
Bearney (townland), 91, 97
Bingley estate (Co. Donegal), 42
British Egg Marketing Board, 88
British Wool Marketing Board, 88
buildings
    dwellings (type and construction), 26, 49–50, 58–9, 62, 70–71, 90–91
    out buildings, 59, 62, 88, 93, 99, 102, 105–7

Camus (townland), 71
Carrigullin (townland), 20, 27, 30, 42, 50, 52, 54, 58, 64, 80, 83, 99, 105
Castlederg, 18, 32, 38, 51, 66, 70, 90
Castlefinn (Co. Donegal), 51, 52
Cattle dealers
    McDermott, brothers (Strabane), 94
    Patterson, Samuel (Lifford), 94
    Robinson, George (Donemana), 94
    Smyth, Francis (Victoria Bridge), 94
Cavanalee
    aqueduct, 30
    Back Burn, 8, 48
    Cavanalee bridge, 20, 21, 43, 49, 89, 91
    farms, size of, 19–20, 22–3, 27, 39, 41, 45, 52–4,
    leases, 8, 19, 26
    meaning of name, translation *Cabhán na Laoigh*, 3
    mill, 27–8, 30–31, 39
    mill pond, 19, 30
    population of, 2, 5, 34–5
    rentals, 23–4, 27, 30, 41, 55–7
    River, 5, 8, 19–20, 22, 23, 24, 28, 30, 32, 41, 54, 80, 89–91
        water turbines, 90
    roads, 20–21, 35, 49, 58, 91
    size of (acres), 6
    Townland Valuation, 23–4
census of 1901, 59–60, 71–2, 76–7, 82

cholera (epidemic of 1832), 40, 44
Clarke, Rev. Edward, 73
    L'Amie, Jean (daughter), 73
conacre letting arrangements, 94, 95, 97, 101–2, 105
cottiers & agricultural labourers, 7, 15, 52, 62–3, 71–2, 101, 110
Crawford, Capt. Patrick, 2
creameries
    Leckpatrick, 102, 104
    Victoria Bridge, 64, 94
crop failures and famine, 7, 33–4, 43, 44, 55, 83
crops
    barley, 62, 95, 97–8
    corn, 27, 40, 52
        kilns, 27, 40, 49
    flax, 7, 10, 12, 38, 40, 48–9, 58, 63
    grass, 38, 47, 95, 97–9, 101, 110
        hay, 10, 12, 47, 52, 62, 95, 98–9, 102
        silage, 95, 97–9, 103
    oats, 3, 10, 12, 38, 40, 52, 62, 95, 98
        straw, 52, 62–3, 95, 98
    peas, 98
    potatoes, 8, 10, 12, 33–4, 38, 40, 47, 52, 62–3, 93, 97, 101–2, 110
        potato inspectors, 101
        spinners, 101
        varieties 63, 101
    turnips, 47, 52, 62–3, 102
    wheat, 62, 95
Cummings (Woodend), 102

dairy farming *see* livestock cattle
Davis estate (Co. Donegal), 42
Department of Agriculture *see* Agriculture
Department of the Environment
    Roads Service, 91
Dergalt (townland), 8, 43
Derry, 1, 44, 64, 67
    Clayton (egg merchant), 68
    newspapers
        Londonderry Sentinel, 83
    port, 67
    railways, 44
    Second World War, 85
    Siege of (1689), 8

Devon Commission, 38
Douglas Bridge, 12, 20, 63
Drumenny (townland), 64
Drumnaboy (townland), 30, 39, 101–2

Edymore
    Back Burn, 3, 4–5, 7, 12, 15, 21, 48, 58, 90
    farms, size of, 14–5, 26–7, 50, 52–4, 58–9, 64, 74,
    leases, 8, 19, 26, 53–4
        Ulster custom, 15, 18, 55–6
    meaning of name, translation *An tÉaden Mór*, 4
    population of, 2, 5, 34–5, 43
    rentals, 18, 23–4, 27, 36–8, 40, 55–7, 74
    roads, 21, 35, 58, 91
    school, 43
    size of (acres), 6
    Townland Valuation, 23–4
Emigration, 15, 36–7, 44, 66, 71, 73, 79, 81–3
    Australia, 81
    Canada, 66, 81, 82
    England, 73
    New Zealand, 82
    Scotland, 68, 82–3
    South Africa, 81–2
    United States, 15, 36, 71, 73, 81
England & Wales
    immigration from, 35, 42
European Economic Community (EEC), 88
European Union, 88–9, 94, 104, 110
    Common Agricultural Policy (CAP), 88–9, 110
    milk quotas, 103–4
Evish (townland), 53, 58, 80–81

facilities/amenities, 89
    coal, 91
    electricity, 86, 89–91
        Electricity Board for Northern Ireland (EBNI), 91
    gas, 89, 91
    mains water supply, 88–91
    oil, 91
    sewage, 89–90
farmers *see* tenants/farmers
farm labour (seasonal), 63, 66

Ferguson
    Harry, 81
    Joe, 81
fertiliser merchants
    Jack, Sydney, 94
    Surplis, Lowry, 94
    Taylor, Thomas, 94
First World War, 84–5
    Battle of the Somme, 84–5
Flight of the Earls, 1
Forbes, Alfred (organist), 74
Foster, John (Speaker of the Irish House of Commons), 10
Fulton, Robert (2) (Bobby), milk roundsman, 52, 65–6, 81, 102

Glentimon Young Farmers' Club, 87
Griffith's Valuation, 34, 41, 45, 50, 54–5

Hearth Tax returns (1664 & 1666), 6, 35
Herdman's Flax Spinning Mill *see* Sion Mills
Home Rule Movement, 76
Humphreys
    Eliza, 71
    Fanny *see* Alexander, Mrs Frances
    Isabella, 70
    Major John *see* Abercorn Estate Agents
    Thomas (T.W.D.) *see* Abercorn Estate Agents

Irish language, 72

James VI of Scotland, I of England, 5–6, 8
Johnson (Leckpatrick), 102

Kee, 101–2
    Donald, 97
    William, 97
Killeter, 32, 70

Land Acts
    Ashbourne Act (Land Purchase Act) 1885, 55
    Land Act 1881, 55
    Land Commission, 55, 56
    Wyndham Act (Irish Land Act) 1903, 55
Land League, 76
Larchmount (townland), 77
Leckpatrick Co-operative Agricultural & Dairy Society Ltd., Artigarvan, 94, 95, 102, 107
Lifford (Co. Donegal), 2, 43, 52, 72, 85, 94
    Bridge, 9, 43
Ligfordrum, 20, 97
linen manufacture, 7, 9–11, 40, 44, 52, 58, 63
    scutch mills, 12
        Maguire's mill, 63
        Ward's mill, 63
Liskinbwee (townland), 5, 30
    School, 43
livestock
    cattle, 8, 10, 12, 19, 22, 36, 38, 40, 50–1, 62, 64, 88–9, 94–5, 102–5, 110
        Artificial Insemination (AI) Scheme, 88, 103
        beef, 105
        breeds, 64, 102–3, 105
        butter, 10, 12, 40, 50–2, 64
        buttermilk, 40
        diseases
            Bovine Tuberculosis, 88
            Brucellosis, 88
            BSE (Bovine Spongiform Encephalopathy), 105
            Warble-fly, 88
        milk, 10, 12, 40, 50, 52, 64, 66, 71–2, 81, 87–90, 94, 99, 102–4, 105, 106, 110
            milking machines/parlours, 64, 66, 88–9, 102–4
    donkeys, 21
    horses, 36, 46, 48, 58, 62, 66, 93, 95, 97, 99, 110
    pigs, 3, 10, 12, 62–4, 87–8, 90, 106
    poultry, 10, 12, 62, 64, 67–8, 107
        breeds, 67
        eggs, 10, 12, 67, 88, 107
    sheep, 88, 89, 94, 99, 102, 106
        clipping, 106
        dipping, 88, 106

Marketing of Eggs Act (1924), 67
Mathew's Bridge, 58
Milk & Milk Products Act Northern Ireland (1934), 66
Milk Marketing Board, 87–8
millers
    James & Miller & Sons, Artigarvan, 95
    Robert Smyth & Sons
        Ballindrait (Co. Donegal), 95
        Strabane, 62, 94
Milltown (townland), 5, 24, 30, 32, 49, 91
Milltown Lodge/House, 24, 26, 32, 70, 71, 90
Ministry of Agriculture *see* Agriculture
Mourne, River, 2, 3, 19, 24, 33, 37, 44, 73
Muster Rolls (1630), 6, 35

Napoleonic Wars, 18, 26
Newtownstewart, 83, 94, 103
    Castle, 1
Nine Years' War, 1

O'Doherty, Sir Cahir of Inishowen, 1
Omagh, 59, 93
    Omagh Show, 93
O'Neill, 1, 5, 110
    Castle, 1
    cattle farming, 3
    Cormac, 3
    Neal, 3
    Sir Art, 3
    Sir Hugh (Earl of Tyrone), 1
    Turlough Luineach, 1, 3
    Turlough MacArt, 3
Orange Order, 44

Pigs Marketing Board, 87
Plantation of Ulster, 1, 5, 6, 27, 42
    Bodley's Survey map (1609), 2
Plumbridge, 20–1, 49, 58, 90, 91
poteen & illicit distilling, 31, 44

quarries, 38, 58
    gravel, 21
    limestone, 27, 58
        kilns, 27, 40
    slate, 27

railways
    Derry to Strabane, 44, 57, 67
    Strabane to Omagh, 44, 57
Raphoe (Co. Donegal), 10, 37, 42
    Bishop of, 52
Royal Irish Constabulary, 83
rundale holdings, 8

Scotland
    immigration from, 1, 6, 8–9, 35–6
    mercenaries, 1
    return to, 8–9
    soldiers, 1–2
Second World War, 48, 49, 63–4, 85, 87, 89, 95, 97–8, 102
    smuggling, 85
    Territorial Army, 85
    US troops, 85
Seed Potato Marketing Board, 88, 101
Sessiagh divisions
    definition, 2
    numbers in each Ballyboe, 3
    Cavanalee
        Alltydyarry, 3
        Corlegaskin, 3
        Crosmic(ck)gillyvane, 3
        Fallagherin, 3
        Knockedaghtan, 3
        Knockganiffe, 3
        Straghnemucke, 3
        Straghrey, 3
        Tempillam, 3
    Edymore
        Altconoleve, 4
        Cooleneshanagh, 5
        Corrikerrygan, 5
        Dromrollaghe, 5, 30
        Gortegaddery, 5
        Lissdownmorry, 5

        Tawnaghenagh, 4
        Tawnaghnehaskelly, 4
        Tawnaghranny, 5
        Tawnalohan, 5
Sinclair, Mr, of Hollyhill, 36
Sion Mills, 44, 77, 81, 87, 90
    Herdman's Flax Spinning Mill, 44, 81, 87
Stewart, Capt. William, 2
Strabane, 1, 3, 5, 6, 9, 18, 20–1, 33, 37, 39, 42–3, 64, 66, 68, 70, 83–5, 91, 93–4, 97, 101–2,
    Agricultural College, 86
    Bridge, 43
    Brown Linen Hall, 9, 44
    Canal, 44, 57
    Castle, 1
    churches, 39, 42–3, 72–5
        Church of Ireland, 7, 9, 38, 70, 72, 74–5
            Smith, Rev. James, 72
        Methodist, 73, 75
        Presbyterian, 9, 39, 72–4, 77
            Clarke, Rev. Edward, 73
                Appointed Moderator, 73
            Crawford, Rev. William, 42
            Gibson, Rev. James, 72
            Goudy, Rev. Alexander, 43
            Russell, Rev. Andrew, 72
            Toland, Rev. Charles, 73
        Roman Catholic, 72–3, 75
    construction of Strabane to Plumbridge Road, 20
    Corporation, 8, 9
    fairs (May and November), 7, 26, 35, 37, 44, 57, 70
    famine, 33, 44
    gas works, 89
    hiring fair, 72
    inn, 36
    July Show, 84
    Market House, 9, 44
    markets, 7, 10, 12, 37, 51, 57, 70, 83, 93–4
        butter, 57, 73
        cattle, 51, 92, 94
        flax, 57
        grain, 57
        linen ,44
        pork, 57
        sheep, 94

McGee, George, burgess of Strabane
    Corporation, 8, 22
Mill, 27, 30–31, 62
    rent, 30–31
newspapers
    Strabane Journal, 43
    Strabane Morning Post, 43
    Strabane Newsletter, 43
orchards, 19
Poor Law Guardians, 37, 76
    Workhouse, 37, 44
population, 8, 43, 57
railway, 44, 57
Rural District Council, 62, 76
schools & education, 42–3
        Church of Ireland School, 75
        County Primary School, 75
        Meetinghouse St Primary School, 37, 75
            teachers
                Miss Anderson (Mrs Fleming), 75
                Miss Black, 75
                Miss Young, 37, 75
        Strabane Academy, 42, 75
        Strabane Grammar School, 24, 70, 90
Second World War
    blackout, 85
Steamship Company, 70
Town Hall, 42
traders, 44, 57
    agricultural contractors
        Russell, Roy, 97
    automobile engineers & agents
        Sweeney, J.H., 67
    blacksmiths, 68
        Duddy
            John, 57
            Patrick, 69
    butter & egg merchants
        Honeyford & Co., 57, 77
    cattle salesmen
        Weir, Alex & Co., 57
    chemists
        Hill, 57
    coal merchants
        Harpur, William, 57

    collector of customs
        Blair, William, 39
    dealers, cattle
        McDermott (brothers), 94
    drapers
        Stevenson, 57
    fish merchants
        Casey, Thomas, 101
    founders
        Stevenson (Strabane Foundry), 48
    grocers
        Colhoun, 68
        Lowry & Rule, 57
    innkeepers
        Knox, 36
    ironmongers
        Harpur, William, 57
        Stevenson, William, 57
    Machinery Salesmen & Auctioneers
        Boggs'
            Jack, 93–4
            Robert, 94
        General Trading Services Ltd., 94
            Linton & Robinson Ltd., 94
    millers (Cavanalee/Strabane mill)
        Barnhill, James, 31
        Doherty, George, 31
        Lowther, Thomas, 31, 39
        Smyly, David, 31
    millers (Strabane)
        Robert Smyth & Sons, 62, 94
    produce merchants
        Bannigans, 63
    saddlers, 68
        Baxter, Jack, 69
        Quinn brothers, 68–9
            John, 69
water supply, 89
    waterworks, 90
Young Farmers' Club, 87

tenants/farmers
    Aiken
        Andrew, 64
        Hamilton, 56
        James, 62
        Margaret, 54

Index

Barnhill
    George, 54
    James, 20, 31
    John, 19, 20, 35
    Joseph, 20
Brown
    Isabella (widow), 18, 37
    William, 18, 35, 37
Carland
    Hugh, 54
Clarke
    Herbert, 66, 86, 89, 91, 97, 103, 104–7, 109
Conway 54, 72
    Daniel, 109
    Hugh and Bridget
        return from USA, 71
    Michael, 109
    Owen, 26–7
    Peter, 109
Crumley, 98, 106
    George, 109
    John, 106, 109
    Samuel, 59
    William, 59
Cunningham, 7–9
    Robert, 6
Cuthbertson
    Thomas, 54
Davis, 20, 42, 45, 70, 76–9, 98–9, 105
    family tree, 79
    Isabella, 79–80
    John (2), died 1944, 79–80, 93
    John (3) (Jackie), 74, 86, 105–6, 109
    John (4), 86–7
    Joseph (1), died late 19th century, 15, 42, 59
    Joseph (2), died 1922, 54, 62, 79, 81–2
    Martha, 79–80,
    Norman, 74, 97
    Robert (1), died 1877, 26, 52, 54, 78
    Robert (2), died 1958, 79–80
    Robert (3), (Bobby), 86–7, 88, 97, 99, 101, 103–4, 109
    Samuel, 79, 109
    Trevor, 79, 109
    William, 74, 79

Devine
    Hugh, 71
Doherty
    George, 31
Dooher
    Charles, 109
    Edward, 22
    Matthew, 22, 23
    Patrick, 109
    Thomas, 71
Finlay, 7, 8, 14, 36
    George, 6
    John, 35, 36
Fulton, 20, 43, 45, 52, 53–4, 58, 62, 63, 64, 66, 70, 72, 75, 76, 81, 90, 98, 102
    family tree, 53
    Jane, died 1883, 41, 52–53, 76, 81
    John (1), died 1855, 18, 42
    John (2), died 1875, 50–2, 75–81
    John (3), died c. 1920, 52
    John (4), (Jack), died 1987, 64, 102
    Samuel (3), died 1962, 102
    William (1), died late 19th century, 42, 52, 76–7
    William (2), died 1930, 52, 55–6, 62, 64, 66, 69, 73, 107
    William (3), died 1985, 64, 66, 90–1, 93, 97, 99, 102, 104–6
    William (4), 86, 88, 90, 105–6, 109
Gallagher, 85
    Neal, 58
Gillilan
    Samuel, 18, 35
Gordon, 73
    Robert, 43, 73, 74
    Victor, 36
Graham, 58–9, 72
    Francis, 55
    James, 41, 54, 75
    Lowther, 82
    Mary, 82
    Thomas, 19, 35, 43
    William, 54
Haghey
    Anne, 45

Haggarty
    John, 22
    Patrick, 21, 23
Hamilton
    Fred, 102
    James, 15
    Robert, 75
    William, 109
Hughey, 85
    Nixon, 64
Hunter
    James, 20
H(o)uston, 19, 20, 21–2, 63, 67, 70, 75, 76, 78, 90, 97, 98, 101, 106, 107
    family tree, 78
    Andrew (1), died 1834, 39, 78
    James (1), died c. 1755, 9, 19, 36, 78
    James (2), died c. 1775, 22, 78
    James (3), died 1805, 78
    James, senior (4), died c. 1860, 43, 45, 78
    James, junior (5), died c. 1860, 42, 78
    James (6), died 1923, 78
    James (7), died 1965, 59, 78, 81
    John (1), died 1880, 39, 42–3, 45, 74, 78
    John (2), died 1970, 78, 81
    Robert (1), died 1895, 78
    Robert (2), died 1952, 58, 62–3, 78, 80–1, 90–1, 97–9
    Robert, (Bertie) (3), 86, 94, 98, 102, 105, 109
    Samuel (Uel) 74, 78, 86, 88, 94, 97–8, 102, 105, 109
    Thomas (2), died 1902, 59, 75, 78
    Thomas (3), died 1912, 41, 54, 62, 73–4, 76–8, 81
    Thomas (5), died 1957, 74, 76, 78, 93, 98–9
Kelly
    Joseph, 109
    Sean, 109
King, 45, 70, 76, 80, 82, 105
    family tree, 80
    Samuel, 52–3, 80–3

Knox, 35
    Alex, 18
    Ezekiel, 18
    George, 18
    Joseph, 41
    Widow, 18
    William, 18
Lowry
    Robert, 54
Lowther
    Galbraith, 31, 37
    Thomas, 19, 30, 31, 39
    Widow, 30–31
    William, 18, 35
Lyon
    William, 23
McCartan
    Donald oge, 6
McColgan
    Donald, 6
    Roger, 21
McCrea
    Alex, 54
    James, 41
    William, 41
McFadden
    Peter, 109
McNamee, 22
    Denis, 22, 23
    John, 23
McNeilans
    John, 36
Magee
    John (younger), 6
Moan
    George, 102
Mutch, 89, 90, 105
    Annie, 94
    George, 80, 83, 94
    Malcolm, 94, 109
Nichol, 7–9
    James, 6

O'Fadachan
    Donaghy boy, 6
O'Haran
    Manus, 6
O'Machry, 7
    Sean, 6
Orr, 35
    George, 15, 18
Porter
    James, 18
    Margaret, 26, 53

Rabb, 7, 8, 14
    John, 6, 35, 38, 42
    John junior, 18
Regan, 72
    Alexander, 71, 81
    James, 71
Sawyer
    Thomas, 15
    William, 15
Simison
    Alex, 15, 36–7
    John junior, 15, 37
    John senior, 15, 35, 37
Smith
    Andrew, 59, 62
Smyly
    David, 31
    Robert, 35
Smyth
    Lowry, 86, 87, 88, 89, 99, 103, 109
    William, 74, 85–87, 89, 90, 93, 97, 101–3, 105–6
Sproule brothers, 109
Stilly
    William, 18, 42
Thompson
    Galbraith, 15, 18, 35
    Joseph, 15
    Nathaniel, 15, 39
Todd
    Alex, 35

Weir
    James, 20
Wilson, 38, 45, 70, 72
    John, 27, 39–41, 43, 52–3, 72
    John, senior, 38
    Robert, 27, 39, 40, 41, 43, 72, 77
    Robert, senior, 18, 37, 38, 40, 41, 43
        will of, 38–41
    Young, 49, 50
    Jane, 49
    John, 49
    Joseph, 49, 50, 54, 59, 62, 71, 81
threshing machine/combine contractors
    Boyd, Hugh (Dysert), 97
    Graham, Houston (Strabane), 63, 97
    Moss, Francis (Dernalebe), 97
    Russell, Roy (Strabane), 97
    Sayers, Bill (Bearney), 97
tithes payable to the Church of Ireland, 7, 26–7, 38, 55
turf & peat, 3, 15, 19–22, 26, 27, 33, 38, 40
typhoid, 77
Tyrone, Earl of *see* Sir Hugh O'Neill

Ulster Custom, 15, 18, 55–6
Ulster Farmers' Union, 87
    North Tyrone, 87
    Victoria Bridge, 87
Ulster Solemn League & Covenant, 76
United Irishmen, 44

Victoria Bridge, 20, 64, 71, 91, 94

Wesley, John, 42
Williamite Wars, 8

Young Farmers' Club
    Glentimon, 87
    Strabane, 87